A MONK OF FIFE

Being the Chronicle written by Norman Leslie of Pitcullo,
concerning marvellous deeds that befell in the realm of France,
in the years of our redemption, MCCCCXXIX-XXXI. Now
first done into English out of the French by

ANDREW LANG

1st WORLD
LIBRARY
Literary Society

A Monk of Fife

Andrew Lang

© 1st World Library, 2007
PO Box 2211
Fairfield, IA 52556
www.1stworldlibrary.com
First Edition

LCCN: 2007934222

Softcover ISBN: 978-1-4218-9694-6
Hardcover ISBN: 978-1-4218-9794-3
eBook ISBN: 978-1-4218-9594-9

Purchase *"A Monk of Fife"*
as a traditional bound book at:
www.1stWorldLibrary.com/purchase.asp?ISBN=978-1-4218-9694-6

1st World Library is a literary, educational organization
dedicated to:

- Creating a free internet library of downloadable ebooks

- Hosting writing competitions and offering book publishing scholarships.

1ˢᵗ World Library Literary Society

Giving Back to the World

"If you want to work on the core problem, it's early school literacy."

-James Barksdale, former CEO of Netscape

"No skill is more crucial to the future of a child, or to a democratic and prosperous society, than literacy."

-Los Angeles Times

"Literacy... means far more than learning how to read and write... The aim is to transmit... knowledge and promote social participation."

-UNESCO

"Literacy is not a luxury, it is a right and a responsibility. If our world is to meet the challenges of the twenty-first century we must harness the energy and creativity of all our citizens."

-President Bill Clinton

"Parents should be encouraged to read to their children, and teachers should be equipped with all available techniques for teaching literacy, so the varying needs and capacities of individual kids can be taken into account."

-Hugh Mackay

TO HENRIETTA LANG

My Dear Aunt,—To you, who read to me stories from the History of France, before I could read them for myself, this Chronicle is affectionately dedicated.

Yours ever,

ANDREW LANG.

PREFACE

Norman Leslie of Pitcullo, whose narrative the reader has in his hands, refers more than once to his unfinished Latin Chronicle. That work, usually known as "The Book of Pluscarden," has been edited by Mr. Felix Skene, in the series of "Historians of Scotland" (vol. vii.). To Mr. Skene's introduction and notes the curious are referred. Here it may suffice to say that the original MS. of the Latin Chronicle is lost; that of six known manuscript copies none is older than 1480; that two of these copies contain a Prologue; and that the Prologue tells us all that has hitherto been known about the author.

The date of the lost Latin original is 1461, as the author himself avers. He also, in his Prologue, states the purpose of his work. At the bidding of an unnamed Abbot of Dunfermline, who must have been Richard Bothwell, he is to abbreviate "The Great Chronicle," and "bring it up to date," as we now say. He is to recount the events of his own time, "with certain other miraculous deeds, which I who write have had cognisance of, seen, and heard, beyond the bounds of this realm. Also, lastly, concerning a certain marvellous Maiden, who recovered the kingdom of France out of the hands of the tyrant, Henry, King of England. The aforesaid Maiden I saw, was conversant with, and was in her company in her said recovery of France, and till her life's end I was ever present." After "I was ever present" the copies add "etc.," perhaps a sign of omission. The monkish author probably said more about the heroine of his youth, and this he copyists have chosen to leave out.

The author never fulfilled this promise of telling, in Latin, the history of the Maid as her career was seen by a Scottish ally and friend. Nor did he ever explain how a Scot, and a foe of England, succeeded in being present at the Maiden's martyrdom in Rouen. At least he never fulfilled his promise, as far as any of the six Latin MSS. of his Chronicle are concerned. Every one of these MSS.—doubtless following their incomplete original—breaks off short in the middle of the second sentence of Chapter xxxii. Book xii. Here is the brief fragment which that chapter contains:—

"In those days the Lord stirred up the spirit of a certain marvellous Maiden, born on the borders of France, in the duchy of Lorraine, and the see of Toul, towards the Imperial territories. This Maiden her father and mother employed in tending sheep; daily, too, did she handle the distaff; man's love she knew not; no sin, as it is said, was found in her, to her innocence the neighbours bore witness . . . "

Here the Latin narrative of the one man who followed Jeanne d'Arc through good and evil to her life's end breaks off abruptly. The author does not give his name; even the name of the Abbot at whose command he wrote "is left blank, as if it had been erased in the original" (Mr. Felix Skene, "Liber Pluscardensis," in the "Historians of Scotland," vii. p. 18). It might be guessed that the original fell into English hands between 1461 and 1489, and that they blotted out the name of the author, and destroyed a most valuable record of their conqueror and their victim, Jeanne d'Arc.

Against this theory we have to set the explanation here

offered by Norman Leslie, our author, in the Ratisbon Scots College's French MS., of which this work is a translation. Leslie never finished his Latin Chronicle, but he wrote, in French, the narrative which follows, decorating it with the designs which Mr. Selwyn Image has carefully copied in black and white.

Possessing this information, we need not examine Mr. W. F. Skene's learned but unconvincing theory that the author of the fragmentary Latin work was one Maurice Drummond, out of the Lennox. The hypothesis is that of Mr. W. F. Skene, and Mr. Felix Skene points out the difficulties which beset the opinion of his distinguished kinsman. Our Monk is a man of Fife.

As to the veracity of the following narrative, the translator finds it minutely corroborated, wherever corroboration could be expected, in the large mass of documents which fill the five volumes of M. Quicherat's "Proces de Jeanne d'Arc," in contemporary chronicles, and in MSS. more recently discovered in French local or national archives. Thus Charlotte Boucher, Barthelemy Barrette, Noiroufle, the Scottish painter, and his daughter Elliot, Capdorat, ay, even Thomas Scott, the King's Messenger, were all real living people, traces of whose existence, with some of their adventures, survive faintly in brown old manuscripts. Louis de Coutes, the pretty page of the Maid, a boy of fourteen, may have been hardly judged by Norman Leslie, but he certainly abandoned Jeanne d'Arc at her first failure.

So, after explaining the true position and character of our monkish author and artist, we leave his book to the judgment which it has tarried for so long.

CHAPTER I

HOW THIS BOOK WAS WRITTEN, AND HOW NORMAN LESLIE FLED OUT OF FIFE

It is not of my own will, nor for my own glory, that I, Norman Leslie, sometime of Pitcullo, and in religion called Brother Norman, of the Order of Benedictines, of Dunfermline, indite this book. But on my coming out of France, in the year of our Lord One thousand four hundred and fifty-nine, it was laid on me by my Superior, Richard, Abbot in Dunfermline, that I should abbreviate the Great Chronicle of Scotland, and continue the same down to our own time. {1} He bade me tell, moreover, all that I knew of the glorious Maid of France, called Jeanne la Pucelle, in whose company I was, from her beginning even till her end.

Obedient, therefore, to my Superior, I wrote, in this our cell of Pluscarden, a Latin book containing the histories of times past, but when I came to tell of matters wherein, as Maro says, "pars magna fui," I grew weary of such rude, barbarous Latin as alone I am skilled to indite, for of the manner Ciceronian, as it is now practised by clerks of Italy, I am not master: my book, therefore, I left unfinished, breaking off in the middle of a sentence. Yet, considering the command laid on me, in the end I am come to this resolve, namely, to write the history of the wars in France, and the history of the blessed Maid (so far at least as I was an eyewitness and partaker thereof), in the French language, being the most commonly understood of all men, and the most delectable. It is not my intent to tell all the story of the Maid, and all her deeds and sayings, for the world would scarcely contain the books that should be written. But what I myself beheld, that I shall relate, especially concerning certain accidents not known to the general, by reason of which ignorance the whole truth can scarce be understood. For, if Heaven visibly sided with France and the Maid, no less did Hell most manifestly take part with our old enemy of England. And often in this life, if we look not the more closely, and with the eyes of faith, Sathanas shall seem to have the upper hand in the battle, with whose very imp and minion I myself was conversant, to my sorrow, as shall be shown.

First, concerning myself I must say some few words, to the end that what follows may be the more readily understood.

I was born in the kingdom of Fife, being, by some five years, the younger of two sons of Archibald Leslie, of Pitcullo, near St. Andrews, a cadet of the great House of Rothes. My mother was an Englishwoman of the Debatable Land, a Storey of Netherby, and of me, in our country speech, it used to be said that I was "a mother's bairn." For I had ever my greatest joy in her, whom I lost ere I was sixteen years of age, and she in me: not that she favoured me unduly, for she was very just, but that, within ourselves, we each knew who was nearest to her heart. She was, indeed, a saintly woman, yet of a merry wit, and she had great pleasure in reading of books, and in romances. Being always, when I might, in her company, I became a clerk insensibly, and without labour I could early read and write, wherefore my father was minded to bring me up for a churchman. For this cause, I was some deal despised by others of my age, and, yet more, because from my mother I had caught the Southron trick of the tongue. They called me "English Norman," and many a battle I have fought on that quarrel, for I am as true a Scot as any, and I hated the English (my own mother's people though they were) for taking and holding captive our King, James I. of worthy memory. My fancy, like that of most boys, was all for the wars, and full of dreams concerning knights and ladies, dragons and enchanters, about which the other lads were fain enough to hear me tell what I had read in romances, though they mocked at me for reading. Yet they oft came ill speed with their jests, for my brother had taught me to use my hands: and to hold a sword I was instructed by our smith, who had been prentice to Harry Gow, the Burn-the-Wind of Perth, and the best man at his weapon in broad Scotland. From him I got many a trick of fence that served my turn later.

But now the evil time came when my dear mother sickened and died, leaving to me her memory and her great chain of gold. A bitter sorrow is her death to me still; but anon my father took to him another wife of the Bethunes of Blebo. I blame myself, rather than this lady, that we dwelt not happily in the same house. My father therefore, still minded to make me a churchman, sent me to Robert of Montrose's new college that stands in the South Street of St. Andrews, a city not far from our house of Pitcullo. But there, like a wayward boy, I took more pleasure in the battles of the "nations"—as of Fife against Galloway and the Lennox; or in games of catch-pull, football, wrestling, hurling the bar, archery, and golf—than in divine learning—as of logic, and Aristotle his analytics.

Yet I loved to be in the scriptorium of the Abbey, and to see the good Father Peter limning the blessed saints in blue, and red, and gold, of which art he taught me a little. Often I would help him to grind his colours, and he instructed me in the laying of them on paper or vellum, with white of egg, and in fixing and burnishing the gold, and in drawing flowers, and figures, and strange beasts and devils, such as we see grinning from the walls of the cathedral. In the French language, too, he learned me, for he had been taught at the great University of Paris; and in Avignon had seen the Pope himself, Benedict XIII., of uncertain memory.

Much I loved to be with Father Peter, whose lessons did not irk me, but jumped with my own desire to read romances in the French tongue, whereof there are many. But never could I have dreamed that, in days to come, this art of painting would win me my bread for a while, and that a Leslie of Pitcullo should be driven by hunger to so base and contemned a handiwork, unworthy, when practised for gain, of my blood.

Yet it would have been well for me to follow even this craft more, and my sports and pastimes less: Dickon Melville had then escaped a broken head, and I, perchance, a broken heart. But youth is given over to vanities that war against the soul, and, among others, to that wicked game of the Golf, now justly cried down by our laws, {2} as the mother of cursing and idleness, mischief and wastery, of which game, as I verily believe, the devil himself is the father.

It chanced, on an October day of the year of grace Fourteen hundred and twenty-eight, that I was playing myself at this accursed sport with one Richard Melville, a student of like age with myself. We were evenly matched, though Dickon was tall and weighty, being great of growth for his age, whereas I was of but scant inches, slim, and, as men said, of a girlish countenance. Yet I was well skilled in the game of the Golf, and have driven a Holland ball the length of an arrow-flight, there or thereby. But wherefore should my sinful soul be now in mind of these old vanities, repented of, I trust, long ago?

As we twain, Dickon and I, were known for fell champions at this unholy sport, many of the other scholars followed us, laying wagers on our heads. They were but a wild set of lads, for, as then, there was not, as now there is, a house appointed for scholars to dwell in together under authority. We wore coloured clothes, and our hair long; gold chains, and whingers {3} in our belts, all of which things are now most righteously forbidden. But I carried no whinger on the links, as considering that it hampered a man in his play. So the game went on, now Dickon leading "by a hole," as they say, and now myself, and great wagers were laid on us.

Now, at the hole that is set high above the Eden, whence you see far over the country, and the river-mouth, and the shipping, it chanced that my ball lay between Dickon's and the hole, so that he could in no manner win past it.

"You laid me that stimy of set purpose," cried Dickon, throwing down his club in a rage; "and this is the third time you have done it in this game."

"It is clean against common luck," quoth one of his party, "and the game and the money laid on it should be ours."

"By the blessed bones of the Apostle," I said, "no luck is more common. To-day to me, to-morrow to thee! Lay it of purpose, I could not if I would."

"You lie!" he shouted in a rage, and gripped to his whinger.

It was ever my father's counsel that I must take the lie from none. Therefore, as his steel was out, and I carried none, I made no more ado, and the word of shame had scarce left his lips when I felled him with the iron club that we use in sand.

"He is dead!" cried they of his party, while the lads of my

own looked askance on me, and had manifestly no mind to be partakers in my deed.

Now, Melville came of a great house, and, partly in fear of their feud, partly like one amazed and without any counsel, I ran and leaped into a boat that chanced to lie convenient on the sand, and pulled out into the Eden. Thence I saw them raise up Melville, and bear him towards the town, his friends lifting their hands against me, with threats and malisons. His legs trailed and his head wagged like the legs and the head of a dead man, and I was without hope in the world.

At first it was my thought to row up the river-mouth, land, and make across the marshes and fields to our house at Pitcullo. But I bethought me that my father was an austere man, whom I had vexed beyond bearing with my late wicked follies, into which, since the death of my mother, I had fallen. And now I was bringing him no college prize, but a blood-feud, which he was like to find an ill heritage enough, even without an evil and thankless son. My stepmother, too, who loved me little, would inflame his anger against me. Many daughters he had, and of gear and goods no more than enough. Robin, my elder brother, he had let pass to France, where he served among the men of John Kirkmichael, Bishop of Orleans—he that smote the Duke of Clarence in fair fight at Bauge.

Thinking of my father, and of my stepmother's ill welcome, and of Robin, abroad in the wars against our old enemy of England, it may be that I fell into a kind of half dream, the boat lulling me by its movement on the waters. Suddenly I felt a crashing blow on my head. It was as if the powder used for artillery had exploded in my mouth, with flash of light and fiery taste, and I knew nothing. Then, how long after I could not tell, there was water on my face, the blue sky and the blue tide were spinning round—they spun swiftly, then slowly, then stood still. There was a fierce pain stounding in my head, and a voice said—

"That good oar-stroke will learn you to steal boats!"

I knew the voice; it was that of a merchant sailor-man with whom, on the day before, I had quarrelled in the market-place. Now I was lying at the bottom of a boat which four seamen, who had rowed up to me and had broken my head as I meditated, were pulling towards a merchant-vessel, or carrick, in the Eden-mouth. Her sails were being set; the boat wherein I lay was towing that into which I had leaped after striking down Melville. For two of the ship's men, being on shore, had hailed their fellows in the carrick, and they had taken vengeance upon me.

"You scholar lads must be taught better than your masters learn you," said my enemy.

And therewith they carried me on board the vessel, the "St. Margaret," of Berwick, laden with a cargo of dried salmon from Eden-mouth. They meant me no kindness, for there was an old feud between the scholars and the sailors; but it seemed to me, in my foolishness, that now I was in luck's way. I need not go back, with blood on my hands, to Pitcullo and my father. I had money in my pouch, my mother's gold chain about my neck, a ship's deck under my foot, and the seas before me. It was not hard for me to bargain with the shipmaster for a passage to Berwick, whence I might put myself aboard a vessel that traded to Bordeaux for wine from that country. The sailors I made my friends at no great cost, for indeed they were the conquerors, and could afford to show clemency, and hold me to slight ransom as a prisoner of war.

So we lifted anchor, and sailed out of Eden-mouth, none of

those on shore knowing how I was aboard the carrick that slipped by the bishop's castle, and so under the great towers of the minster and St. Rule's, forth to the Northern Sea. Despite my broken head—which put it comfortably into my mind that maybe Dickon's was no worse—I could have laughed to think how clean I had vanished away from St. Andrews, as if the fairies had taken me. Now having time to reason of it quietly, I picked up hope for Dickon's life, remembering his head to be of the thickest. Then came into my mind the many romances of chivalry which I had read, wherein the young squire has to flee his country for a chance blow, as did Messire Patroclus, in the Romance of Troy, who slew a man in anger over the game of the chess, and many another knight, in the tales of Charlemagne and his paladins. For ever it is thus the story opens, and my story, methought, was beginning to-day like the rest.

Now, not to prove more wearisome than need be, and so vex those who read this chronicle with much talk about myself, and such accidents of travel as beset all voyagers, and chiefly in time of war, I found a trading ship at Berwick, and reached Bordeaux safe, after much sickness on the sea. And in Bordeaux, with a very sore heart, I changed the links of my mother's chain that were left to me—all but four, that still I keep—for money of that country; and so, with a lighter pack than spirit, I set forth towards Orleans and to my brother Robin.

On this journey I had good cause to bless Father Peter of the Abbey for his teaching me the French tongue, that was of more service to me than all my Latin. Yet my Latin, too, the little I knew, stood me in good stead at the monasteries, where often I found bed and board, and no small kindness; I little deeming that, in time to come, I also should be in religion, an old man and weary, glad to speak with travellers concerning the news of the world, from which I am now these ten years retired. Yet I love even better to call back memories of these days, when I took my part in the fray. If this be a sin, may God and the Saints forgive me, for if I have fought, it was in a rightful cause, which Heaven at last has prospered, and in no private quarrel. And methinks I have one among the Saints to pray for me, as a friend for a friend not unfaithful. But on this matter I submit me to the judgment of the Church, as in all questions of the faith.

Andrew Lang

CHAPTER II

HOW NORMAN LESLIE MET NOIROUFLE THE CORDELIER, CALLED BROTHER THOMAS IN RELIGION: AND OF MIRACLES WROUGHT BY BROTHER THOMAS

The ways were rude and long from Bordeaux town to Orleans, whither I had set my face, not knowing, when I left my own country, that the city was beleaguered by the English. For who could guess that lords and knights of the Christian faith, holding captive the gentle Duke of Orleans, would besiege his own city?—a thing unheard of among the very Saracens, and a deed that God punished. Yet the news of this great villainy, namely, the leaguer of Orleans, then newly begun, reached my ears on my landing at Bordeaux, and made me greatly fear that I might never meet my brother Robin alive. And this my doubt proved but too true, for he soon after this time fell, with many other Scottish gentlemen and archers, deserted shamefully by the French and by Charles de Bourbon, Comte de Clermont, at the Battle of the Herrings. But of this I knew nothing—as, indeed, the battle was not yet fought—and only pushed on for France, thinking to take service with the Dauphin against the English. My journey was through a country ruinous enough, for, though the English were on the further bank of the Loire, the partisans of the Dauphin had made a ruin round themselves and their holds, and, not being paid, they lived upon the country.

The further north I held, by ways broken and ruined with rains and suns, the more bare and rugged grew the whole land. Once, stopping hard by a hamlet, I had sat down to munch such food as I carried, and was sharing my meal with a little brown herd-boy, who told me that he was dinnerless. A few sheep and lean kine plucked at such scant grasses as grew among rocks, and herbs useless but sweet-scented, when suddenly a horn was blown from the tower of the little church. The first note of that blast had not died away, when every cow and sheep was scampering towards the hamlet and a kind of "barmkyn" {4} they had builded there for protection, and the boy after them, running with his bare legs for dear life. For me, I was too amazed to run in time, so lay skulking in the thick sweet-smelling herbs, whence I saw certain men-at-arms gallop to the crest of a cliff hard by, and ride on with curses, for they were not of strength to take the barmkyn.

Such was the face of France in many counties. The fields lay weedy and untilled; the starving peasant-folk took to the highway, every man preying on his neighbour. Woods had grown up, and broken in upon the roads. Howbeit, though robbers harboured therein, none of them held to ransom a wandering poor Scots scholar.

Slowly I trudged, being often delayed, and I was now nearing Poictiers, and thought myself well on my road to Chinon, where, as I heard, the Dauphin lay, when I came to a place where the road should have crossed a stream—not wide, but strong, smooth, and very deep. The stream ran through a glen; and above the road I had long noted the towers of a castle. But as I drew closer, I saw first that the walls were black with fire and roofless, and that carrion birds

Andrew Lang

were hovering over them, some enemy having fallen upon the place: and next, behold, the bridge was broken, and there was neither ford nor ferry! All the ruin was fresh, the castle still smouldering, the kites flocking and yelling above the trees, the planks of the bridge showing that the destruction was but of yesterday.

This matter of the broken bridge cost me little thought, for I could swim like an otter. But there was another traveller down by the stream who seemed more nearly concerned. When I came close to him, I found him standing up to his waist in the water, taking soundings with a long and heavy staff. His cordelier's frock was tucked up into his belt, his long brown legs, with black hairs thick on them, were naked. He was a huge, dark man, and when he turned and stared at me, I thought that, among all men of the Church and in religion whom I had ever beheld, he was the foulest and most fierce to look upon. He had an ugly, murderous visage, fell eyes and keen, and a right long nose, hooked like a falcon's. The eyes in his head shone like swords, and of all eyes of man I ever saw, his were the most piercing and most terrible. On his back he carried, as I noticed at the first, what I never saw on a cordelier's back before, or on any but his since—an arbalest, and he had bolts enough in his bag, the feathers showing above.

"Pax vobiscum," he cried, in a loud, grating voice, as he saw me, and scrambled out to shore.

"Et cum anima tua," I answered.

"Nom de Dieu!" he said, "you have bottomed my Latin already, that is scarce so deep as the river here. My malison on them that broke the bridge!" Then he looked me over fiercely.

"Burgundy or Armagnac?" he asked.

I thought the question strange, as a traveller would scarce care to pronounce for Burgundy in that country. But this was a man who would dare anything, so I deemed it better to answer that I was a Scot, and, so far, of neither party.

"Tug-mutton, wine-sack!" he said, these being two of many ill names which the French gave our countrymen; for, of all men, the French are least grateful to us, who, under Heaven and the Maid, have set their King on his throne again.

The English knew this, if the French did not; and their great King, Harry the Fifth, when he fell ill of St. Fiacre's sickness, after plundering that Scots saint's shrine of certain horse-shoes, silver-gilt, said well that, "go where he would, he was bearded by Scots, dead or alive." But the French are not a thankful people.

I had no answer very ready to my tongue, so stepped down silent to the water-edge, and was about taking off my doublet and hose, meaning to carry them on my head and swim across. But he barred the way with his staff, and, for me, I gripped to my whinger, and watched my chance to run in under his guard. For this cordelier was not to be respected, I deemed, like others of the Order of St. Francis, and all men of Holy Church.

"Answer a civil question," he said, "before it comes to worse: Armagnac or Burgundy?"

"Armagnac," I answered, "or anything else that is not English. Clear the causeway, mad friar!"

At that he threw down his staff.

"I go north also," he said, "to Orleans, if I may, for the foul 'manants' and peasant dogs of this country have burned the castle of Alfonse Rodigo, a good knight that held them in right good order this year past. He was worthy, indeed, to ride with that excellent captain, Don Rodrigo de Villandradas. King's captain or village labourer, all was fish that came to his net, and but two days ago I was his honourable chaplain. But he made the people mad, and a great carouse that we kept gave them their opportunity. They have roasted the good knight Alfonse, and would have done as much for me, his almoner, frock and all, if wine had any mastery over me. But I gave them the slip. Heaven helps its own! Natheless, I would that this river were between me and their vengeance, and, for once, I dread the smell of roast meat that is still in my nostrils—pah!"

And here he spat on the ground.

"But one door closes," he went on, "and another opens, and to Orleans am I now bound, in the service of my holy calling."

"There is, indeed, cause enough for the shriving of souls of sinners, Father, in that country, as I hear, and a holy man like you will be right welcome to many."

"They need little shriving that are opposite my culverin," said this strange priest. "Though now I carry but an arbalest, the gun is my mistress, and my patron is the gunner's saint, St. Barbara. And even with this toy, methinks I have the lives of a score of goddams in my bolt-pouch."

I knew that in these wild days many clerics were careless as to that which the Church enjoins concerning the effusion of blood—nay, I have named John Kirkmichael, Bishop of Orleans, as having himself broken a spear on the body of the

Duke of Clarence. The Abbe of Cerquenceaux, also, was a valiant man in religion, and a good captain, and, all over France, clerics were gripping to sword and spear. But such a priest as this I did not expect to see.

"Your name?" he asked suddenly, the words coming out with a sound like the first grating of a saw on stone.

"They call me Norman Leslie de Pitcullo," I answered. "And yours?"

"My name," he said, "is Noiroufle"—and I thought that never had I seen a man so well fitted with a name;—"in religion, Brother Thomas, a poor brother of the Order of the mad St. Francis of Assisi."

"Then, Brother Thomas, how do you mean to cross this water which lies between you and the exercise of your holy calling? Do you swim?"

"Like a stone cannon-ball, and, for all that I can find, the cursed water has no bottom. Cross!" he snarled. "Let me see you swim."

I was glad enough to be quit of him so soon, but I noticed that, as I stripped and packed my clothes to carry in a bundle on my head, the holy man set his foot in the stirrup of his weapon, and was winding up his arbalest with a windlass, a bolt in his mouth, watching at the same time a heron that rose from a marsh on the further side of the stream. On this bird, I deemed, he meant to try his skill with the arbalest.

"Adieu, Brother Thomas," I said, as I took the water; and in a few strokes I was across and running up and down on the bank to get myself dry. "Back!" came his grating voice— "back! and without your clothes, you wine-sack of Scotland, or I shoot!" and his arbalest was levelled on me.

I have often asked myself since what I should have done, and what was the part of a brave man. Perchance I might have dived, and swum down-stream under water, but then I had bestowed my bundle of clothes some little way off, and Brother Thomas commanded it from his side of the stream. He would have waited there in ambush till I came shivering back for hose and doublet, and I should be in no better case than I was now. Meanwhile his weapon was levelled at me, and I could see the bolt-point set straight for my breast, and glittering in a pale blink of the sun. The bravest course is ever the best. I should have thrown myself on the earth, no doubt, and so crawled to cover, taking my chance of death rather than the shame of obeying under threat and force. But I was young, and had never looked death in the face, so, being afraid and astonished, I made what seemed the best of an ill business, and, though my face reddens yet at the thought of it, I leaped in and swam back like a dog to heel.

"Behold me," I said, making as brave a countenance as I might in face of necessity.

"Well done, Norman Leslie de Pitcullo," he snarled, baring his yellow teeth. "This is the obedience which the young owe to the Church. Now, ferry me over; you are my boat."

"You will drown, man," I said. "Not while you swim."

Then, unbuckling his frock, he packed it as he had seen me do, bade me put it on my head, and so stepped out into the water, holding forth his arm to put about my neck. I was for teaching him how to lay it on my shoulder, and was bidding him keep still as a plank of wood, but he snarled—

"I have sailed on a boat of flesh before to-day."

To do him justice, he kept still as a log of wood, and so, yielding partly to the stream, I landed him somewhat further down than the place where my own clothes were lying. To them he walked, and very quietly picking up my whinger and my raiment that he gathered under his arm, he concealed himself in a thick bush, albeit it was leafless, where no man could have been aware of him. This amazed me not a little, for modesty did not seem any part of his nature.

"Now," says he, "fetch over my arbalest. Lying where I am you have no advantage to shoot me, as, nom de Dieu! I would have shot you had you not obeyed. And hark ye, by the way, unwind the arbalest before you cross; it is ever well to be on the safe side. And be sure you wet not the string." He pushed his face through the bush, and held in his mouth my naked whinger, that shone between his shining eyes.

Now again I say it, I have thought over this matter many a time, and have even laughed aloud and bitterly, when I was alone, at the figure of me shivering there, on a cold February day, and at my helpless estate. For a naked man is no match for a man with a whinger, and he was sitting on my clothes. So this friar, unworthy as he was of his holy calling, had me at an avail on every side, nor do I yet see what I could do but obey him, as I did. And when I landed from this fifth voyage, he laughed and gave me his blessing, and, what I needed more, some fiery spirits from a water-gourd, in which Father Thomas carried no water.

"Well done, my son," he said, "and now we are comrades. My life was not over safe on yonder side, seeing that the 'manants' hate me, and respect not my hood, and two are better company than one, where we are going."

This encounter was the beginning of many evils, and often now the picture shines upon my eyes, and I see the grey water, and hear the cold wind whistle in the dry reeds of the river-bank whereon we sat.

The man was my master, Heaven help me! as surely as Sathanas was his. And though, at last, I slipped his clutches, as you shall hear (more readily than, I trow, he will scape his lord in the end, for he still lives), yet it was an ill day that we met—an ill day for me and for France. Howbeit we jogged on, he merrily enough singing a sculdudery song, I something surly, under a grey February sky, with a keen wind searching out the threadbare places in our raiment. My comrade, as he called himself, told me what passages he chose in the history of his life: how he came to be frocked (but 'cucullus non facit monachum'), and how, in the troubles of these times, he had discovered in himself a great aptitude for the gunner's trade, of which he boasted not a little. He had been in one and another of these armed companies that took service with either side, for hire, being better warriors and more skilled than the noblesse, but a curse to France: for, in peace or war, friend or foe, they plundered all, and held all to ransom. With Rodrigo de Villandradas, that blood-hound of Spain, he had been high in favour, but when Rodrigo went to harry south and east, he had tarried at Ruffec, with another thief of that nation, Alfonse Rodigo. All his talk, as we went, was of slaying men in fight; whom he slew he cared not much, but chiefly he hated the English and them of Burgundy. To him, war was what hunting and shooting game is to others; a cruel and bloody pastime, when Christians are the quarry!

"John the Lorrainer, and I, there are no others to be named with us at the culverin," he would brag. "We two against an army, give us good cover, and powder and leaden balls enough. Hey! Master John and I must shoot a match yet, against English targets, and of them there are plenty under Orleans. But if I make not the better speed, the town will have fallen, or yielded, rescue or no rescue, and of rescue there is no hope at all. The devil fights for the English, who will soon be swarming over the Loire, and that King of Bourges of ours will have to flee, and gnaw horse's fodder, oats and barley, with your friends in Scotland."

This was one of the many ungenerous taunts which the French made often against us Scots, that have been their ancient and leal brethren in arms since the days of King Achaius and Charlemagne.

"The Dauphin," he went on, "for King he is none, and crowned he will never be, should be in Orleans, leading his men; and lo! he is tied to the belt of fat La Tremouille, and is dancing of ballets at Chinon—a murrain on him, and on them that make his music!" Then he fell to cursing his King, a thing terrible to hear, and so to asking me questions about myself. I told him that I had fled my own country for a man-slaying, hoping, may Heaven forgive me! to make him think the higher of me for the deed.

"So we all begin," said he; "a shrewd blow, or a fair wench; a death, or a birth unlawful, 'tis all one forth we are driven to the world and the wars. Yet you have started well,—well enough, and better than I gave your girl's face credit for. Bar steel and rope, you may carry some French gold back to stinking Scotland yet."

He gave me so much credit as this for a deed that deserved none, but rather called for rebuke from him, who, however unworthy, was in religion, and wore the garb of the Blessed Francis. But very far from fortifying me in virtuous courses, as was his bounden duty, there was no wickedness that he did not try to teach me, till partly I hated him, and partly, I fear, I admired one so skilled in evil. The truth is, as I said, that this man, for that time, was my master. He was learned

Andrew Lang

in all the arts by which poor and wandering folk can keep their bellies full wandering by the way. With women, ugly and terrible of aspect as he was, he had a great power: a pious saying for the old; a way with the young which has ever been a mystery to me, unless, as some of the learned think, all women are naturally lovers of wickedness, if strength and courage go with it. What by wheedling, what by bullying, what by tales of pilgrimages to holy shrines (he was coming from Jerusalem by way of Rome, so he told all we met), he ever won a welcome.

Other more devilish cantrips he played, one of them at the peasant's house where we rested on the first night of our common travel. The Lenten supper which they gave us, with no little kindness, was ended, and we were sitting in the firelight, Brother Thomas discoursing largely of his pilgrimages, and of his favour among the high clergy. Thus, at I know not what convent of the Clarisses, {5} in Italy, the holy Sisters had pressed on him a relic of Monsieur St. Aignan, the patron of the good town of Orleans. To see this relic, the farmer, his wife, and his sons and daughters crowded eagerly; it was but a little blackened finger bone, yet they were fain to touch it, as is the custom. But this he would not yet allow.

"Perchance some of you," he said, "are already corrupt, not knowing it, with the poisonous breath of that damnable Hussite heresy, which is blowing from the east like wind of the pestilence, and ye may have doubts concerning the verity of this most holy and miraculous relic?"

They all crossed themselves, protesting that no such wicked whisper of Sathanas had ever come into their minds, nor had they so much as heard of Huss and his blasphemies.

"Nay," said Brother Thomas, "I could scarcely blame you if

it were partly as I said. For in this latter time of the world, when I have myself met Jews flocking to Babylon expecting the birth of Antichrist, there be many false brethren, who carry about feigned relics, to deceive the simple. We should believe no man, if he be, as I am, a stranger, unless he shows us a sign, such as now I will show you. Give me, of your grace, a kerchief, or a napkin." The goodwife gave him a clean white napkin from her aumbry, and he tore it up before their eyes, she not daring to stay his hand.

"Now note this holy relic and its wonderful power," he said, holding the blackened bone high in his left hand, and all our eyes were fixed on it. "Now mark," he said again, passing it over the napkin; and lo! there was a clean white napkin in his hands, and of the torn shreds not a trace!

We were still gaping, and crossing ourselves with blessings on this happy day and our unworthy eyes that beheld a miracle, when he did a thing yet more marvellous, if that might be, which I scarce expect any man will believe. Going to the table, and catching up a glass vessel on which the goodwife set great store, he threw it against the wall, and we all plainly heard it shiver into tinkling pieces. Then, crossing the room into the corner, that was dusky enough, he faced us, again holding the blessed relic, whereon we stared, in holy fear. Then he rose, and in his hand was the goodwife's glass vessel, without crack or flaw! {6}

"Such," he said, "are the properties of this miraculous relic; there is nothing broken but it will mend, ay, a broken limb, as I can prove on my own sinful body,"—thrusting out his great brown leg, whereon, assuredly, were signs of a fracture; "ay, a broken leg, or, my dear daughters, a broken heart." At this, of course, they were all eager to touch the blessed relic with their poor rings of base metal, such as they wear who are not rich. Nay, but first, he said, they must give their mites for a convent of the Clarisses, that was building at Castres, by the care of the holy Colette, whom he might call his patroness, unworthy as he was.

Then he showed us a safe-conduct, signed with that blessed woman's own hand, such as she was wont to give to the religious of the Order of St. Francis. By virtue of this, he said (and, by miracle, for once he said truly, as I had but too good cause to learn), he could go freely in and out among the camps of French, English, and Burgundians.

You may conceive how joyous they were in that poor cottage, on a night so blessed, and how Brother Thomas told us of the holy Colette, that famous nun and Mother in Christ, as he that had often been in her company. He had seen her body lifted in the air while she remained in a pious ecstasy, her mind soaring aloft and her fleshly body following it some way.

He had often watched that snow-white beast which followed her, such a creature as is known in no country of the sinful world, but is a thing of Paradise. And he had tried to caress this wondrous creature of God, but vainly, for none but the holy sister Colette may handle it. Concerning her miracles of healing, too, he told us, all of which we already knew for very truth, and still know on better warranty than his.

Ye may believe that, late and at last, Brother Thomas had his choice of the warmest place to sleep in—by the "four," as is the wont of pilgrims, for in his humility this holy man would not suffer the farmer's wife and the farmer to give him their bed, as they desired. I, too, was very kindly entreated by the young lads, but I could scarcely sleep for marvelling at these miracles done by one so unworthy; and great, indeed, I deemed, must be the virtue of that relic which wrought such signs in the hands of an evil man. But I have since held that he feigned all by art magic and very sorcery, for, as we wended next morning on our road, he plainly told me, truly or falsely, that he had picked up the blackened finger-bone out of the loathly ashes of the dead in the burned castle near Ruffec.

Wherefore I consider that when Brother Thomas sold the grace of his relic, by the touching of rings, he dealt in a devilish black simony, vending to simple Christians no grace but that of his master, Sathanas. Thus he was not only evil (if I guess aright, which I submit to the judgment of my ecclesiastical superiors, and of the Church), but he had even found out a new kind of wickedness, such as I never read of in any books of theology wherein is much to be learned. I have spoken with some, however, knights and men of this world, who deemed that he did but beguile our eyes by craft and sleight-of-hand.

This other hellish art he had, by direct inspiration, as I hold, of his master Behemoth, that he could throw his voice whither he would, so that, in all seeming, it came from above, or from below, or from a corner of a room, fashioning it to resemble the voice of whom he would, yet none might see his lips move. With this craft he would affray the peasants about the fire in the little inns where we sometimes rested, when he would be telling tales of bogles and eldritch fantasies, and of fiends that rout and rap, and make the tables and firkins dance. Such art of speech, I am advised, is spoken of by St. Jerome, in his comment on the holy prophet the saint Isaiah, and they that use it he calls "ventriloqui," in the Latin, or "belly-speakers," and he takes an unfavourable sense of them and their doings. So much I have from the learned William de Boyis, Prior of Pluscarden, where now I write; with whom I have conversed of these matters privately, and he thinks this art a thing that men may learn by practice, without dealing in nigromancy and the black magic. This question I am content to leave, as is fitting, to the judgment of my superiors. And indeed, as at that time, Brother Thomas spake not in his belly except to make sport and affray the simple people, soon turning their fears to mirth. Certainly the country folk never misdoubted him, the women for a holy man, the men for a good fellow; though all they of his own cloth shrank from him, and I have seen them cross themselves in his presence, but to no avail. He would say a word or two in their ears, and they straightway left the place where he might be. None the less, with his tales and arts, Brother Thomas commonly so wrought that we seldom slept "a la belle etoile" in that bitter spring weather, but we ordinarily had leave to lie by the hearth, and got a supper and a breakfast. The good peasants would find their hen-roosts the poorer often, for all that he could snap up was to him fortune of war.

I loved these manners little, but leave him I could not. His eye was ever on me; if I stirred in the night he was awake and watching me, and by day he never let me out of a bolt's flight. To cut the string of his wicked weapon was a thought often in my mind, but he was too vigilant. My face was his passport, he said; my face, indeed, being innocent enough, as was no shame to me, but an endless cause of mirth and mockery to him. Yet, by reason of the serviceableness of the man in that perilous country, and my constant surprise and wonder at what he did and said, and might do next (which no man could guess beforehand), and a kind of foolish pride in his very wickedness, so much beyond what I had ever dreamed of, and for pure fear of him also, I found myself following with him day by day, ever thinking to escape, and never escaping.

I have since deemed that, just as his wickedness was to a boy (for I was little more), a kind of charm, made up of a sort of admiring hate and fear, so my guilelessness (as it seemed to him) also wrought on him strangely. For in part it made sport for him to see my open mouth and staring eyes at the spectacle of his devilries, and in part he really hated me, and hated my very virtue of simplicity, which it was his desire and delight to surprise and corrupt.

On these strange terms, then, now drawn each to other, and now forced apart, we wended by Poictiers towards Chinon, where the Dauphin and his Court then lay. So we fared northwards, through Poitou, where we found evil news enough. For, walking into a village, we saw men, women, and children, all gathered, gaping about one that stood beside a horse nearly foundered, its legs thrust wide, its nostrils all foam and blood. The man, who seemed as weary as his horse, held a paper in his hands, which the priest of that parish took from him and read aloud to us. The rider was a royal messenger, one Thomas Scott of Easter Buccleuch, in Rankel Burn, whom I knew later, and his tidings were evil. The Dauphin bade his good towns know that, on the 12th of February, Sir John Stewart, constable of the Scottish forces in France, had fallen in battle at Rouvray, with very many of his company, and some Frenchmen. They had beset a convoy under Sir John Fastolf, that was bringing meat to the English leaguered about Orleans. But Fastolf had wholly routed them (by treachery, as we later learned of the Comte de Clermont), and Sir John Stewart, with his brother Sir William, were slain. Wherefore the Dauphin bade the good towns send him money and men, or all was lost.

Such were the evil tidings, which put me in sore fear for my brother Robin, one that, in such an onfall, would go far, as beseemed his blood. But as touching his fortunes, Thomas Scott could tell me neither good nor bad, though he knew Robin, and gave him a good name for a stout man-at-arms. It was of some comfort to me to hear a Scots tongue; but, for the rest, I travelled on with a heavier heart, deeming that Orleans must indeed fall ere I could seek my brother in that town.

CHAPTER III

WHAT BEFELL OUTSIDE OF CHINON TOWN

My old nurse, when I was a child, used to tell me a long story of a prince who, wandering through the world, made friends with many strange companions. One she called Lynx-eye, that could see through a mountain; one was Swift-foot, that could outrun the wind; one was Fine-ear, that could hear the grass growing; and there was Greedy-gut, that could swallow a river. All these were very serviceable to this gracious prince, of I know not what country, in his adventures; and they were often brought into my mind by the companions whom we picked up on the grass-grown roads.

These wanderers were as strange as the friends of the prince, and were as variously, but scarce as honourably, gifted. There was the one-armed soldier, who showed his stump very piteously when it was a question of begging from a burgess, but was as well furnished with limbs as other men when no burgess was in sight. There was a wretched woman violer, with her jackanapes, and with her husband, a hang-dog ruffian, she bearing the mark of his fist on her eye, and commonly trailing far behind him with her brat on her back. There was a blind man, with his staff, who might well enough answer to Keen-eye, that is, when no strangers were in sight. There was a layman, wearing cope and stole and selling indulgences, but our captain, Brother Thomas, soon banished him from our company, for that he divided the trade. Others there were, each one of them a Greedy-gut, a crew of broken men, who marched with us on the roads; but we never entered a town or a house with these discreditable attendants.

Now, it may seem strange, but the nearer we drew to Chinon and the Court, the poorer grew the country, for the Court and the men-at-arms had stripped it bare, like a flight of locusts. For this reason the Dauphin could seldom abide long at one place, for he was so much better known than trusted that the very cordwainer would not let him march off in a new pair of boots without seeing his money, and, as the song said, he even greased his old clouted shoon, and made them last as long as he might. For head-gear he was as ill provided, seeing that he had pawned the fleurons of his crown. There were days when his treasurer at Tours (as I myself have heard him say) did not reckon three ducats in his coffers, and the heir of France borrowed money from his very cook. So the people told us, and I have often marvelled how, despite this poverty, kings and nobles, when I have seen them, go always in cloth of gold, with rich jewels. But, as you may guess, near the Court of a beggar Dauphin the country-folk too were sour and beggarly.

We had to tighten our belts before we came to the wood wherein cross-roads meet, from north, south, and east, within five miles of the town of Chinon. There was not a white coin among us; night was falling, and it seemed as if we must lie out under the stars, and be fed, like the wolves we heard howling, on wind. By the roadside, at the crossways, but not in view of the road, a council of our ragged regiment was held in a deep ditch. It would be late ere we reached the town, gates would scarce open for us, we could not fee the warders, houses would be shut and dark; the King's archers were apt to bear them unfriendly to wandering men with the devil dancing in their pouches. Resource we saw none; if there was a cottage, dogs, like wolves for hunger and fierceness, were baying round it. As for Brother Thomas, an evil bruit had gone before us concerning a cordelier that the fowls and geese were fain to follow, as wilder things, they say, follow the blessed St. Francis. So there sat Brother Thomas at the cross-roads, footsore, hungry, and sullen, in the midst of us, who dared not speak, he twanging at the string of his arbalest. He called himself our Moses, in his blasphemous way, and the blind man having girded at him for not leading us into the land of plenty, he had struck the man till he bled, and now stood stanching his wound.

Suddenly Brother Thomas ceased from his twanging, and holding up his hand for silence, leaned his ear to the ground. The night was still, though a cold wind came very stealthily from the east.

"Horses!" he said.

"It is but the noise of the brook by the way," said the blind man, sullenly.

Brother Thomas listened again.

"No, it is horses," he whispered. "My men, they that ride horses can spare somewhat out of their abundance to feed the poor." And with that he began winding up his arbalest hastily. "Aymeric," he said to one of our afflicted company, "you draw a good bow for a blind man; hide yourself in the opposite ditch, and be ready when I give the word 'Pax vobiscum.' You, Giles," he spoke to the one-armed soldier, "go with him, and, do you hear, aim low, at the third man's horse. From the sound there are not more than five or six of them. We can but fail, at worst, and the wood is thick behind us, where none may pursue. You, Norman de Pitcullo, have your whinger ready, and fasten this rope tightly to yonder birch-tree stem, and then cross and give it a turn or two about that oak sapling on the other side of the way. That trap will bring down a horse or twain. Be quick, you Scotch wine-bag!"

I had seen many ill things done, and, to my shame, had held my peace. But a Leslie of Pitcullo does not take purses on the high-road. Therefore my heart rose in sudden anger, I having all day hated him more and more for his bitter tongue, and I was opening my mouth to cry "A secours!"—a warning to them who were approaching, when, quick as lightning, Brother Thomas caught me behind the knee-joints, and I was on the ground with his weight above me. One cry I had uttered, when his hand was on my mouth.

"Give him the steel in his guts!" whispered the blind man.

"Slit his weasand, the Scotch pig!" said the one-armed soldier.

They were all on me now.

"No, I keep him for better sport," snarled Brother Thomas. "He shall learn the Scots for 'ecorcheurs' (flayers of men) "when we have filled our pouches."

With that he crammed a great napkin in my mouth, so that I could not cry, made it fast with a piece of cord, trussed me with the rope which he had bidden me tie across the path to trip the horses, and with a kick sent me flying to the bottom of the ditch, my face being turned from the road.

I could hear Giles and Aymeric steal across the way, and the rustling of boughs as they settled on the opposite side. I could hear the trampling hoofs of horses coming slowly and wearily from the east. At this moment chanced a thing that has ever seemed strange to me: I felt the hand of the violer woman laid lightly and kindly on my hair. I had ever pitied her, and, as I might, had been kind to her and her bairn; and now, as it appears, she pitied me. But there could be no help in her, nor did she dare to raise her voice and give an alarm. So I could but gnaw at my gag, trying to find scope for my tongue to cry, for now it was not only the travellers that I would save, but my own life, and my escape from a death of torment lay on my success. But my mouth was as dry as a kiln, my tongue was doubled back till I thought that I should have choked. The night was now deadly still, and the ring of the weary hoofs drew nearer and nearer. I heard a stumble, and the scramble of a tired horse as he recovered himself; for the rest, all was silent, though the beating of my own heart sounded heavy and husky in my ears.

Closer and closer the travellers drew, and soon it was plain that they rode not carelessly, nor as men who deemed themselves secure, for the tramp of one horse singled itself out in front of the others, and this, doubtless, was ridden by an "eclaireur," sent forward to see that the way ahead was safe. Now I heard a low growl of a curse from Brother Thomas, and my heart took some comfort. They might be warned, if the Brother shot at the foremost man; or, at worst, if he was permitted to pass, the man would bear swift tidings to Chinon, and we might be avenged, the travellers and I, for I now felt that they and I were in the same peril.

The single rider drew near, and passed, and there came no cry of "Pax vobiscum" from the friar. But the foremost rider had, perchance, the best horse, and the least wearied, for there was even too great a gap between him and the rest of his company.

And now their voices might be heard, as they talked by the way, yet not so loud that, straining my ears as I did, I could hear any words. But the sounds waxed louder, with words spoken, ring of hoofs, and rattle of scabbard on stirrup, and so I knew, at least, that they who rode so late were men armed. Brother Thomas, too, knew it, and cursed again very low.

Nearer, nearer they came, then almost opposite, and now, as I listened to hear the traitorous signal of murder—"Pax vobiscum"—and the twang of bow-strings, on the night there rang a voice, a woman's voice, soft but wondrous clear, such as never I knew from any lips but hers who then spoke; that voice I heard in its last word, "Jesus!" and still it is sounding in my ears.

That voice said—

"Nous voila presqu'arrives, grace a mes Freres de Paradis."

Instantly, I knew not how, at the sound of that blessed voice, and the courage in it, I felt my fear slip from me, as when we awaken from a dreadful dream, and in its place came happiness and peace. Scarce otherwise might he feel who dies in fear and wakes in Paradise.

On the forest boughs above me, my face being turned from the road, somewhat passed, or seemed to pass, like a soft golden light, such as in the Scots tongue we call a "boyn," that ofttimes, men say, travels with the blessed saints. Yet some may deem it but a glancing in my own eyes, from the blood flying to my head; howsoever it be, I had never seen the like before, nor have I seen it since, and, assuredly, the black branches and wild weeds were lit up bare and clear.

The tramp of the horses passed, there was no cry of "Pax

Andrew Lang

vobiscum," no twang of bows, and slowly the ring of hoofs died away on the road to Chinon. Then came a rustling of the boughs on the further side of the way, and a noise of footsteps stealthily crossing the road, and now I heard a low sound of weeping from the violer woman, that was crouching hard by where I lay. Her man struck her across the mouth, and she was still.

"You saw it? Saints be with us! You saw them?" he whispered to Brother Thomas.

"Fool, had I not seen, would I not have given the word? Get you gone, all the sort of you, there is a fey man in this company, be he who he will. Wander your own ways, and if ever one of you dogs speak to me again, in field, or street, or market, or ever mention this night . . . ye shall have my news of it. Begone! Off!"

"Nay, but, Brother Thomas, saw'st thou what we saw? What sight saw'st thou?"

"What saw I? Fools, what should I have seen, but an outrider, and he a King's messenger, sent forward to warn the rest by his fall, if he fell, or to raise the country on us, if he passed, and if afterward they passed us not. They were men wary in war, and travelling on the Dauphin's business. Verily there was no profit in them."

"And that was all? We saw other things."

"What I saw was enough for me, or for any good clerk of St. Nicholas, and of questions there has been more than enough. Begone! scatter to the winds, and be silent."

"And may we not put the steel in that Scotch dog who delayed us? Saints or sorcerers, their horses must have come down but for him."

Brother Thomas caught me up, as if I had been a child, in his arms, and tossed me over the ditch-bank into the wood, where I crashed on my face through the boughs.

"Only one horse would have fallen, and that had brought the others on us. The Scot is safe enough, his mouth is well shut. I will have no blood to-night; leave him to the wolves. And now, begone with you: to Fierbois, if you will; I go my own road—alone."

They wandered each his own way, sullen and murmuring, starved and weary. What they had seen or fancied, and whether, if the rest saw aught strange, Brother Thomas saw nought, I knew not then, and know not till this hour. But the tale of this ambush, and of how they that lay in hiding held their hands, and fled—having come, none might say whence, and gone, whither none might tell—is true, and was soon widely spoken of in the realm of France.

The woods fell still again, save for the babble of the brook, and there I lay, bound, and heard only the stream in the silence of the night.

There I lay, quaking, when all the caitiffs had departed, and the black, chill night received me into itself. At first my mind was benumbed, like my body; but the pain of my face, smarting with switch and scratch of the boughs through which I had fallen, awoke me to thought and fear. I turned over to lie on my back, and look up for any light of hope in the sky, but nothing fell on me from heaven save a cold rain, that the leafless boughs did little to ward off. Scant hope or comfort had I; my whole body ached and shuddered, only I did not thirst, for the rain soaked through the accursed napkin on my mouth, while the dank earth, with its graveyard smell, seemed to draw me down into itself, as it drags a rotting leaf. I was buried before death, as it were, even if the wolves found me not and gave me other sepulture; and now and again I heard their long hunting cry, and at every patter of a beast's foot, or shivering of the branches, I thought my hour was come—and I unconfessed! The road was still as death, no man passing by it. This night to me was like the night of a man laid living in the tomb. By no twisting and turning could I loosen the rope that Brother Thomas had bound me in, with a hand well taught by cruel practice. At last the rain in my face grew like a water-torture, always dropping, and I half turned my face and pressed it to the ground.

Whether I slept by whiles, or waked all night, I know not, but certainly I dreamed, seeing with shut eyes faces that came and went, shifting from beauty such as I had never yet beheld, to visages more and more hideous and sinful, ending at last in the worst—the fell countenance of Noiroufle. Then I woke wholly to myself, in terror, to find that he was not there, and now came to me some of that ease which had been born of the strange, sweet voice, and the strange words, "Mes Freres de Paradis."

"My brethren of Paradise"; who could she be that rode so late in company of armed men, and yet spoke of such great kinsfolk? That it might be the holy Colette, then, as now, so famous in France for her miracles, and good deeds, and her austerities, was a thought that arose in me. But the holy Sister, as I had heard, never mounted a horse in her many wanderings, she being a villein's daughter, but was carried in a litter, or fared in a chariot; nor did she go in company with armed men, for who would dare to lay hands on her? Moreover, the voice that I had heard was that of a very young girl, and the holy Sister Colette was now entered into the vale of years. So my questioning found no answer.

And now I heard light feet, as of some beast stirring and scratching in the trees overhead, and there with a light jingling noise. Was it a squirrel? Whatever it was, it raced about the tree, coming nearer and going further away, till it fell with a weight on my breast, and, shivering with cold, all strained like a harp-string as I was, I could have screamed, but for the gag in my mouth. The thing crawled up my body, and I saw two red eyes fixed on mine, and deemed it had been a wild cat, such as lives in our corries of the north—a fell beast if brought to bay, but otherwise not hurtful to man.

There the red eyes looked on me, and I on them, till I grew giddy with gazing, and half turned my head with a stifled sob. Then there came a sharp cry which I knew well enough, and the beast leaped up and nestled under my breast, for this so dreadful thing was no worse than the violer woman's jackanapes, that had slipped its chain, or, rather, had drawn it out of her hand, for now I plainly heard the light chain jingle. This put me on wondering whether they had really departed; the man, verily, thirsted for my life, but he would have slain me ere this hour, I thought, if that had been his purpose. The poor beast a little helped to warm me with the heat of his body, and he was a friendly creature, making me feel less alone in the night. Yet, in my own misery, I could not help but sorrow for the poor woman when she found her jackanapes gone, that was great part of her living: and I knew what she would have to bear for its loss from the man that was her master.

As this was in my mind, the first grey stole into the sky so that I could see the black branches overhead; and now there awoke the cries of birds, and soon the wood was full of their sweet jargoning. This put some hope into my heart; but the morning hours were long, and colder than the night, to one wet to the bone with the rains. Now, too, I comforted myself with believing that, arrive what might, I was wholly quit of

Brother Thomas, whereat I rejoiced, like the man in the tale who had sold his soul to the Enemy, and yet, in the end, escaped his clutches by the aid of Holy Church. Death was better to me than life with Brother Thomas, who must assuredly have dragged me with him to the death that cannot die. Morning must bring travellers, and my groaning might lead them to my aid. And, indeed, foot-farers did come, and I did groan as well as I could, but, like the Levite in Scripture, they passed by on the other side of the way, fearing to meddle with one wounded perchance to the death, lest they might be charged with his slaying, if he died, or might anger his enemies, if he lived.

The light was now fully come, and some rays of the blessed sun fell upon me, whereon I said orisons within myself, commanding my case to the saints. Devoutly I prayed, that, if I escaped with life, I might be delivered from the fear of man, and namely of Brother Thomas. It were better for me to have died by his weapon at first, beside the broken bridge, than to have lived his slave, going in dread of him, with a slave's hatred in my heart. So now I prayed for spirit enough to defend my honour and that of my country, which I had borne to hear reviled without striking a blow for it. Never again might I dree this extreme shame and dishonour. On this head I addressed myself, as was fitting, to the holy Apostle St. Andrew, our patron, to whom is especially dear the honour of Scotland.

Then, as if he and the other saints had listened to me, I heard sounds of horses' hoofs, coming up the road from Chinon way, and also voices. These, like the others of the night before, came nearer, and I heard a woman's voice gaily singing. And then awoke such joy in my heart as never was there before, and this was far the gladdest voice that ever yet I heard, for, behold, it was the speech of my own country, and the tune I knew and the words.

"O, we maun part this love, Willie,
That has been lang between;
There's a French lord coming over sea
To wed me wi' a ring;
There's a French lord coming o'er the sea
To wed and take me hame!"

"And who shall the French lord be, Elliot?" came another voice, a man's this time, "though he need not cross the sea for you, the worse the luck. Is it young Pothon de Xaintrailles? Faith, he comes often enough to see how his new penoncel fares in my hands, and seems right curious in painting."

It may be deemed strange that, even in this hour, I conceived in my heart a great mislike of this young French lord, how unjustly I soon well understood.

"O, nae French lord for me, father,
O, nae French lord for me,
But I'll ware my heart on a true-born Scot,
And wi' him I'll cross the sea."

"Oh, father, lo you, I can make as well as sing, for that is no word of the old ballant, but just came on to my tongue!"

They were now right close to me, and, half in fear, half in hope, I began to stir and rustle in the grass, for of my stifled groaning had hitherto come no profit. Then I heard the horses stop.

"What stirring is that in the wood, father? I am afraid," came the girl's voice.

"Belike a fox shifting his lair. Push on, Maid Elliot." The horses advanced, when, by the blessing of the saints, the jackanapes woke in my breast.

The creature was used to run questing with a little wooden bowl he carried for largesse, to beg of horsemen for his mistress. This trick of his he did now, hearing the horses' tramp. He leaped the ditch, and I suppose he ran in front of the steeds, shaking his little bowl, as was his wont.

"Oh, father," sounded the girl's voice, "see the little jackanapes! Some travelling body has lost him. Let me jump down and catch him. Look, he has a little coat on, made like a herald's tabard, and wears the colours of France. Here, hold my reins."

"No, lass. Who can tell where, or who, his owner is? Take you my reins, and I will bring you the beast."

I heard him heavily dismount.

"It will not let itself be caught by a lame man," he said; and he scrambled up the ditch bank, while the jackanapes fled to me, and then ran forward again, back and forth.

"Nom Dieu, whom have we here?" cried the man, in French.

I turned, and made such a sound with my mouth as I might, while the jackanapes nestled to my breast.

"Why do ye not speak, man?" he said again; and I turned my eyes on him, looking as pitifully as might be out of my blood-bedabbled face.

He was a burly man, great of growth, with fresh red cheeks, blue eyes, reddish hair, and a red beard, such as are many in the Border marches of my own country, the saints bless them for true men! Withal he dragged his leg in walking, which he did with difficulty and much carefulness. He "hirpled," as we say, towards me very warily; then, seeing the rope bound about me, and the cloth in my mouth, he drew his dagger, but not to cut my bonds. He was over canny for that, but he slit the string that kept the cursed gag in my mouth, and picked it out with his dagger point; and, oh the blessed taste of that first long draught of air, I cannot set it down in words! "What, in the name of all the saints, make you here, in this guise?" he asked in French, but with a rude Border accent.

"I am a kindly Scot," I said in our own tongue, "of your own country. Give me water." And then a dwawm, as we call it, or fainting-fit, came over me.

When I knew myself again, I was lying with my head in a maiden's lap, and well I could have believed that the fairies had carried me to their own land, as has befallen many, whereof some have returned to earth with the tale, and some go yet in that unearthly company.

"Gentle demoiselle, are you the gracious Queen of Faerie?" I asked, as one half-wakened, not knowing what I said. Indeed this lady was clad all in the fairy green, and her eyes were as blue as the sky above her head, and the long yellow locks on her shoulders were shining like the sun.

"Father, he is not dead," she said, laughing as sweet as all the singing-birds in March—"he is not dead, but sorely wandering in his mind when he takes Elliot Hume for the Fairy Queen."

"Faith, he might have made a worse guess," cried the man. "But now, sir, now that your bonds are cut, I see nothing better for you than a well-washed face, for, indeed, you are by ordinary 'kenspeckle,' and no company for maids."

With that he brought some water from the burn by the road, and therewith he wiped my face, first giving me to drink. When I had drunk, the maid whom he called Elliot got up, her face very rosy, and they set my back against a tree, which I was right sorry for, as indeed I was now clean out of fairyland and back in this troublesome world. The horses stood by us, tethered to trees, and browsed on the budding branches.

"And now, maybe," he said, speaking in the kindly Scots, that was like music in my ear—"now, maybe, you will tell us who you are, and how you came into this jeopardy."

I told him, shortly, that I was a Scot of Fife; whereto he answered that my speech was strangely English. On this matter I satisfied him with the truth, namely, that my mother was of England. I gave my name but not that of our lands, and showed him how I had been wandering north, to take service with the Dauphin, when I was set upon, and robbed and bound by thieves, for I had no clearness as to telling him all my tale, and no desire to claim acquaintance with Brother Thomas.

"And the jackanapes?" he asked, whereto I had no better answer than that I had seen the beast with a wandering violer on the day before, and that she having lost it, as I supposed, it had come to me in the night.

The girl was standing with the creature in her arms, feeding it with pieces of comfits from a pouch fastened at her girdle.

"The little beast is not mine to give," I went on, seeing how she had an affection to the ape, "but till the owner claims it, it is all the ransom I have to pay for my life, and I would fain see it wear the colours of this gentle maid who saved me. It has many pretty tricks, but though to-day I be a beggar, I trow she will not let it practise that ill trick of begging."

"Sooner would I beg myself, fair sir," she said, with such a courtly reverence as surprised me; for though they seemed folks well to see in the world, they were not, methought, of noble blood, nor had they with them any company of palfreniers or archers.

"Elliot, you feed the jackanapes and let our countryman hunger," said the man; and, blushing again, she made haste to give me some of the provision she had made for her journey.

So I ate and drank, she waiting on me very gently; but now, being weary of painful writing, and hearing the call to the refectory, and the brethren trampling thither, I must break off, for, if I be late, they will sconce me of my ale. Alas! it is to these little cares of creature comforts that I am come, who have seen the face of so many a war, and lived and fought on rat's flesh at Compiegne.

CHAPTER IV

IN WHAT COMPANY NORMAN LESLIE ENTERED CHINON; AND HOW HE DEMEANED HIMSELF TO TAKE SERVICE

Not seemly, was it, that I should expect these kind people, even though they were of my own country, to do more for me than they had already done. So, when I had eaten and drunk, I made my obeisance as if I would be trudging towards Chinon, adding many thanks, as well I might.

"Nay, countryman," said the man, "for all that I can see, you may as well bide a while with us; for, indeed, with leave of my graceless maid, I think we may even end our wild-goose chase here and get us back to the town."

Seeing me marvel, perhaps, that any should have ridden some four miles or five, and yet speak of returning, he looked at the girl, who was playing with the jackanapes, and who smiled at him as he spoke. "You must know," said he, "that though I am the father of your Fairy Queen, I am also one of the gracious Princess's obedient subjects. No mother has she, poor wench," he added, in a lower voice; "and faith, we men must always obey some woman—as it seems now that the King himself must soon do and all his captains."

"You speak," I said, "of the gracious Queen of Sicily and Jerusalem?"—a lady who was thought to be of much avail, as was but right, in the counsels of her son-in-law, the Dauphin, he having married her gentle daughter.

"Ay; Queen Yolande is far ben {7} with the King—would he had no worse counsellors!" said he, smiling; "but I speak of a far more potent sovereign, if all that she tells of herself be true. You have heard, or belike you have not heard, of the famed Pucelle—so she calls herself, I hope not without a warranty—the Lorrainer peasant lass, who is to drive the English into the sea, so she gives us all fair warning?"

"Never a word have I heard, or never marked so senseless a bruit if I heard it; she must be some moon-struck wench, and in her wits wandering."

"Moon-struck, or sun-struck, or saint-struck, she will strike down our ancient enemy of England, and show you men how it is not wine and wickedness that make good soldiers!" cried the girl whom he called Elliot, her face rose-red with anger; and from her eyes two blue rays of light shot straight to mine, so that I believe my face waxed wan, the blood flying to my heart.

"Listen to her! look at her!" said her father, jestingly. "Elliot, if your renowned maid can fright the English as you have affrayed a good Scot, the battle is won and Orleans is delivered."

But she had turned her back on us pettishly, and was talking in a low voice to her jackanapes. As for me, if my face had been pale before, it now grew red enough for shame that I had angered her, who was so fair, though how I had sinned I knew not. But often I have seen that women, and these the best, will be all afire at a light word, wherein the touchiest man-at-arms who ever fought on the turn of a straw could pick no honourable quarrel.

"How have I been so unhappy as to offend mademoiselle?" I asked, in a whisper, of her father, giving her a high title, in very confusion.

"Oh, she will hear no bourde nor jest on this Pucelle that all the countryside is clashing of, and that is bewitching my maid, methinks, even from afar. My maid Elliot (so I call her from my mother's kin, but her true name is Marion, and the French dub her Heliote) hath set all her heart and her hope on one that is a young lass like herself, and she is full of old soothsayings about a virgin that is to come out of an oak-wood and deliver France—no less! For me, I misdoubt that Merlin, the Welsh prophet on whom they set store, and the rest of the soothsayers, are all in one tale with old Thomas Rhymer, of Ercildoune, whose prophecies our own folk crack about by the ingle on winter nights at home. But be it as it may, this wench of Lorraine has, these three-quarters of a year, been about the Sieur Robert de Baudricourt, now commanding for the King at Vaucouleurs, away in the east, praying him to send her to the Court. She has visions, and hears voices—so she says; and she gives Baudricourt no peace till he carries her to the King. The story goes that, on the ill day of the Battle of the Herrings, she, being at Vaucouleurs—a hundred leagues away and more,—saw that fight plainly, and our countrymen fallen, manlike, around the Constable, and the French flying like hares before a little pack of English talbots. When the evil news came, and was approved true, Baudricourt could hold her in no longer, and now she is on the way with half a dozen esquires and archers of his command. The second-sight she may have—it is common enough, if you believe the red-shanked Highlanders; but if maiden she set forth from Vaucouleurs, great miracle it is if maiden she comes to Chinon." He whispered this in a manner that we call "pauky," being a free man with his tongue.

"This is a strange tale enough," I said; "the saints grant that the Maid speaks truly!"

"But yesterday came a letter of her sending to the King," he went on, "but never of her writing, for they say that she knows not 'A' from 'B,' if she meets them in her voyaging. Now, nothing would serve my wilful daughter Elliot (she being possessed, as I said, with love for this female mystery), but that we must ride forth and be the first to meet the Maid on her way, and offer her shelter at my poor house, if she does but seem honest, though methinks a hostelry is good enough for one that has ridden so far, with men for all her company. And I, being but a subject of my daughter's, as I said, and this a Saint's Day, when a man may rest from his paints and brushes, I even let saddle the steeds, and came forth to see what ferlies Heaven would send us."

"Oh, a lucky day for me, fair sir," I answered him, marvelling to hear him speak of paint and brushes, and even as I spoke a thought came into my mind. "If you will listen to me, sir," I said, "and if the gentle maid, your daughter, will pardon me for staying you so long from the road, I will tell you that, to my thinking, you have come over late, for that yesterday the Maiden you speak of rode, after nightfall, into Chinon."

Now the girl turned round on me, and, in faith, I asked no more than to see her face, kind or angry. "You tell us, sir, that you never heard speak of the Maid till this hour, and now you say that you know of her comings and goings. Unriddle your riddle, sir, if it pleases you, and say how you saw and knew one that you never heard speech of."

She was still very wroth, and I knew not whether I might not anger her yet more, so I louted lowly, cap in hand, and said—

"It is but a guess that comes into my mind, and I pray you be not angry with me, who am ready and willing to believe in this Maid, or in any that will help France, for, if I be not wrong, last night her coming saved my life, and that of her own company."

"How may that be, if thieves robbed and bound you?"

"I told you not all my tale," I said, "for, indeed, few would have believed the thing that had not seen it. But, upon my faith as a gentleman, and by the arm-bone of the holy Apostle Andrew, which these sinful eyes have seen, in the church of the Apostle in his own town, somewhat holy passed this way last night; and if this Maid be indeed sent from heaven, that holy thing was she, and none other."

"Nom Dieu! saints are not common wayfarers on our roads at night. There is no 'wale' of saints in this country," said the father of Elliot; "and as this Pucelle of Lorraine must needs pass by us here, if she is still on the way, even tell us all your tale."

With that I told them how the "brigands" (for so they now began to call such reivers as Brother Thomas) were, to my shame, and maugre my head, for a time of my own company. And I told them of the bushment that they laid to trap travellers, and how I had striven to give a warning, and how they bound me and gagged me, and of the strange girl's voice that spoke through the night of "mes Freres de Paradis," and of that golden "boyn" faring in the dark, that I thought I saw, and of the words spoken by the blind man and the soldier, concerning some vision which affrayed them, I know not what.

At this tale the girl Elliot, crossing herself very devoutly, cried aloud—

"O father, did I not tell you so? This holy thing can have been no other but that blessed Maiden, guarded by the dear saints in form visible, whom this gentleman, for the sin of keeping evil company, was not given the grace to see. Oh, come, let us mount and ride to Chinon, for already she is within the walls; had we not ridden forth so early, we must have heard tell of it."

It seemed something hard to me that I was to have no grace to behold what others, and they assuredly much more sinful men than myself, had been permitted to look upon, if this damsel was right in that she said. And how could any man, were he himself a saint, see what was passing by, when his head was turned the other way? Howbeit, she called me a gentleman, as indeed I had professed myself to be, and this I saw, that her passion of anger against me was spent, as then, and gone by, like a shower of April.

"Gentleman you call yourself, sir," said her father; "may I ask of what house?"

"We are cadets of the house of Rothes," I answered. "My father, Leslie of Pitcullo, is the fourth son of the third son of the last laird of Rothes but one; and, for me, I was of late a clerk studying in St. Andrews."

"I will not ask why you left your lore," he said; "I have been young myself, and, faith, the story of one lad varies not much from the story of another. If we have any spirit, it drives us out to fight the foreign loons in their own country, if we have no feud at home. But you are a clerk, I hear you say, and have skill enough to read and write?"

"Yea, and, if need were, can paint, in my degree, and do fair lettering on holy books, for this art was my pleasure, and I learned it from a worthy monk in the abbey."

"O day of miracles!" he cried. "Listen, Elliot, and mark how finely I have fallen in luck's way! Lo you, sir, I also am a gentleman in my degree, simple as you see me, being one of the Humes of Polwarth; but by reason of my maimed leg, that came to me with scars many, from certain shrewd blows got at Verneuil fight, I am disabled from war. A murrain on the English bill that dealt the stroke! To make up my ransom (for I was taken prisoner there, where so few got quarter) cost me every crown I could gather, so I even fell back on the skill I learned, like you, when I was a lad, from a priest in the Abbey of Melrose. Ashamed of my craft I am none, for it is better to paint banners and missals than to beg; and now, for these five years, I am advanced to be Court painter to the King himself, thanks to John Kirkmichael, Bishop of Orleans, who is of my far-away kin. A sore fall it is, for a Hume of Polwarth; and strangely enough do the French scribes write my name—'Hauves Poulvoir,' and otherwise, so please you; but that is ever their wont with the best names in all broad Scotland. Lo you, even now there is much ado with banner-painting for the companies that march to help Orleans, ever and again."

"When the Maiden marches, father, you shall have banner-painting," said the girl.

"Ay, lass, when the Maid marches, and when the lift falls and smoors the laverocks we shall catch them in plenty. {8} But, Maid or no Maid, saving your presence, sir, I need what we craftsmen (I pray you again to pardon me) call an apprentice, and I offer you, if you are skilled as you say, this honourable post, till you find a better."

My face grew red again with anger at the word "apprentice," and I know not how I should have answered an offer so unworthy of my blood, when the girl broke in—

"Till this gentleman marches with the flower of France against our old enemy of England, you should say, father, and helps to show them another Bannockburn on Loire-side."

"Ay, well, till then, if it likes you," he said, smiling. "Till then there is bed, and meat, and the penny fee for him, till that great day."

"That is coming soon!" she cried, her eyes raised to heaven, and so fair she looked, that, being a young man and of my complexion amorous, I could not bear to be out of her company when I might be in it, so stooped my pride to agree with him.

"Sir," I said, "I thank you heartily for your offer. You come of as good a house as mine, and yours is the brag of the Border, as mine is of the kingdom of Fife. If you can put your pride in your pouch, faith, so can I; the rather that there is nothing else therein, and so room enough and to spare. But, as touching what this gentle demoiselle has said, I may march also, may I not, when the Maid rides to Orleans?"

"Ay, verify, with my goodwill, then you may," he cried, laughing, while the lass frowned.

Then we clapped hands on it, for a bargain, and he did not insult me by the offer of any arles, or luck penny.

The girl was helped to horse, setting her foot on my hand, that dirled as her little shoe sole touched it; and the jackanapes rode on her saddle-bow very proudly. For me, I ran as well as I might, but stiffly enough, being cold to the

Andrew Lang

marrow, holding by the father's stirrup-leather and watching the lass's yellow hair that danced on her shoulders as she rode foremost. In this company, then, so much better than that I had left, we entered Chinon town, and came to their booth, and their house on the water-side. Then, of their kindness, I must to bed, which comfort I sorely needed, and there I slept, in fragrant linen sheets, till compline rang.

CHAPTER V

OF THE FRAY ON THE DRAWBRIDGE
AT CHINON CASTLE

During supper, to which they called me, my master showed me the best countenance that might be, and it was great joy to me to eat off clean platters once again, on white linen strewn with spring flowers. As the time was Lent, we had fare that they called meagre: fish from the Vienne water, below the town, and eggs cooked in divers fashions, all to the point of excellence, for the wine and fare of Chinon are famous in France. As my duty was, I waited on my master and on the maid Elliot, who was never silent, but babbled of all that she had heard since she came into the town; as to where the Pucelle had lighted off her horse (on the edge-stone of a well, so it seemed), and where and with what goodwife she lodged, and how as yet no message had come to her from the castle and the King; and great joy it was to watch and to hear her. But her father mocked, though in a loving manner; and once she wept at his bourdes, and shone out again, when he fell on his knees, offering her a knife and baring his breast to the stroke, for I have never seen more love between father and child, my own experience being contrary. Yet to my sisters my father was ever debonnair; for, as I have often marked, the mothers love the sons best and the sons the mothers, and between father and daughters it is the same. But of my mother I have spoken in the beginning of this history.

When supper was ended, and all things made orderly, I had no great mind for my bed, having slept my fill for that time. But the maid Elliot left us early, which was as if the light had been taken out of the room.

Beside the fire, my master fell to devising about the state of the country, as burgesses love to do. And I said that, if I were the Dauphin, Chinon Castle should not hold me long, for my "spur would be in my horse's side, and the bridle on his mane," {9} as the old song of the Battle of Harlaw runs, and I on the way to Orleans. Thereto he answered, that he well wished it were so, and, mocking, wished that I were the Dauphin.

"Not that our Dauphin is a coward, the blood of Saint Louis has not fallen so low, but he is wholly under the Sieur de La Tremouille, who was thrust on him while he was young, and still is his master, or, as we say, his governor. Now, this lord is one that would fain run with the hare and hunt with the hounds, and this side of him is Burgundian and that is Armagnac, and on which of the sides his heart is, none knows. At Azincour, as I have heard, he played the man reasonably well. But he waxes very fat for a man-at-arms, and is fond of women, and wine, and of his ease. Now, if once the King ranges up with the Bastard of Orleans, and Xaintrailles, and the other captains, who hate La Tremouille, then his power, and the power of the Chancellor, the Archbishop of Rheims, is gone and ended. So these two work ever to patch up a peace with Burgundy, but, seeing that the duke has his father's death to avenge on our King, they may patch and better patch, but no peace will come of it. And the captains cry 'Forward!' and the archbishop and La Tremouille cry 'Back!' and in the meantime Orleans will fall, and the Dauphin may fly whither he will, for France is lost. But, for myself, I would to the saints that I and my lass were home again, beneath the old thorn-tree at Polwarth on the green, where I have been merry lang syne."

With that word he fell silent, thinking, I doubt not, of his home, as I did of mine, and of the house of Pitcullo and the ash-tree at the door, and the sea beyond the ploughed land of the plain. So, after some space of silence, he went to his bed, and I to mine, where for long I lay wakeful, painting on the dark the face of Elliot, and her blue eyes, and remembering her merry, changeful ways.

Betimes in the morning I was awakened by the sound of her moving about through the house, and having dressed and gone forth from my little chamber, I found her in the house-place, she having come from early Mass. She took little heed of me, giving me some bread and wine, the same as she and her father took; and she was altogether less gay and wilful than she had been, and there seemed to be something that lay heavy on her mind. When her father asked her if the gossips at the church door had given her any more tidings of the Maid, she did but frown, and soon left the chamber, whence my master led me forth into his booth, and bade me show him my hand in writing. This pleased him not ill, and next I must grind colours to his liking; and again he went about his business, while I must mind the booth, and be cap in hand to every saucy page that came from the castle with an order from his lord.

Full many a time my hand was on my whinger, and yet more often I wished myself on the free road again, so that I were out of ill company, and assuredly the Lorrainer Maid, whatever she might be, was scarcely longing more than I for the day when she should unfurl her banner and march, with me at her back, to Orleans. For so irksome was my servitude, and the laying of colours on the ground of banners for my master to paint, and the copying of books of Hours and Missals, and the insolence of customers worse born than myself, that I could have drowned myself in the Vienne water but for the sight of Elliot. Yet she was become staid enough, and betimes sad; as it seemed that there was no good news of her dear Maid, for the King would not see her, and all men (it appeared), save those who had ridden with her, mocked the Pucelle for a bold ramp, with a bee in her bonnet. But the two gentlemen that had been her escort were staunch. Their names were Jean de Metz and Bertrand de Poulengy, good esquires.

Of me Elliot made ofttimes not much more account than of her jackanapes, which was now in very high favour, and waxing fat, so that, when none but her father could hear her, she would jest and call him La Tremouille.

Yet I, as young men will, was forward in all ways to serve her, and to win her grace and favour. She was fain to hear of Scotland, her own country, which she had never seen, and I was as fain to tell her. And betimes I would say how fair were the maidens of our own country, and how any man that saw her would know her to be a Scot, though from her tongue, in French, none might guess it. And, knowing that she loved wildflowers, I would search for them and bring them to her, and would lead her to speak of romances which she loved, no less than I, and of pages who had loved queens, and all such matters as young men and maids are wont to devise of; and now she would listen, and at other seasons would seem proud, and as if her mind were otherwhere. Young knights many came to our booth, and looked ill-pleased when I served them, and their eyes were ever on the inner door, watching for Elliot, whom they seldom had sight of.

So here was I, in a double service, who, before I met Brother

Thomas, had been free of heart and hand. But, if my master's service irked me, in that other I found comfort, when I could devise with Elliot, as concerning our country and her hopes for the Maid. But my own hopes were not high, nor could I mark any sign that she favoured me more than another, though I had the joy to be often in her company. And, indeed, what hope could I have, being so young, and poor, and in visible station no more than any 'prentice lad? My heart was much tormented in these fears, and mainly because we heard no tidings that the Maid was accepted by the Dauphin, and that the day of her marching, and of my deliverance from my base craft of painting, was at hand.

It so fell out, how I knew not, whether I had shown me too presumptuous for an apprentice, or because of any other reason, that Elliot had much forborne my company, and was more often in church at her prayers than in the house, or, when in the house, was busy in divers ways, and I scarce ever could get word of her. Finding her in this mood, I also withdrew within myself, and was both proud and sorely unhappy, longing more than ever to take my own part in the world as a man-at-arms. Now, one day right early, I being alone in the chamber, copying a psalter, Elliot came in, looking for her father. I rose at her coming, doffing my cap, and told her, in few words, that my master had gone forth. Thereon she flitted about the chamber, looking at this and that, while I stood silent, deeming that she used me in a sort scarce becoming my blood and lineage.

Suddenly she said, without turning round, for she was standing by a table gazing at the pictures in a Book of Hours—

"I have seen her!"

"The Pucelle?—do you speak of her, gentle maid?"

"I saw her and spoke to her, and heard her voice"; and here her own broke, and I guessed that she was near to weeping. "I went up within the castle precinct, to the tower Coudraye," she said, "for I knew that she lodged hard by, with a good woman who dwells there. I passed into the chapel of St. Martin on the cliff, and there heard the voice of one praying before the image of Our Lady. The voice was even as you said that day—the sweetest of voices. I knelt beside her, and prayed aloud for her and for France. She rested her hand on my hair—her hair is black, and cut 'en ronde' like a man's. It is true that they say, she dresses in man's garb. We came forth together, and I put my hand into hers, and said, 'I believe in you; if none other believes, yet do I believe.' Then she wept, and she kissed me; she is to visit me here to-morrow, la fille de Dieu—"

She drew a long sob, and struck her hand hard on the table; then, keeping her back ever towards me, she fled swiftly from the room. I was amazed—so light of heart as she commonly seemed, and of late disdainful—to find her in this passion. Yet it was to me that she had spoken—to me that she had opened her heart. Now I guessed that, if I was ever to win her, it must be through this Pucelle, on whom her mind was so strangely bent. So I prayed that, if it might be God's will, He would prosper the Maid, and let me be her loyal servitor, and at last bring me to my desire.

Something also I dreamed, as young men will who have read many romances, of myself made a knight for great feats of arms, and wearing in my salade my lady's favour, and breaking a spear on Talbot, or Fastolf, or Glasdale, in some last great victory for France.

Then shone on my eyesight, as it were, the picture of these two children, for they were little more, Elliot and the Maid, kneeling together in the chapel of St. Martin, the gold hair and the black blended; and what were they two alone against this world and the prince of this world? Alas, how much, and again how little, doth prayer avail us! These thoughts were in my mind all day, while serving and answering customers, and carrying my master's wares about the town, and up to the castle on the cliff, where the soldiers and sentries now knew me well enough, and the Scots archers treated me kindly. But as for Elliot, she was like her first self again, and merrier than common with her father, to whom, as far as my knowledge went, she said not a word about the meeting in the crypt of St. Martin's chapel, though to me she had spoken so freely. This gave me some hope; but when I would have tried to ask her a question, she only gazed at me in a manner that abashed me, and turned off to toy with her jackanapes. Whereby I went to my bed perplexed, and with a heavy heart, as one that was not yet conversant with the ways of women—nay, nor ever, in my secular life, have I understood what they would be at. Happier had it been for my temporal life if I had been wiser in woman's ways. But commonly, when we have learned a lesson, the lore comes too late.

Next day my master had business at the castle with a certain lord, and took me thither to help in carrying his wares. This castle was a place that I loved well, it is so old, having first been builded when the Romans were lords of the land; and is so great and strong that our bishop's castle of St. Andrews seems but a cottage compared to it. From the hill-top there is a wide prospect over the tower and the valley of the Vienne, which I liked to gaze upon. My master, then, went in by the drawbridge, high above the moat, which is so deep that, I trow, no foeman could fill it up and cross it to assail the walls. My master, in limping up the hill, had wearied himself, but soon passed into the castle through the gateway of the bell-tower, as they call it, while I waited for him on the further end of the bridge, idly dropping morsels of bread to the swans that swam in the moat below.

On the drawbridge, standing sentinel, was a French man-at-arms, a young man of my own age, armed with a long fauchard, which we call a bill or halberd, a weapon not unlike the Lochaber axes of the Highlandmen. Other soldiers, French, Scottish, Spaniards, Germans, a mixed company, were idling and dicing just within the gate.

I was throwing my last piece of crust to a swan, my mind empty of thought, when I started out of my dream, hearing that rare woman's voice which once I had heard before. Then turning quickly, I saw, walking between two gentlemen, even those who had ridden with her from Vaucouleurs, one whom no man could deem to be other than that much-talked-of Maid of Lorraine. She was clad very simply, like the varlet of some lord of no great estate, in a black cap with a little silver brooch, a grey doublet, and black and grey hose, trussed up with many points; a sword of small price hung by her side. {10} In stature she was something above the common height of women, her face brown with sun and wind, her eyes great, grey, and beautiful, beneath black brows, her lips red and smiling. In figure she seemed strong and shapely, but so slim—she being but seventeen years of age—that, were it not for her sweet girl's voice, and for the beauty of her grey eyes, she might well have passed for a page, her black hair being cut "en ronde," as was and is the fashion among men-at-arms. Thus much have I written concerning her bodily aspect, because many have asked me what manner of woman was the blessed Maid, and whether she was beautiful. I gazed at her like one moon-struck, then, remembering my courtesy, I doffed my cap, and louted low; and she bowed, smiling graciously like a great lady, but with such an air as if her mind was far away.

She passed, with her two gentlemen, but the French sentinel barred the way, holding his fauchard thwartwise.

"On what business come you, and by what right?" he cried, in a rude voice.

"By the Dauphin's gracious command, to see the Dauphin," said one of the gentlemen right courteously. "Here is his own letter, and you may know the seal, bidding La Pucelle to come before him at this hour."

The fellow looked at the seal, and could not but acknowledge the arms of France thereon. He dropped his fauchard over his shoulder, and stood aside, staring impudently at the Maiden, and muttering foul words.

"So this is the renowned Pucelle," he cried; "by God's name" . . . and here he spoke words such as I may not set down in writing, blaspheming God and the Maid.

She turned and looked at him, but as if she saw him not; and then, a light of joy and love transfiguring her face, she knelt down on the drawbridge, folding her hands, her face bowed, and so abode while one might count twenty, we that beheld her being amazed. Then she rose and bent as if in salutation to one we saw not; next, addressing herself to the sentinel, she said, very gently—

"Sir, how canst thou take in vain the name of God, thou that art in this very hour to die?"

So speaking, she with her gentlemen went within the gate, while the soldier stood gazing after her like a man turned to stone.

The Maid passed from our sight, and then the sentinel, coming to himself, turned in great wrath on me, who stood hard by.

"What make you gaping here, you lousy wine-sack of Scotland?" he cried; and at the word, my prayer which I had made to St. Andrew in my bonds came into my mind, namely, that I should not endure to hear my country defamed.

I stopped not to think of words, wherein I never had a ready wit, but his were still in his mouth when I had leaped within his guard, so that he might not swing out his long halberd.

"Blasphemer and liar!" I cried, gripping his neck with my left hand, while with two up-cuts of my right I sent his lies down his throat in company, as I deem, with certain of his teeth.

He dropped his halberd against the wooden fence of the bridge, and felt for his dagger. I caught at his right hand with mine; cries were in my ears—St. Denis for France! St. Andrew for Scotland!—as the other men on guard came running forth to see the sport.

We gripped and swayed for a moment, then the staff of his fauchard coming between his legs, he tripped and fell, I above him; our weight soused against the low pales of the bridge side, that were crazy and old; there was a crash, and I felt myself in mid-air, failing to the moat far below us. Down and down I whirled, and then the deep water closed over me.

CHAPTER VI

HOW NORMAN LESLIE ESCAPED
OUT OF CHINON CASTLE

Down and down I sank, the water surging up into my nostrils
and sounding in my ears; but, being in water, I was safe if it
were but deep enough. Presently I struck out, and, with a
stroke or two, came to the surface. But no sooner did my
head show above, and I draw a deep breath or twain, looking
for my enemy, than an arbalest bolt cleft the water with a
clipping sound, missing me but narrowly. I had but time to
see that there was a tumult on the bridge, and swords out (the
Scots, as I afterwards heard, knocking up the arbalests that
the French soldiers levelled at me). Then I dived again, and
swam under water, making towards the right and the castle
rock, which ran sheer down to the moat. This course I chose
because I had often noted, from the drawbridge, a jutting
buttress of rock, behind which, at least, I should be out of
arrow-shot. My craft was to give myself all the semblance of
a drowning man, throwing up my arms, when I rose to see
whereabout I was and to take breath, as men toss their limbs
who cannot swim. On the second time of rising thus, I saw
myself close to the jut of rock. My next dive took me behind
it, and I let down my feet, close under the side of this natural
buttress, to look around, being myself now concealed from
the sight of those who were on the bridge.

Andrew Lang

To my surprise I touched bottom, for I had deemed that the water was very deep thereby. Next I found that I was standing on a step of hewn stone, and that a concealed staircase, cut in the rock, goes down, in that place, to the very bottom of the moat; for what purpose I know not, but so it is. {11} I climbed up the steps, shook myself, and wrung the water out of my hair, looking about the while for any sign of my enemy, who had blasphemed against my country and the Maiden. But there was nothing to see on the water save my own cloth cap floating. On the other side of the fosse, howbeit, men were launching a pleasure-boat, which lay by a stair at the foot of the further wall of the fosse. The sight of them made me glad to creep further up the steps that rounded a sharp corner, till I came as far as an iron wicket-gate, which seemed to cut off my retreat. There I stopped, deeming that the wicket must be locked. The men were now rowing the boat into the middle of the water, so, without expecting to find the gate open, I tried the handle. It turned, to my no little amazement; the gate swang lightly aside, as if its hinges had been newly oiled, and I followed the staircase, creeping up the slimy steps in the half-dark. Up and round I went, till I was wellnigh giddy, and then I tripped and reeled so that my body struck against a heavy ironed door. Under my weight it yielded gently, and I stumbled across the threshold of a room that smelled strangely sweet and was very warm, being full of the sun, and the heat of a great fire.

"Is that you, Robin of my heart?" said a girl's voice in French; and, before I could move, a pair of arms were round my neck. Back she leaped, finding me all wet, and not the man she looked for; and there we both stood, in a surprise that prevented either of us from speaking.

She was a pretty lass, with brown hair and bright red cheeks, and was dressed all in white, being, indeed, one of the laundresses of the castle; and this warm room, fragrant with lavender, whereinto I had stumbled, was part of the castle laundry. A mighty fire was burning, and all the tables were covered with piles and flat baskets of white linen, sweet with scented herbs.

Back the maid stepped towards the door, keeping her eyes on mine; and, as she did not scream, I deemed that none were within hearing: wherein I was wrong, and she had another reason for holding her peace.

"Save me, gentle maid, if you may," I cried at last, falling on my knees, just where I stood: "I am a luckless man, and stand in much peril of my life."

"In sooth you do," she said, "if Robert Lindsay of the Scottish Archers finds you here. He loves not that another should take his place at a tryst."

"Maiden," I said, beginning to understand why the gate was unlocked, and wherefore it went so smooth on its hinges, "I fear I have slain a man, one of the King's archers. We wrestled together on the drawbridge, and the palisade breaking, we fell into the moat, whence I clomb by the hidden stairs."

"One of the archers!" cried she, as pale as a lily, and catching at her side with her hand. "Was he a Scot?"

"No, maid, but I am; and I pray you hide me, or show me how to escape from this castle with my life, and that speedily."

"Come hither!" she said, drawing me through a door into a small, square, empty room that jutted out above the moat. "The other maids are at their dinner," she went on, "and I all alone—the season being Lent, and I under penance, and thinking of no danger."

For which reason, I doubt not, namely that the others had gone forth, she had made her tryst at this hour with Robin Lindsay. But he, if he was, as she said, one of the Scottish archers that guarded the gate, was busy enough belike with the tumult on the bridge, or in seeking for the body of mine enemy.

"How to get you forth I know not," she said, "seeing that from yonder room you pass into the kitchen and thence into the guard-room, and thence again by a passage in the wall behind the great hall, and so forth to the court, and through the gate, and thereby there is no escape: for see you the soldiers must, and will avenge their comrade."

Hearing this speech, I seemed to behold myself swinging by a tow from a tree branch, a death not beseeming one of gentle blood. Up and down I looked, in vain, and then I turned to the window, thinking that, as better was not to be, I might dive thence into the moat, and take my chance of escape by the stairs on the further side. But the window was heavily barred. Yet again, if I went forth by the door, and lurked on the postern stair, there was Robin Lindsay's dirk to reckon with, when he came, a laggard, to his love-tryst.

"Stop! I have it," said the girl; and flying into the laundry, she returned with a great bundle of white women's gear and a gown of linen, and a woman's white coif, such as she herself wore.

In less time than a man would deem possible, she had my wet hair, that I wore about my shoulders, as our student's manner was, tucked up under the cap, and the clean white smock over my wet clothes, and belted neatly about my middle.

"A pretty wench you make, I swear by St. Valentine," cried she, falling back to look at me, and then coming forward to pin up something about my coif, with her white fingers.

I reckoned it no harm to offer her a sisterly kiss.

"'Tis lucky Robin Lindsay is late," cried she, laughing, "though even were he here, he could scarce find fault that one maid should kiss another. Now," she said, snatching up a flat crate full of linen, "carry these, the King's shirts, and sorely patched they are, on your head; march straight through the kitchen, then through the guard-room, and then by the door on the left into the long passage, and so into the court, and begone; they will but take you for a newly come blanchisseuse. Only speak as little as may be, for your speech may betray you." She kissed me very kindly on both cheeks, for she was as frank a lass as ever I met, and a merry. Then, leading me to the door of the inner room, she pushed it open, the savoury reek of the kitchen pouring in.

"Make good speed, Margot!" she cried aloud after me, so that all could hear; and I walked straight up the King's kitchen, full as it was of men and boys, breaking salads, spitting fowls, basting meat (though it was Lent, but doubtless the King had a dispensation for his health's sake), watching pots, tasting dishes, and all in a great bustle and clamour. The basket of linen shading my face, I felt the more emboldened, though my legs, verily, trembled under me as I walked. Through the room I went, none regarding me, and so into the guard-room, but truly this was another matter. Some soldiers were dicing at a table, some drinking, some brawling over the matter of the late tumult, but all stopped and looked at me.

"A new face, and, by St. Andrew, a fair one!" said a voice in the accent of my own country.

Andrew Lang

"But she has mighty big feet; belike she is a countrywoman of thine," quoth a French archer; and my heart sank within me as the other cast a tankard at his head.

"Come, my lass," cried another, a Scot, with a dice-box in his hand, catching at my robe as I passed, "kiss me and give me luck," and, striking up my basket of linen, so that the wares were all scattered on the floor, he drew me on to his knee, and gave me a smack that reeked sorely of garlic. Never came man nearer getting a sore buffet, yet I held my hand. Then, making his cast with the dice, he swore roundly, when he saw that he had thrown deuces.

"Lucky in love, unlucky in gaming. Lug out your losings," said his adversary with a laugh; and the man left hold of my waist and began fumbling in his pouch. Straightway, being free, I cast myself on the floor to pick up the linen, and hide my face, which so burned that it must have seemed as red as the most modest maid might have deemed seemly.

"Leave the wench alone; she is new come, I warrant, and has no liking for your wantonness," said a kind voice; and, glancing up, I saw that he who spoke was one of the gentlemen who had ridden with the Maiden from Vaucouleurs. Bertrand de Poulengy was his name; belike he was waiting while the King and the nobles devised with the Maiden privately in the great hall.

He stooped and helped me to pick up my linen, as courteously as if I had been a princess of the blood; and, because he was a gentleman, I suppose, and a stranger, the archers did not meddle with him, save to break certain soldiers' jests, making me glad that I was other than I appeared.

"Come," he said, "my lass, I will be your escort; it seems that Fortune has chosen me for a champion of dames."

With these words he led the way forth, and through a long passage lit from above, which came out into the court at the stairs of the great hall.

Down these stairs the Maiden herself was going, her face held high and a glad look in her eyes, her conference with the King being ended. Poulengy joined her; they said some words which I did not hear, for I deemed that it became me to walk forward after thanking him by a look, and bending my head, for I dared not trust my foreign tongue.

Before I reached the gateway they had joined me, which I was glad of, fearing more insolence from the soldiers. But these men held their peace, looking grave, and even affrighted, being of them who had heard the prophecy of the Maiden and seen its fulfilment.

"Have ye found the body of that man?" said Poulengy to a sergeant-at-arms.

"Nay, sir, we deem that his armour weighed him down, for he never rose once, though that Scot's head was seen thrice and no more. Belike they are good, peaceful friends at the bottom of the fosse together."

"Of what man speak you?" asked the Maiden of Poulengy.

"Of him that blasphemed as we went by an hour ago. Wrestling with a Scot on some quarrel, they broke the palisade, and—lo! there are joiners already mending it. 'Tis old and frail. The gentle Dauphin is over poor to keep the furnishings of his castle as a king should do."

The Maiden grew wan as sun-dried grass in summer when she heard this story told. Crossing herself, she said—

"Alas! I warned him, but he died unconfessed. I will do what I may to have Masses said for the repose of his soul, poor man: and he so young!"

With that she wept, for she wept readily, even for a less thing than such a death as was that archer's.

We had now crossed the drawbridge, whereat my heart beat more lightly, and the Maiden told Poulengy that she would go to the house where she lodged, near the castle.

"And thence," she said, "I must fare into the town, for I have promised to visit a damsel of my friends, one Heliote Poulvoir, if I may find my way thither. Know you, gentle damsel," she said to me, "where she abides? Or perchance you can lead me thither, if it lies on your way."

"I was even going thither, Pucelle," I said, mincing in my speech; whereat she laughed, for of her nature she was merry.

"Scots are Heliote and her father, and a Scot are not you also, damsel? your speech betrays you," she said; "you all cling close together, you Scots, as beseems you well, being strangers in this sweet land of France"; and her face lighted up as she spoke the name she loved, and my heart worshipped her with reverence.

"Farewell," she cried to Poulengy, smiling graciously, and bowing with such a courtesy as a queen might show, for I noted it myself, as did all men, that this peasant girl had the manners of the Court, being schooled, as I deem, by the greatest of ladies, her friends St. Margaret and St. Catherine.

Then, with an archer, who had ridden beside her from Vaucouleurs, following after her as he ever did, the Maiden and I began to go down the steep way that led to the town. Little she spoke, and all my thought was to enter the house before Elliot could spy me in my strange disguise.

Andrew Lang

CHAPTER VII

CONCERNING THE WRATH OF ELLIOT, AND THE JEOPARDY OF NORMAN LESLIE

The while we went down into the city of Chinon, a man attired as a maid, a maiden clad as a man—strange companions!—we held but little converse. Her mind, belike, was on fire with a great light of hope, of which afterwards I learned, and the end of the days of trouble and of men's disbelief seemed to her to be drawing near. We may not know what visions of victory and of auxiliary angels, of her King crowned, and fair France redeemed and at peace, were passing through her fancy. Therefore she was not fain to talk, being at all times a woman of few words; and in this, as in so many other matters, unlike most of her sex.

On my side I had more than enough to think of, for my case and present jeopardy were enough to amaze older and wiser heads than mine. For, imprimis, I had slain one of the King's guards; and, moreover, had struck the first blow, though my adversary, indeed, had given me uttermost provocation. But even if my enemies allowed me to speak in my own defence, which might scarcely be save by miracle, it was scantly possible for me to prove that the other had insulted me and my country. Some little hope I had that Sir Patrick Ogilvie, now constable of the Scottish men-at-arms in France, or Sir

Hugh Kennedy, or some other of our knights, might take up my quarrel, for the sake of our common blood and country, we Scots always backing each the other when abroad. Yet, on the other hand, it was more probable that I might be swinging, with a flock of crows pecking at my face, before any of my countrymen could speak a word for me with the King.

It is true that they who would most eagerly have sought my life deemed me already dead, drowned in the fosse, and so would make no search for me. Yet, as soon as I went about my master's affairs, as needs I must, I would be known and taken; and, as we say in our country proverb, "my craig would ken the weight of my hurdies." {12} None the less, seeing that the soldiers deemed me dead, I might readily escape at once from Chinon, and take to the roads again, if but I could reach my master's house unseen, and get rid of this foolish feminine gear of cap and petticoat which now I wore to my great shame and discomfort.

But on this hand lay little hope; for, once on the road, I should be in a worse jeopardy than ever before, as an apprentice fled from my master, and, moreover, with blood on my hands. Moreover, I could ill brook the thought of leaving Elliot, to whom my heart went forth in love, and of missing my chance to strike a blow in the wars for the Maiden, and against the English; of which reward I had the promise from my master. Fortune, and fame, and love, if I were to gain what every young man most desires, were only to be won by remaining at Chinon; but there, too, the face of death was close to mine—as, indeed, death, or at least shame and poverty, lay ambushed for me on all sides.

Here I sadly remembered how, with a light heart, I had left St. Andrews, deeming that the story of my life was now about to begin, as it did for many young esquires of Greece and other lands, concerning whom I had read in romances. Verily in the tale of my adventures hitherto there had been more cuffs than crowns, more shame than honour; and, as to winning my spurs, I was more in point to win a hempen rope, and in my end disgrace my blood.

Now, as if these perils were not enough to put a man beside himself, there was another risk which, even more than these, took up my thoughts. Among all my dangers and manifold distresses, this raised its head highest in my fancy, namely, the fear that my love should see me in my outlandish guise, clad in woman's weeds, and carrying on my head a woman's burden. It was not so much that she must needs laugh and hold me in little account. Elliot laughed often, so that now it was not her mirth, to which she was ever ready, but her wrath (whereto she was ready also) that I held in awful regard. For her heart and faith, in a marvellous manner passing the love of women, were wholly set on this maid, in whose company I now fared. And, if the Maid went in men's attire (as needs she must, for modesty's sake, who was about men's business, in men's company), here was I attending her in woman's gear, as if to make a mock of her, though in my mind I deemed her no less than a sister of the saints. And Elliot was sure to believe that I carried myself thus in mockery and to make laughter; for, at that time, there were many in France who mocked, as did that soldier whose death I had seen and caused. Thus I stood in no more danger of death, great as was that risk, than in jeopardy of my mistress's favour, which, indeed, of late I had been in some scant hope at last to win. Thus, on all hands, I seemed to myself as sore bestead as ever man was, and on no side saw any hope of succour.

I mused so long and deep on these things, that the thought which might have helped me came to me too late, namely, to tell all my tale to the Maiden herself, and throw me on her mercy. Nay, even when at last and late this light shone on my mind, I had shame to speak to her, considering the marvellous thing which I had just beheld of her, in the fulfilment of her prophecy. But now my master's house was in sight, at the turning from the steep stairs and the wynd, and there stood Elliot on the doorstep, watching and waiting for the Maid, as a girl may wait for her lover coming from the wars.

There was no time given me to slink back and skulk in the shadow of the corner of the wynd; for, like a greyhound in speed, Elliot had flown to us and was kneeling to the Maid, who, with a deep blush and some anger in her face—for she loved no such obeisances—bade her rise, and so kissed and embraced her, as young girls use among themselves when they are friends and fain of each other. I had turned myself to go apart into the shadow of the corner, as secretly as I might, when I ran straight into the arms of the archer that followed close behind us. On this encounter he gave a great laugh, and, I believe, would have kissed me; but, the Maiden looking round, he stood erect and grave as a soldier on guard, for the Maiden would suffer no light loves and daffing.

"Whither make you, damsel, in such haste?" she cried to me. "Come, let me present you to this damsel, my friend—and one of your own country-women. Elliot, ma mie," she said to my mistress, "here is this kind lass, a Scot like yourself, who has guided me all the way from the castle hither, and, faith, the way is hard to find. Do you thank her for me, and let her sit down in your house: she must be weary with the weight of her basket and her linen"—for these, when she spoke to me, I had laid on the ground. With this she led me up to Elliot by the hand, who began to show me very gracious countenance, and to thank me, my face burning all the while with confusion and fear of her anger.

Suddenly a new look, such as I had never seen before on her face in her light angers, came into her eyes, which grew hard and cold, her mouth also showing stiff; and so she stood, pale, gazing sternly, and as one unable to speak. Then—

"Go out of my sight," she said, very low, "and from my father's house! Forth with you for a mocker and a gangrel loon!"—speaking in our common Scots,—"and herd with the base thieves from whom you came, coward and mocking malapert!"

The storm had fallen on my head, even as I feared it must, and I stood as one bereft of speech and reason.

The Maid knew no word of our speech, and this passion of Elliot's, and so sudden a change from kindness to wrath, were what she might not understand.

"Elliot, ma mie," she said, very sweetly, "what mean you by this anger? The damsel has treated me with no little favour. Tell me, I pray, in what she has offended."

But Elliot, not looking at her, said to me again, and this time tears leaped up in her eyes—"Forth with you! begone, ere I call that archer to drag you before the judges of the good town."

I was now desperate, for, clad as I was, the archer had me at an avail, and, if I were taken before the men of the law, all would be known, and my shrift would be short.

"Gracious Pucelle," I said, in French, turning to the Maiden, "my life, and the fortune of one who would gladly fight to the death by your side, are in your hands. For the love of the blessed saints, your sisters, and of Him who sends you on your holy mission, pray this demoiselle to let me enter the house with you, and tell my tale to you and her. If I satisfy you not of my honour and good intent, I am ready, in this hour, to go before the men of law, and deliver myself up to their justice. For though my life is in jeopardy, I dread death less than the anger of this honourable demoiselle. And verily this is a matter of instant life or death."

So saying, I clasped my hands in the manner of one in prayer, setting all my soul into my speech, as a man desperate.

The Maiden had listened very gravely, and sweetly she smiled when my prayer was ended.

"Verily," she said to me, "here is deeper water than I can fathom. Elliot, ma mie, you hear how gently, and in what distress, this fair lass beseeches us."

"Fair lass!" cried Elliot: and then broke off between a sob and a laugh, her hand catching at her side.

"If you love me," said the Maid, looking on her astonished, and not without anger—"if you love me, as you have said, you that are the first of my comforters, and, till this day, my only friend in your strange town, let the lass come in and tell us her tale. For, even if she be distraught, and beside herself, as I well deem, I am sent to be a friend of all them that suffer. Moreover, ma mie, I have glad tidings for you, which I am longing to speak, but speak it I will never, while the lass goes thus in terror and fear of death or shame."

In saying these last words, the fashion of her countenance was changed to a sweet entreaty and command, such as few could have beheld and denied her what she craved, and she laid her hand lightly on Elliot's shoulder.

"Come," said Elliot, "be it as you will; come in with me; and you"—turning to myself—"do you follow us."

They passed into the house, I coming after, and the archer waiting at the door.

"Let none enter," said the Maiden to her archer, "unless any come to me from the King, or unless it be the master of the house."

We passed into the chamber where my master was wont to paint his missals and psalters when he would be alone. Then Elliot very graciously bade the Maiden be seated, but herself stood up, facing me.

"Gracious Maiden, and messenger of the holy saints," she said, "this lass, as you deem her, is no woman, but a man, my father's apprentice, who has clad himself thus to make of you a mockery and a laughing-stock, because that you, being a maid, go attired as a man, by the will of Them who sent you to save France. Have I said enough, and do I well to be angry?" and her eyes shone as she spoke.

The Maiden's brows met in wrath; she gazed upon me steadfastly, and I looked—sinful man that I am!—to see her hand go to the hilt of the sword that she wore. But, making no motion, she only said—

"And thou, wherefore hast thou mocked at one who did thee no evil, and at this damsel, thy master's daughter?"

"Gentle Maiden," I said, "listen to me for but a little moment. It may be, when thou hast heard all, that thou wilt still be wroth with me, though not for mockery, which was never in my mind. But the gentle damsel, thy friend, will assuredly pardon me, who have already put my life in peril for thy sake, and for the sake of our dear country of Scotland and her good name."

"Thy life in peril for me! How mean you? I stood in no danger, and I never saw your face before."

"Yet hast thou saved my life," I said; "but of that we may devise hereafter. I am, indeed, though a gentleman by blood and birth, the apprentice of the father of this damsel, thy friend, who is himself a gentleman and of a good house, but poverty drives men to strange shifts. This day I went with my master to the castle, and I was on the drawbridge when thou, with the gentlemen thy esquires, passed over it to see the King. On that bridge a man-at-arms spoke to thee shameful words, blaspheming the holy name of God. No sooner hadst thou gone by than he turned on me, reviling my native country of Scotland. Then I, not deeming that to endure such taunts became my birth and breeding, struck him on his lying mouth. Then, as we wrestled on the bridge, we both struck against the barrier, which was low, frail, and old, so that it gave way under our weight, and we both fell into the moat. When I rose he was not in sight, otherwise I would have saved him by swimming, for I desire to have the life of no man on my hands in private quarrel. But the archers shot at me from the drawbridge, so that I had to take thought for myself. By swimming under the water I escaped, behind a jutting rock, to a secret stair, whence I pushed my way into a chamber of the castle. Therein was a damsel, busy with the linen, who, of her goodwill, clad me in this wretched apparel above my own garb, and so, for that time, saved my life, and I passed forth unknown; but yet hath caused me to lose what I prize more highly than life—that is, the gracious countenance of this gentle lady, thy friend and my master's daughter, whom it is my honour and duty in all things to please and serve. Tell me, then, do I merit your wrath as a jester and a mock-maker, or does this gentle lady

Andrew Lang

well to be angry with her servitor?"

The Maiden crossed herself, and murmured a prayer for the soul of him who had died in the moat. But Elliot instantly flew to me, and, dragging off my woman's cap, tore with her fair hands at the white linen smock about my neck and waist, so that it was rent asunder and fell on the floor, leaving me clad in my wet doublet and hose.

At this sight, without word spoken, she broke out into the merriest laughter that ever I heard, and the most welcome; and the Maid too, catching the malady of her mirth, laughed low and graciously, so that to see and hear her was marvel.

"Begone!" cried Elliot—"begone, and shift thy dripping gear"; and, as I fled swiftly to my chamber, I heard her laughter yet, though there came a sob into it; but for the Maid, she had already stinted in her mirth ere I left the room.

In this strange and unseemly fashion did I first come into the knowledge of this admirable Maid—whom, alas! I was to see more often sad than merry, and weeping rather than laughing, though, even in her utmost need, her heart could be light and her mirth free: a manner that is uncommon even among brave men, but, in women, never known by me save in her. For it is the way of women to be very busy and seriously concerned about the smallest things, whereat a man only smiles. But she, with her life at stake, could pluck gaiety forth of danger, if the peril threatened none but herself. These manners of hers I learned to know and marvel at in the later days that came too soon; but now in my chamber, I shifted my wet raiment for dry with a heart wondrous light. My craig {13} was in peril, as we say, neither less nor more than half an hour agone, but I had escaped the anger of Elliot; and even, as I deemed, had won more of her good countenance, seeing that I had struck a blow for Scotland and for her friend. This thought made me great cheer in my heart; as I heard, from the room below, the voices of the two girls devising together very seriously for nigh the space of an hour. But, knowing that they might have matters secret between themselves to tell of, for the Maiden had said that she brought good tidings, I kept coy and to myself in my little upper chamber. To leave the house, indeed, was more than my life was worth. Now to fly and hide was what I could not bring myself to venture; here I would stay where my heart was, and take what fortune the saints might send. So I endured to wait, and not gladden myself with the sight of Elliot, and the knowledge of how I now stood with her. To me this was great penance, but at last the voices ceased, and, looking secretly from the window, I saw the Maiden depart, her archer following her.

Now I could no longer bridle in my desire to be with Elliot, and learn whether I was indeed forgiven, and how I stood in her favour. So, passing down the stair that led from my cubicle, I stood at the door of the room wherein she was and knocked twice. But none answered, and, venturing to enter, I heard the sound of a stifled sob. She had thrown herself on a settle, her face turned to the wall, and the afternoon sun was shining on her yellow hair, which lay loose upon her shoulders.

I dared to say no word, and she only made a motion of her hand towards me, that I should begone, without showing me the light of her countenance. On this I went forth stealthily, my heart again very heavy, for the Maiden had spoken of learning good tidings; and wherefore should my mistress weep, who, an hour agone, had been so merry? Difficult are the ways of women, a language hard to be understood, wherefore "love," as the Roman says, "is full of anxious fears."

Much misdoubting how I fared in Elliot's heart, and devising within myself what this new sorrow of Elliot's might signify, I half forgot my own danger, yet not so much as to fare forth of the doors, or even into the booth, where customers might come, and I be known. Therefore I passed into a room behind the booth, where my master was wont to instruct me in my painting; and there, since better might not be, I set about grinding and mixing such colours as I knew that he required.

I had not been long about this task, when I heard him enter the booth from without, whence he walked straight into my workroom. I looked up from my colours, whereat his face, which was ruddy, grew wan, he staggered back, and, being lame, reeled against the wall. There he brought up, crossing himself, and making the sign of the cross at me.

"Avaunt!" he said, "in the name of this holy sign, whether thou art a wandering spirit, or a devil in a dead man's semblance."

"Master," I said, "I am neither spirit nor devil. Was it ever yet heard that brownie or bogle mixed colours for a painter? Nay, touch me, and see whether I am not of sinful Scots flesh and blood"; and thereon I laughed aloud, knowing what caused his fear, and merry at the sight of it, for he had ever held tales of "diablerie," and of wraiths and freits and fetches, in high scorn.

He sat him down on a chair and gaped upon me, while I could not contain myself from laughing.

"For God's sake," said he, "bring me a cup of red wine, for my wits are wandering. Deil's buckie," he said in the Scots, "will water not drown you? Faith, then, it is to hemp that you were born, as shall shortly be seen."

I drew him some wine from a cask that stood in the corner, on draught. He drank it at one venture, and held out the cup for more, the colour coming back into his face.

"Did the archers tell me false, then, when they said that you had fired up at a chance word, and flung yourself and the sentinel into the moat? And where have you been wasting your time, and why went you from the bridge ere I came back, if the archers took another prentice lad for Norman Leslie?"

"They told you truth," I said.

"Then, in the name of Antichrist—that I should say so!—how scaped you drowning, and how came you here?"

I told him the story, as briefly as might be.

"Ill luck go with yon second-sighted wench that has bewitched Elliot, and you too, for all that I can see. Never did I think to be frayed with a bogle, {14} and, as might have been deemed, the bogle but a prentice loon, when all was done. To my thinking all this fairy work is no more true than that you are a dead man's wraith. But they are all wild about it, at the castle, where I was kept long, doing no trade, and listening to their mad clatter."

He took out of his pouch a parcel heedfully wrapped in soft folds of silk.

"Here is this Book of Hours," he said, "that I have spent my eyesight, and gold, purple, and carmine, and cobalt upon, these three years past; a jewel it is, though I say so. And I had good hope to sell it to Hugh Kennedy, for he has of late had luck in taking two English knights prisoners at Orleans—the only profitable trade that men now can drive,—and the good knight dearly loves a painted book of devotion; especially if, like this of mine, it be adorned with the loves of Jupiter, and the Swan, and Danae, and other heathen pliskies. We were chaffering over the price, and getting near a bargain, when in comes Patrick Ogilvie with a tale of this second-sighted Maid, and how she had been called to see the King, and of what befell. First, it seems, she boded the death of that luckless limb of a sentinel, and then you took it upon you to fulfil her saying, and so you and he were drowned, and I left prenticeless. Little comfort to me it was to hear Kennedy and Ogilvie praise you for a good Scot and true, and say that it was great pity of your death."

At this hearing my heart leaped for joy, first, at my own praise from such good knights, and next, because I saw a blink of hope, having friends at Court. My master went on—

"Next, Ogilvie told how he had been in hall, with the Dauphin, the Chancellor Tremouille, and some scores of knights and nobles, a great throng. They were all waiting on this Lorrainer wench, for the Dauphin had been told, at last, that she brought a letter from Baudricourt, but before he would not see her. This letter had been kept from him, I guess by whom, and there was other clash of marvels wrought by her, I know not what. So their wisdom was set on putting her to a kind of trial, foolish enough! A young knight was dressed in jewels and a coronet of the King's, and the King was clad right soberly, and held himself far back in the throng, while the other stood in front, looking big. So the wench comes in, and, walking straight through the press of knights, with her head high, kneels to the King, where he stood retired, and calls him 'gentle Dauphin'!

"'Nay, ma mie,' says he, "tis not I who am the Dauphin, but his Highness yonder,'—pointing to the young knight, who showed all his plumage like a muircock in spring.

"Nay, gentle Dauphin," she answers, so Ogilvie said, "it is to thee that I am sent, and no other, and I am come to save the good town of Orleans, and to lead thee to thy sacring at Rheims."

"Here they were all struck amazed, and the King not least, who then had some words apart with the girl. And he has given her rooms in the Tour Coudraye within the castle; and the clergy and the doctors are to examine her straitly, whether she be from a good airt, {15} or an ill, and all because she knew the King, she who had never seen him before. Why should she never have seen him—who warrants me of it?—she dwelling these last days nigh the castle! Freits are folly, to my thinking, and fools they that follow them. Lad, you gave me a gliff; pass me another stoup of wine! Freits, forsooth!"

I served him, and he sat and chuckled in his chair, being pleasured by the thought of his own wisdom. "Not a word of this to Elliot, though," he said suddenly; "when there is a woman in a house—blessings on her!—it is anything for a quiet life! But, 'nom Dieu!' what with the fright you gave me, sitting there, whereas I deemed you were meat for eels and carp, and what with thy tale—ha, ha!—and my tale, and the wine, maybe, I forgot your own peril, my lad. Faith, your neck is like to be longer, if we be not better advised."

Hearing him talk of that marvellous thing, wrought through inspiration by the Maid—whereat, as his manner was, he mocked, I had clean forgotten my own jeopardy. Now this was instant, for who knew how much the archer might have guessed, that followed with the Maid and me, and men-at-arms might anon be at our door.

"It may be," said I, "that Sir Patrick Ogilvie and Sir Hugh Kennedy would say a word for me in the King's ear."

Andrew Lang

"Faith, that is our one chance, and, luckily for you, the lad you drowned, though in the King's service, came hither in the following of a poor knight, who might take blood-ransom for his man. Had he been La Tremouille's man, you must assuredly have fled the country."

He took up his Book of Hours, with a sigh, and wrapped it again in its silken parcel.

"This must be your price with Kennedy," he said, "if better may not be. It is like parting with the apple of my eye, but, I know not well how, I love you, my lad, and blood is thicker than water. Give me my staff; I must hirple up that weary hill again, and you, come hither."

He led me to his own chamber, where I had never been before, and showed me how, in the chimney-neuk, was a way into a certain black hole of little ease, wherein, if any came in search for me, I might lie hidden. And, fetching me a cold fish (Lenten cheer), a loaf, and a stoup of wine, whereof I was glad enough, he left me, groaning the while at his ill-fortune, but laden with such thanks as I might give for all his great kindness.

There then, I sat, when I had eaten, my ears pricked to listen for the tramp of armed men below and the thunder of their summons at the door. But they came not, and presently my thought stole back to Elliot, who, indeed, was never out of my mind then—nay, nor now is. But whether that memory be sinful in a man of religion or not, I leave to the saints and to good confession. Much I perplexed myself with marvelling why she did so weep; above all, since I knew what hopeful tidings she had gotten of her friend and her enterprise. But no light came to me in my meditations. I did not know then that whereas young men, and many lasses too, are like the Roman lad who went with his bosom bare, crying "Aura veni," and sighing for the breeze of Love to come, other maidens are wroth with Love when he creeps into their hearts, and would fain cast him out—being in a manner mad with anger against Love, and against him whom they desire, and against themselves. This mood, as was later seen, was Elliot's, for her heart was like a wild bird trapped, that turns with bill and claw on him who comes to set it free. Moreover, I have since deemed that her passion of faith in the Maid made war on her love for me; one breast being scantly great enough to contain these two affections, and her pride taking, against the natural love, the part of the love which was divine.

But all these were later thoughts, that came to me in musing on the sorrows of my days; and, like most wisdom, this knowledge arrived too late, and I, as then, was holden in perplexity.

CHAPTER VIII

OF CERTAIN QUARRELS THAT CAME
ON THE HANDS OF NORMAN LESLIE

Belike I had dropped asleep, outwearied with what had befallen me, mind and body, but I started up suddenly at the sound of a dagger-hilt smitten against the main door of the house, and a voice crying, "Open, in the name of the Dauphin." They had come in quest of me, and when I heard them, it was as if a hand had given my heart a squeeze, and for a moment my breath seemed to be stopped. This past, I heard the old serving-woman fumbling with the bolts, and peering from behind the curtain of my casement, I saw that the ways were dark, and the narrow street was lit up with flaring torches, the lights wavering in the wind. I stepped to the wide ingle, thinking to creep into the secret hiding-hole. But to what avail? It might have served my turn if my escape alive from the moat had only been guessed, but now my master must have told all the story, and the men-at-arms must be assured that I was within. Thinking thus, I stood at pause, when a whisper came, as if from within the ingle—

"Unbar the door, and hide not."

It must be Elliot's voice, speaking through some tube contrived in the ingle of the dwelling-room below or otherwise. Glad at heart to think that she took thought of me, I unbarred the door, and threw myself into a chair before the fire, trying to look like one unconcerned. The bolts were now drawn below; I heard voices, rather Scots than French, to my sense. Then the step of one man climbed up the stair, heavily, and with the tap of a staff keeping tune to it. It was my master. His face was pale, and falling into a chair, he wiped the sweat from his brow. "Unhappy man that I am!" he said, "I have lost my apprentice."

I gulped something down in my throat ere I could say, "Then it is death?"

"Nay," he said, and smiled. "But gliff for gliff, {16} you put a fear on me this day, and now we are even."

"Yet I scarce need a cup of wine for my recovery, master," I said, filling him a beaker from the flagon on the table, which he drained gladly, being sore wearied, so steep was the way to the castle, and hard for a lame man. My heart was as light as a leaf on a tree, and the bitterness of shameful death seemed gone by.

"I have lost my prentice another way," he said, setting down the cup on the table. "I had much a do to see Kennedy, for he was at the dice with other lords. At length, deeming there was no time to waste, I sent in the bonny Book of Hours, praying him to hear me for a moment on a weighty matter. That brought him to my side; he leaped at the book like a trout at a fly, and took me to his own chamber. There I told him your story. When it came to the wench in the King's laundry, and Robin Lindsay, and you clad in girl's gear, and kissed in the guard-room, he struck hand on thigh and laughed aloud.

"Then I deemed your cause as good as three parts won, and

he could not hold in, but led me to a chamber where were many lords, dicing and drinking: Tremouille, Ogilvie, the Bishop of Orleans—that holy man, who has come to ask for aid from the King,—La Hire, Xaintrailles, and I know not whom. There I must tell all the chronicle again; and some said this, and some that, and Tremouille mocks, that the Maid uttered her prophecy to no other end but to make you fulfil it, and slay her enemy for the sake of her 'beaux yeux.' The others would hear nothing of this, and, indeed, though I am no gull, I wot that Tremouille is wrong here, and over cunning; he trusts neither man nor woman. Howsoever it be, he went with the story to the King, who is keen to hear any new thing. And, to be short, the end of it is this: that you have your free pardon, on these terms, namely, that you have two score of masses said for the dead man, and yourself take service under Sir Hugh Kennedy, that the King may not lose a man-at-arms."

Never, sure, came gladder tidings to any man than these to me. An hour ago the rope seemed tight about my neck; one day past, and I was but a prentice to the mean craft of painting and limning, arts good for a monk, or a manant, but, save for pleasure, not to be melled or meddled with by a man of gentle blood. And now I was to wear arms, and that in the best of causes, under the best of captains, one of my own country—a lord in Ayrshire.

"Ay, even so," my master said, marking the joy in my face, "you are right glad to leave us—a lass and a lameter. {17} Well, well, such is youth, and eld is soon forgotten."

I fell on my knees at his feet, and kissed his hands, and I believe that I wept.

"Sir," I said, "you have been to me as a father, and more than it has been my fortune to find my own father. Never would I leave you with my will, and for the gentle demoiselle, your daughter—" But here I stinted, since in sooth I knew not well what words to say.

"Ay, we shall both miss you betimes; but courage, man! After all, this new life beseems you best, and, mark me, a lass thinks none the worse of a lad because he wears not the prentice's hodden grey, but a Scots archer's green, white, and red, and Charles for badge on breast and sleeve, and a sword by his side. And as for the bonny Book of Hours—'Master,' I said with shame, 'was that my ransom?'

"Kennedy would have come near my price, and strove to make me take the gold. But what is bred in the bone will out; I am a gentleman born, not a huckster, and the book I gave him freely. May it profit the good knight in his devotions! But now, come, they are weary waiting for us; the hour waxes late, and Elliot, I trow, is long abed. You must begone to the castle."

In the stairs, and about the door, some ten of Sir Hugh's men were waiting, all countrymen of my own, and the noise they made and their speech were pleasant to me. They gave me welcome with shouts and laughter, and clasped my hands: "for him that called us wine-sacks, you have given him water to his wine, and the frog for his butler," they said, making a jest of life and death. But my own heart for the nonce was heavy enough again, I longing to take farewell of Elliot, which might not be, nor might she face that wild company. Howbeit, thinking it good to have a friend at court, I made occasion to put in the hand of the old serving-woman all of such small coins as I had won in my life servile, deeming myself well quit of such ill-gotten gear. And thereafter, with great mirth and noise, they set forth to climb the hill towards the castle, where I was led, through many a windy passage, to the chamber of Sir Hugh Kennedy. There were torches lit, and the knight, a broad-shouldered, fair-haired man, with a stern, flushed face, was turning over and gazing at his new Book of Hours, like a child busy with a fresh toy. He laid the book down when we entered, and the senior of the two archers who accompanied me told him that I was he who had been summoned.

"Your name?" he asked; and I gave it.

"You are of gentle blood?" And I answering "Yes," he replied, "Then see that you are ready to shed it for the King. Your life that was justly forfeit, is now, by his Royal mercy, returned to you, to be spent in his service. Rutherford and Douglas, go take him to quarters, and see that to-morrow he is clad as beseems a man of my command. Now good night to you—but stay! You, Norman Leslie, you will have quarrels on your hand. Wait not for them, but go to meet them, if they are with the French men-at-arms, and in quarrel see that you be swift and deadly. For the townsfolk, no brawling, marauding, or haling about of honest wenches. Here we are strangers, and my men must be respected."

He bowed his head: his words had been curt, no grace or kindness had he shown me of countenance. I felt in my heart that to him I was but a pawn in the game of battle. Now I seemed as far off as ever I was from my foolish dream of winning my spurs; nay, perchance never had I sunk lower in my own conceit. Till this hour I had been, as it were, the hinge on which my share of the world turned, and now I was no more than a wheel in the carriage of a couleuvrine, an unconsidered cog in the machine of war. I was to be lost in a multitude, every one as good as myself, or better; and when I had thought of taking service, I had not foreseen the manner of it and the nature of the soldier's trade. My head, that I had carried high, somewhat drooped, as I saluted, imitating my companions, and we wheeled forth of the room.

"Hugh has taken the pride out of you, lad, or my name is not Randal Rutherford," said the Border man who had guided me. "Faith, he has a keen tongue and a short way with him, but there are worse commanders. And now you must to your quarters, for the hour is late and the guard-room shut."

He led me to our common sleeping-place, where, among many snoring men-at-arms in a great bare hall, a pallet was laid for me, and my flesh crept as I remembered how this was the couch of him whom I had slain. Howbeit, being well weary, despite the strangeness of the place, after brief orisons I slept sound till a trumpet called us in the morning.

Concerning the strangeness of this waking, to me who had been gently nurtured, and the rough life, and profane words which I must hear (not, indeed, that they had been wholly banished from our wild days at St. Andrews), it is needless that I should tell. Seeing that I was come among rude neighbours, I even made shift to fall back, in semblance, on such manners as I had used among the students before I left Scotland, though many perils, and the fear wherein I stood of Brother Thomas, and the company of the maid Elliot, had caused me half to forget my swaggering ways. So, may God forgive me! I swore roundly; I made as if I deemed lightly of that Frenchman's death, and, in brief, I so bore me that, ere noon (when I behoved to go into Chinon with Randal Rutherford, and there provide me with the rich apparel of our company), I had three good quarrels on my hand.

First, there was the man-at-arms who had kissed me in the guard-room. He, in a "bourde" and mockery, making pretence that he would repeat his insult, got that which was owing him, and with interest, for indeed he could see out of neither of his squint eyes when I had dealt with him. And for this cause perforce, if he needed more proof of my manhood than the weight of my fist, he must tarry for the demonstration which he desired.

Then there was Robin Lindsay, and at his wrath I make no marvel, for the tale of how he came late to tryst, and at second-hand (with many such rude and wanton additions as soldiers use to make), was noised abroad all over the castle. His quarrel was no matter for fisticuffs; so, being attired in helmet, vambrace rere-brace, gauntlets, and greaves out of the armoury, where many such suits were stored, I met him in a certain quiet court behind the castle, where quarrels were usually voided. And now my practice of the sword at home and the lessons of our smith came handily to my need. After much clashing of steel and smiting out of sparks, I chanced, by an art known to me, to strike his sword out of his hand. Then, having him at an avail, I threw down my own blade, and so plainly told him the plain truth, and how to his mistress I owed my life, which I would rather lose now at his hand than hear her honour blamed, that he forgave me, and we embraced as friends. Neither was this jest anew cast up against either of us, men fearing to laugh, as we say, with the wrong side of their mouths.

After this friendly bout at point and edge, Robin and Randal Rutherford, being off duty, must needs carry me to the Tennis Court, where Tremouille and the King were playing two young lords, and that for such a stake as would have helped to arm a hundred men for the aid of Orleans. It was pretty to see the ball fly about basted from the walls, and the players bounding and striking; and, little as I understood the game, so eager was I over the sport, that a gentleman within the "dedans" touched me twice on the shoulder before I was aware of him.

"I would have a word with you, sir, if your grace can spare me the leisure."

"May it not be spoken here?" I asked, for I was sorry to lose the spectacle of the tennis, which was new to me, and is a pastime wherein France beats the world. Pity it is that many players should so curse and blaspheme God and His saints!

"My business," replied the stranger, "is of a kind that will hardly endure waiting."

With that I rose and followed him out into the open courtyard, much marvelling what might be toward.

"You are that young gentleman," said my man, "for a gentleman I take you to be, from your aspect and common report, who yesterday were the death of Gilles de Puiseux?"

"Sir, to my sorrow, and not by my will, I am he, and but now I was going forth to have certain masses said for his soul's welfare": which was true, Randal Rutherford having filled my purse against pay-day.

"I thank you, sir, for your courtesy, and perchance may have occasion to do the like gentle service for you. Gilles de Puiseux was of my blood and kin; he has none other to take up his feud for him in this place, and now your quickness of comprehension will tell you that the business wherewith I permit myself to break your leisure will brook no tarrying. Let me say that I take it not upon me to defend the words of my cousin, who insulted a woman, and, as I believe, a messenger from the blessed Saints that love France."

I looked at him in some amazement. He was a young man of about my own years, delicately and richly clad in furs, silks, and velvets, a great gold chain hanging in loops about his neck, a gold brooch with an ancient Roman medal in his cap. But the most notable thing in him was his thick golden hair, whence La Hire had named him "Capdorat," because he was so blond, and right keen in war, and hardy beyond others. And here he was challenging me, who stood before him in a prentice's hodden grey!

"Sir," I said, "I could wish you a better quarrel, but not more courtesy. Many a gentleman seeing me such as I am, would bid me send, ere he crossed swords with me, to my own country for my bor-brief, {18} which I came away in too great haste to carry with me. Nay, I was but now to set forth and buy me a sword and other accoutrements; natheless, from the armoury here they may equip me with sword and body armour."

"Of body-armour take no thought," he answered, "for this quarrel is of a kind that must needs be voided in our smocks"; he meaning that it was "a outrance," till one of us fell.

Verily, now I saw that this was not to be a matter of striking sparks from steel, as Robin and I had done, but of life and death.

"I shall be the more speedily at your service," I made answer; and as I spoke Randal and Robin came forth from the "dedans," the sport being over. They joined me, and I told them in few words my new business, my adversary tarrying, cap in hand, till I had spoken, and then proclaiming himself Aymar de Puiseux, a gentleman of Dauphine, as indeed my friends knew.

"I shall wait on you, with your leave, at the isle in the river, where it is of custom, opposite the booths of the gold-workers," quoth he, "about the hour of noon"; and so, saluting us, he went, as he said, to provide himself with friends.

"Blood of Judas!" quoth Robin, who swore terribly in his speech, "you have your hands full, young Norman. He is but now crept out of the rank of pages, but when the French and English pages fought a valliance of late, under Orleans, none won more praise than he, who was captain of the French party."

"He played a good sword?" I asked.

"He threw a good stone! Man, it was a stone bicker, and they had lids of baskets for targes."

"And he challenges me to the field," I said hotly, "By St. Andrew! I will cuff his ears and send him back to the other boys."

"Norman, my lad, when were you in a stone bicker last?" quoth Randal; and I hung my head, for it was not yet six months gone since the sailors and we students were stoning each other in North Street.

"Yet he does play a very good sword, and is cunning of fence, for your comfort," said Randal. So I hummed the old lilt of the Leslies, whence, they say, comes our name—

    Between the less lea and the mair,
    He slew the knight and left him there;—

for I deemed it well to show a good face. Moreover, I had some conceit of myself as a swordsman, and Randal was laughing like a foolbody at my countenance.

"Faith, you will make a spoon or spoil a horn, and—let me have my laugh out—you bid well for an archer," said Randal; and Robin counselling me to play the same prank on the French lad's sword as late I had done on his own, they

Andrew Lang

took each of them an arm of mine, and so we swaggered down the steep ways into Chinon.

First I would go to the tailor and the cordwainer, and be fitted for my new splendours as an archer of the guard.

They both laughed at me again, for, said they very cheerfully, "You may never live to wear these fine feathers."

But Randal making the reflection that, if I fell, there would be none to pay the shopmaster, they both shouted with delight in the street, so that passers-by turned and marvelled at them. Clearly I saw that to go to fight a duel is one thing, and to go and look on is another, and much more gay, for my heart had no desire of all this merriment. Rather would I have recommended my case to the saints, and chiefly to St. Andrew, for whose cause and honour I was about to put my life in jeopardy. But shame, and the fear of seeming fearful, drove me to jest with the others—such risks of dying unconfessed are run by sinful men!

Howbeit, they helped me to choose cloth of the best colour and fashion, laughing the more because I, being short of stature and slim, the tailor, if I fell, might well find none among the archers to purchase that for which, belike, I should have no need.

"We must even enlist the Pucelle in our guard, for she might wear this apparel," quoth Randal.

Thus boisterously they bore themselves, but more gravely at the swordsmith's, where we picked out a good cut-and-thrust blade, well balanced, that came readily to my hand. Then, I with sword at side, like a gentleman, we made to the river, passing my master's booth, where I looked wistfully at the windows for a blink of Elliot, but saw none that I knew, only, from an open casement, the little jackanapes mopped and mowed at me in friendly fashion. Hard by the booth was a little pier, and we took boat, and so landed on the island, where were waiting for us my adversary and two other gentlemen. Having saluted each other, we passed to a smooth grassy spot, surrounded on all sides by tall poplar trees. Here in places daffodils were dancing in the wind; but otherwhere the sward was much trampled down, and in two or three spots were black patches that wellnigh turned my courage, for I was not yet used to the sight of men's blood, here often shed for little cause.

The friends of us twain adversaries, for enemies we could scarce be called, chose out a smooth spot with a fair light, the sun being veiled, and when we had stripped to our smocks, we drew and fell to work. He was very quick and light in his movements, bounding nimbly to this side or that, but I, using a hanging guard, in our common Scots manner, did somewhat perplex him, to whom the fashion was new. One or two scratches we dealt each other, but, for all that, I could see we were well matched, and neither closed, as men rarely do in such a combat, till they are wroth with hurts and their blood warm. Now I gashed his thigh, but not deeply, and with that, as I deemed, his temper fired, for he made a full sweep at my leg above the knee. This I have always reckoned a fool's stroke, as leaving the upper part of the body unguarded, and avoiding with my right leg, I drove down with all my force at his head. But, even as I struck, came a flash and the sudden deadness of a deep wound, for he had but feinted, and then, avoiding me so that I touched him not, he drove his point into my breast. Between the force of my own blow and this stab I fell forward on my face, and thence rolled over on my back, catching at my breast with my hands, as though to stop the blood, but, in sooth, not well knowing what I did.

He had thrown down his sword, and now was kneeling by my side.

"I take you to witness," he said, "that this has befallen to my great sorrow, and had I been where this gentleman was yesterday, and heard my cousin blaspheme, I would myself have drawn on him, but—" And here, as I later heard, he fainted from loss of blood, my sword having cut a great vein; and I likewise lost sense and knowledge. Nor did I know more till they lifted me and laid me on a litter of poplar boughs, having stanched my wound as best they might. In the boat, as they ferried us across the river, I believe that I fainted again; and so, "between home and hell," as the saying is, I lay on my litter and was carried along the street beside the water. Folk gathered around us as we went. I heard their voices as in a dream, when lo! there sounded a voice that I knew right well, for Elliot was asking of the people "who was hurt?" At this hearing I hove myself up on my elbow, beckoning with my other hand; and I opened my mouth to speak, but, in place of words, came only a wave of blood that sickened me, and I seemed to be dreaming, in my bed, of Elliot and her jackanapes; and then feet were trampling, and at length I was laid down, and so seemed to fall most blessedly asleep, with a little hand in mine, and rarely peaceful and happy in my heart, though wherefore I knew not. After many days of tossing on the waves of the world, it was as if I had been brought into the haven where I would be. Of what was passing I knew or I remember nothing. Later I heard that a good priest had been brought to my bedside, and perchance there was made some such confession as the Church, in her mercy, accepts from sinful men in such case as mine. But I had no thought of life or death, purgatory or paradise; only, if paradise be rest among those we love, such rest for an unknown while, and such sense of blissful companionship, were mine. But whether it was well to pass through and beyond this scarce sensible joy, or whether that peace will ever again be mine and unending, I leave with humility to them in whose hands are Christian souls.

Andrew Lang

CHAPTER IX

OF THE WINNING OF ELLIOT

The days of fever and of dreams went by and passed, leaving me very weak, but not ignorant of where I was, and of what had come and gone. My master had often been by my bedside, and Elliot now and again; the old housewife also watched me by night, and gave me drink when I thirsted. Most of the while I deemed I was at home, in the house of Pitcullo; yet I felt there was something strange, and that there was pain somewhere in the room. But at length, as was said, I came to knowledge of things, and could see Elliot and remember her, when she knelt praying by my bed, as oft she did, whiles I lay between life and death. I have heard speak of men who, being inflamed with love, as I had been, fell into a fever of the body, and when that passed, lo! their passion had passed with it, and their longing. And so it seemed to be with me. For some days I was not permitted to utter a word, and later, I was as glad in Elliot's company as you may have seen a little lad and lass, not near come to full age, who go playing together with flowers and such toys. So we were merry together, the jackanapes keeping us company, and making much game and sport.

Perchance these were my most blessed days, as of one who had returned to the sinless years, when we are happier than we know, and not yet acquainted with desire. Now and again Rutherford and Lindsay would come to visit me, seeming strangely still and gentle, speaking little, but looking at me with kind eyes, and vowing that my tailor should yet be paid for his labour. Capdorat also came, for he had but suffered a flesh wound with much loss of blood, and we showed each other the best countenance. So time went by, while I grew stronger daily; and now it was ordained by the leech, a skilful man, that I might leave my bed, and be clothed, and go about through the house, and eat stronger food, whereof I had the greatest desire, and would ever be eating like a howlet. {19} Now, when I was to rise, I looked that they should bring me my old prentice's gabardine and hose, but on the morning of that day Elliot came, bearing in her arms a parcel of raiment very gay and costly.

"Here is your fine clothing new come from the tailor's booth," she cried merrily. "See, you shall be as bright as spring, in green, and white, and red!"

There was the bonnet, with its three coloured plumes, and the doublet, with Charles wrought in silver on the arm and breast, and all other things seemly—a joy to mine eyes.

She held them up before me, her face shining like the return of life, with a happy welcome; and my heart beat to see and hear her as of old it was wont to do.

"And wherefore should not I go to the wars," she cried, "and fight beside the Maid? I am as tall as she, if scantly so strong, and brave—oh, I am very brave Glacidas, I bid you beware!" she said, putting the archer's bonnet gallantly cocked on her beautiful head, and drawing forth the sword from his scabbard, as one in act to fight, but in innocent unwarlike wise.

There she stood before me in the sunlight, like the Angel of Victory, all glad and fair, and two blue rays from her eyes shot into my heart, and lo! I was no more a child, but a man again and a lover.

"O Elliot," I said, ere ever I wist what I was saying, and I caught her left hand into mine—"O Elliot, I love you! Give me but your love, and I shall come back from the wars a knight, and claim my love to be my lady."

She snatched her hand suddenly, as if angered, out of mine, and therewith, being very weak, I gave a cry, my wound fiercely paining me. Then her face changed from rose-red to lily-white, she dropped on her knees by my bed, and her arms were about my neck, and all over my face her soft, sweet-scented hair and her tears.

"Oh, I have slain you, I have slain you, my love!" she sobbed, making a low, sweet moan, as a cushat in the wild wood, for I lay deadly still, being overcome with pain and joy. And there I was, my love comforting me as a mother comforts her child.

I moved my hand, to take hers in mine—her little hand; and so, for a space, there was silence between us, save for her kind moaning, and in my heart was such gladness as comes but once to men, and may not be spoken in words of this world.

There was silence between us; then she rose very gently and tossed back her hair, showing her face wet with tears, but rosy-red with happiness and sweet shame. Had it not been for that chance hurt, how long might I have wooed ere I won her? But her heart was molten by my anguish.

"Hath the pain passed?" she whispered.

"Sweet was the pain, my love, and sweetly hast thou healed it with thy magic."

Then she kissed me, and so fled from the room, as one abashed, and came not back that day, when, indeed, I did not rise, nor for two days more, being weaker than we had deemed. But happiness is the greatest leech on earth, and does the rarest miracles of healing; so in three days' space I won strength to leave my bed and my room, and could sit by the door, at noon, in the sun of spring, that is warmer in France than in our own country.

Now it could not be but that Elliot and I must meet, when her father was in town about his affairs, or busy in the painting-room, and much work he had then on his hands. But Elliot was right coy, hiding herself from me, who watched warily, till one day, when my master was abroad, I had the fortune to find her alone in the chamber, putting spring flowers in a very fair vessel of glass. I made no more ado, but coming in stealthily, I caught her boldly about the body, saying—

"Yield you, rescue or no rescue, and strive not against me, lest you slay a wounded man-at-arms."

For very fear, as I believe, lest she might stir my wound again, she was still as a bird that lies in your hands when once you have caught it. And all that passes of kiss and kind word between happy lovers passed between us, till I prayed of her grace, that I might tell her father how things stood, for well I had seen by his words and deeds that he cherished me as a son. So she granted this, and we fell to devising as to what was to be in days to come. Lackland was I, and penniless, save for my pay, if I got it; but we looked to the common fortune of young men-at-arms, namely, spoil of war and the ransom of prisoners of England or Burgundy. For I had set up my resolve either to die gloriously, or to win great wealth and honour, which, to a young man and a lover, seem things easily come by. Nor could my master look for a great fortune in marriage, seeing that, despite his gentle birth, he lived but as a burgess, and by the work of his hands.

As we thus devised, she told me how matters now were in the country, of which, indeed, I still knew but little, for, to a man sick and nigh upon death, nothing imports greatly that betides beyond the walls of his chamber. What I heard was this: namely, that, about Orleans, the English ever pressed the good town more closely, building new bastilles and other great works, so as to close the way from Blois against any that came thence of our party with victual and men-at-arms. And daily there was fighting without the walls, wherein now one side had the better, now the other; but food was scant in Orleans, and many were slain by cannon-shots. Yet much was spoken of a new cannonier, lately come to aid the men of Orleans, and how he and John of Lorraine slew many of the hardiest of the English with their couleuvrines.

At this telling I bethought me of Brother Thomas, but spoke no word concerning him, for my mistress began very gladly to devise of her dear Maid, concerning whom, indeed, she could never long be silent. "Faithless heart and fickle," I said in a jest, "I believe you love that Maid more than you love me, and as she wears sword at side, like a man, I must even challenge her to fight in the island."

Here she stayed my speech in the best manner and the most gracious, laughing low, so that, verily, I was clean besotted with love, and marvelled that any could be so fair as she, and how I could have won such a lady.

"Beware how you challenge my Maid," said she at last, "for she fights but on horseback, with lance and sperthe, {20} and the Duc d'Alencon has seen her tilt at the ring, and has given her the best steed in his stables, whereon she shall soon lead her army to Orleans."

"Then I must lay by my quarrel, for who am I to challenge my captain? But, tell me, hath she heard any word of thee and me?"

Elliot waxed rosy, and whispered—

"We had spoken together about thee, ere she went to Poictiers to be examined and questioned by the doctors of law and learning, after thou wert wounded." Concerning this journey to Poictiers I knew nothing, but I was more concerned to hear what the Maid had said about Elliot and me. For seeing that the Maid herself was vowed (as men deemed) to virginity, it passed into my mind that she might think holy matrimony but a low estate, and might try to set my mistress's heart on following her own example. And then, I thought, but foolishly, Elliot's love for me might be weaker than her love for the Maid.

"Yes," my lady went on, "I could not but open my heart about thee and me, to one who is of my own age, and so wise, unlike other girls. Moreover, I scarce knew well whether your heart was like disposed with my heart. Therefore I devised with her more than once or twice."

Hiding her face on my breast, she spoke very low; and as my fancy had once seen the children, the dark head and the golden, bowed together in prayer for France and the Dauphin, so now I saw them again, held close together in converse, and that strange Maid and Prophetess listening, like any girl, to a girl's tale of the secrets of her heart.

"And what counsel gave the Maid?" I said; "or had she any prophecy of our fortune?"

"Nay, on such matters she knows no more than you or I, or knows but seldom, nor seeks to learn from her counsel. Only she is bidden that she must rescue Orleans, and lead the Dauphin to his sacring at Rheims. But she wished me well, and comforted me that your heart was even as my own, as she saw on that day when you wore woman's gear and slew him that blasphemed her. And of you she spoke the best words, for that you, who knew her not, took her part against her enemy. And for your wound she sorrowed much, not knowing, more than I who am simple, whether it would turn to life or death. And if to life, then, if she could but persuade the doctor and clergy and the King's counsellors to let her go, she said that you should follow with her to the wars, and she, if so the saints pleased, would be the making of your fortune, you and I being her first friends."

"The saints fight for her!" I said, "for we have done our part thus far, and I would that I may be well ere she raises her standard."

But here Elliot turned right pale, at the thought of my going to the wars, she holding my face off and gazing steadily upon me with wistful eyes.

"O God, send that the Maid go speedily!" she cried, "for as now you are not fit to bear arms."

"Thou wouldst not have me lag behind, when the Maid's banner is on the wind?"

"Nay," she said, but slowly, "thee and all that I have would I give for her and for her cause, and for the saints. But now thou must not go,"—and her eyes yearned upon me—"now that I could overthrow thee if we came to war."

So here she laughed again, being like the weather without—a

changeful thing of shower and shine.

Thus we continued devising, and she told me that, some days after my wounding, the Maid had held converse apart with the King, and then gave him to wit of certain marvellous matters, that none might know save by heavenly inspiration. But what these matters might be none could tell, save the King and the Maiden only.

That this was sooth I can affirm, having myself been present in later years, when one that affected to be the very Pucelle, never slain, or re-arisen by miracle, came before the King, and truly she had beguiled many. Then the King said, "Welcome Pucelle, ma mie, thou art welcome if thou hast memory of that secret thing which is between thee and me." Whereon this false woman, as one confounded, fell on her knees and confessed her treason.

This that Elliot told me, therefore, while the sun shone into the chamber through the bare vine-tendrils, was sooth, and by this miracle, it seems, the Maid had at last won the ear of the King. So he bade carry her to Poictiers, where the doctors and the learned were but now examining into her holy life, and her knowledge of religion, being amazed by the wisdom of her answers. The noble ladies about her, too, and these mendicant friars that were sent to hold inquisition concerning her at Domremy, had found in her nothing but simplicity and holy maidenhood, pity and piety. But, as for a sign of her sending, and a marvel to convince all men's hearts, that, she said, she would only work at Orleans. So now she was being accepted, and was to raise her standard, as we had cause to believe.

"But," said Elliot, "the weeks go by, and much is said, and men and victual are to be gathered, and still they tarry, doing no great deed. Oh, would that to-day her standard were on the wind! for to-day, and for these many days, I must have you here, and tend you till you be fit to bear arms."

Therewith she made me much good cheer; then, very tenderly taking her arms from about me, lest I should be hurt again, she cried—

"But we speak idly, and thou hast not seen the standard, and the banner, and the pennon of the Maid that my father is painting."

Then I must lean on her shoulder, as, indeed, I still had cause to do, and so, right heedfully, she brought me into the painting-chamber. There, upon great easels, were stretched three sheets of "bougran," {21} very white and glistering—a mighty long sheet for the standard, a smaller one, square, for the banner, and the pennon smaller yet, in form of a triangle, as is customary.

The great standard, in the Maiden's wars, was to be used for the rallying of all her host; the pennon was a signal to those who fought around her, as guards of her body; and about the banner afterwards gathered, for prayer and praise, those men, confessed and clean of conscience, whom she had called and chosen.

These cloths were now but half painted, the figures being drawn, by my master's hands, and the ground-colours laid; but some portions were quite finished, very bright and beautiful. On the standard was figured God the Father, having the globe in His hand; two angels knelt by Him, one holding for His blessing the lily of France. The field was to be sown with fleurs-de-lys, and to bear the holy names: Jhesu—Maria. On the banner was our Lord crucified between the Holy Virgin and St. John. And on the pennon was wrought the Annunciation, the angel with a lily kneeling to the Blessed Virgin. On the standard, my master, later, fashioned the chosen blazon of the Maid—a dove argent, on a field azure. But the blazon of the sword supporting the crown, between two lilies, that was later given to her and her house, she did not use, as her enemies said she did, out of pride and vainglory, mixing her arms with holy things, even at Rheims at the sacring. For when she was at Rheims, no armorial bearings had yet been given to her. Herein, then, as always, they lied in their cruel throats; for, as the Psalmist says, "Quare fremuerunt gentes?"

All these evil tongues, and all thought of evil days, were far from us as we stood looking at the work, and praising it, as well we might, for never had my master wrought so well. Now, as I studied on the paintings, I well saw that my master had drawn the angel of the pennon in the likeness of his own daughter Elliot. Wonderful it was to see her fair face and blue eyes, holy and humble, with the gold halo round her head.

"Ah, love," I said, "that banner I could follow far, pursuing fame and the face of my lady!"

With that we fell into such dalliance and kind speech as lovers use, wholly rapt from the world in our happiness.

Even then, before we so much as heard his step at the door, my master entered, and there stood we, my arm about her neck and hers about my body, embracing me.

He stood with eyes wide open, and gave one long whistle.

"Faith!" he cried, "our surgery hath wrought miracles! You are whole beyond what I looked for; but surely you are deaf, for my step is heavy enough, yet, me thinks, you heard me not."

Elliot spoke no word, but drawing me very heedfully to a settle that was by the side of the room, she fled without looking behind her.

"Sir," I said, as soon as she was gone, "I need make no long story—"

"Faith, no!" he answered, standing back from the banner and holding his hands at each side of his eyes, regarding his work as limners do. "You twain, I doubt not, were smitten senseless by these great masterpieces, and the thought of the holy use to which they were made."

"That might well have been, sir, but what we had covenanted to tell you this day we have told unwittingly, methinks, already. I could not be in your daughter's company, and have the grace of her gentle ministerings—"

"But you must stand senseless before her father's paintings? Faith, you are a very grateful lad! But so it is, and I am not one of those blind folk who see not what is under their eyes. And now, what now? Well, I can tell you. You are to be healed, and follow these flags to war, and win your spurs, and much wealth by ransoms, and so make my lass your lady. Is it not so?"

I was abashed by his "bourdes," and could say nought, for, being still very weak, the tears came into my eyes. Then he drew near me, limping, and put his hand on my shoulder, but very gently, saying—

"Even so be it, my son, as better may not be. 'Tis no great match, but I looked, in this country, for nothing nobler or more wealthy. That my lass should be happy, and have one to fend for her, there is my affair, and I am not one of those fathers who think to make their daughters glad by taking from them their heart's desire. So cheer up! What, a man-at-arms weeping! Strange times, when maids lead men-at-arms and men-at-arms weep at home!"

With these words he comforted me, and made me welcome, for indeed he was a kind man and a wise; so many there are that cause shrewd sorrow when there should be joy in their houses! This was never his way, and wise do I call him, for all that has come and gone.

In a little time, when I had thanked him, and shown him, I trow, how he stood in my love, he bade me go to my chamber and be at rest, saying that he must take thought as to how matters stood.

"For you are not yet fit to bear arms, nor will be for these many days. Nor is it seemly, nor our country's custom, that my maid should dwell here in the house with you, as things are between you, and I must consider of how I may bestow her till you march with your troop, if marching there is to be."

This I dared not gainsay, and so I went to my chamber with a heart full of grief and joy, for these hours that are all of gladness come rarely to lovers, and to me were scantly measured. Perchance it was for my soul's welfare, to win me from the ways of the world.

But to Elliot and me that night bore no joy, but sorrow, albeit passing. At supper we met, indeed, but she stayed with us not long after supper, when my master, with a serious countenance, told me how he had taken counsel with a very holy woman, of his own kin, widow of an archer, and how she was going on pilgrimage to our Lady of Puy en Velay, by reason of the jubilee, for this year Good Friday and the Annunciation fell on the same day.

"To-morrow she sets forth, and whatsoever prayer can do for France and the King shall be done. Always, after this day of jubilee, they say that strange and great matters come to pass. That there will be strange matters I make no doubt, for when before, save under holy Deborah in Scripture, did men follow a woman to war? May good come of it! However it fall out, Elliot is willing to go on pilgrimage, for she is very devout. Moreover, she tells me that it had been in her mind before, for the mother of that Maid is to be at Puy, praying for her daughter, as, certes, she hath great need, if ever woman had. And Elliot is fain to meet her and devise with her about the Maid. And for you, you still need our nursing, and the sooner you win strength, the nearer you are to that which you would win. Still, I am sorry, lad, for I remember my courting days and the lass's mother, blessings on her!"

To all this I could make no answer but that his will was mine; and so the day ended in a mingling of gladness and sorrow.

CHAPTER X

HOW NORMAN LESLIE WAS
OUT OF ALL COMFORT

My brethren the good Benedictine Fathers here in Pluscarden Priory, are wont betimes to be merry over my penitents, for all the young lads and lasses in the glen say they are fain to be shriven by old Father Norman and by no other.

This that my brethren report may well be true, and yet I take no shame in the bruit or "fama." For as in my hot youth I suffered sorrows many from love, so now I may say, like that Carthaginian queen in Maro, "miseris succurrere disco." The years of the youth of most women and men are like a tourney, or jousts courteous, and many fall in the lists of love, and many carry sorer wounds away from Love's spears, than they wot of who do but look on from the safe seats and secure pavilions of age. Though all may seem but a gentle and joyous passage of arms, and the weapons that they use but arms of courtesy, yet are shrewd blows dealt and wounds taken which bleed inwardly, perchance through a whole life long. To medicine these wounds with kind words is, it may be, part of my poor skill as a healer of souls in my degree, and therefore do the young resort to Father Norman.

Some confessors there be who laugh within their hearts at

these sorrows of lovers, as if they were mere "nugae" and featherweights: others there are who wax impatient, holding all love for sin in some degree, and forgetting that Monseigneur St. Peter himself was a married man, and doubtless had his own share of trouble and amorous annoy when he was winning the lady his wife, even as other men. But if I be of any avail (as they deem) in the healing of hearts, I owe my skill of that surgery to remembrance of the days of my youth, when I found none to give me comfort, save what I won from a book that my master had in hand to copy and adorn, namely, "The Book of One Hundred Ballades, containing Counsel to a Knight, that he should love loyally"; this counsel offered by Messire Lyonnet de Coismes, Messire Jehan de Mailly, the Sieur d'Yvry, and many other good knights that were true lovers. Verily, in sermons of preachers and lives of holy men I found no such comfort.

Almost the sorest time of my sorrowing was for very grief of heart when Elliot set forth on pilgrimage to Puy en Velay, for we were but newly come together; "twain we were with one heart," as a maker sang whom once I met in France ere I came back to Scotland; sweetly could he make, but was a young clerk of no godly counsel, and had to name Maitre Francoys Villon. Our heart was one, the heart of Elliot and mine own, and lo! here, in a day, it was torn asunder and we were set apart by the wisdom of men.

I remember me how I lay wakeful on the night before the day when Elliot should depart. Tossing and turning, I lay till the small fowls brake forth with their songs, and my own thought seemed to come and go, and come again in my head, like the "ritournelle" of the birds. At last I might not endure, but rose and attired myself very early, and so went down into the chamber. Thither presently came Elliot, feigning wonder to find me arisen, and making pretence that she was about her housewiferies, but well I wot that she might sleep no more than I. The old housewife coming and going through the room, there we devised, comforting each other with hopes and prayers; indeed we sorely wanted comfort, because never till we were wed, if ever that should be, might we have such solace of each other's presence as we desired. Then I brought from the workshop a sheet of vellum and colours, and the painting tools, and so fashioned a little picture of her, to wear within the breast of my doublet. A rude thing it was and is, for what gold, however finely handled, could match with her golden hair, whereof, at my desire, she gave me a lock; and of all worldly gear from my secular life, these and the four links of my mother's chain alone are still mine, and where my heart is there is my treasure. And she, too, must clip a long curl of my hair, for as yet it was not cut "en ronde," as archers use to wear it, but when she came again, she said she would find me shrewdly shaven, and then would love me no longer. Then she laughed and kissed me, and fell to comforting me for that she would not be long away.

"And in three months or four," she said, "the King will be sacred at Rheims, and the Maid will give you red wine to drink in Paris town, and the English will be swept into the sea, and then we shall have peace and abundance."

"And then shall we be wedded, and never part," I cried; whereat she blushed, bidding me not be over bold, for her heart might yet change, and so laughed again; and thus we fleeted the time, till her father came and sent her about disposing such things as she must take with her. Among these she was set on carrying her jackanapes, to make her merry on the road, though here I was of another counsel. For in so great a gathering there must be many gangrel folk, and among them, peradventure, the violer woman, who would desire to have the creature given back to her. But, if it were so, Elliot said she would purchase the jackanapes, "for I am no lifter of other men's cattle, as all you Scots are, and I am fain to own my jackanapes honestly."

So she carried him with her, the light chain about her wrist, and he riding on her saddle-bow, for presently, with many banners waving and with singing of hymns, came the troop who wended together on pilgrimage. Many townsfolk well armed were there to guard their women; the flags of all the crafts were on the wind; the priests carried blessed banners; so with this goodly company, and her confessor, and her father's old kinswoman, Elliot rode away. The jackanapes was screeching on her saddle-bow, her yellow hair was lifted on her shoulder with the light breeze; her father rode the first two stages with them. Merry enough they seemed that went, and the bells were chiming, but I was left alone, my heart empty, or only full of useless longings. I betook myself, therefore, to a chapel hard by, and there made my orisons for their safety and for good speed to the Maid and her holy enterprise.

Thereafter there was no similitude for me and my unhappy estate, save that of a dog who has lost his master in a strange place, and goes questing everywhere, and comfortless. Then Randal Rutherford, coming to visit me, found me such a lackmirth, he said, and my wits so distraught, that a love-sick wench were better company for a man-at-arms.

"Cheer up, man," he said. "Look at me, did I not leave my heart at Branxholme Mains with Mally Grieve, and so in every town where I have been in garrison, and do you see me cast down? Off with this green sickness, or never will you have strength to march with the Maid, where there is wealth to be won, and golden coronets, and gaudy stones, such as Saunders Macausland took off the Duke of Clarence at Bauge. Faith, between the wound Capdorat gave you and this arrow of Dan Cupid's in your heart, I believe you will not be of strength to carry arms till there is not a pockpudding left in broad France. Come forth, and drain a pot or two of wine, or, if the leech forbids it, come, I will play you for all that is owing between you and me."

With that he lugged out his dice and fetched a tablier, but presently vowed that it was plain robbery, for I could keep no count of the game. Therewith he left me, laughing and mocking, and saying that I had been bolder with Robin Lindsay's lass.

Being alone and out of all comfort, I fell to wandering in the workroom, and there lit, to my solace, on that blessed book of the hundred ballades, which my master was adorning with pictures, and with scarlet, blue, and gold. It set forth how a young knight, in sorrow of love, was riding between Pont de Ce and Angiers, and how other knights met him and gave him counsel. These lines I read, and getting them by rote, took them for my device, for they bid the lover thrust himself foremost in the press, and in breach, mine, and escalade.

> S'en assault viens, devant te lance,
> En mine, en eschielle, en tous lieux
> Ou proesce les bons avance,
> Ta Dame t'en aimera mieux.

But reading soon grew a weariness to me, as my life was, and my master coming home, bade me be of better cheer.

"By St. Andrew," quoth he, "this is no new malady of thine, but well known to leeches from of old, and never yet was it mortal! Remede there is none, save to make ballades and rondels, and forget sorrow in hunting rhymes, if thou art a maker. Thou art none? Nay, nor ever was I, lad; but I have had this disease, and yet you see me whole and well. Come, lend me a hand at painting in these lilies; it passes not thy skill."

So I wrought some work whereof I have reason to be proud, for these lilies were carried wheresoever blows and honour were to be won, ay, and where few might follow them. Meanwhile, my master devised with me about such sights as he had seen on the way, and how great a concourse was on pilgrimage to Puy, and how, if prayers availed, the cause of France was won; "and yet, in England too, wives are praying for their lords, and lasses for their lads in France. But ours is the better quarrel."

So that weary day went by, one of the longest that I have known, and other days, till now the leech said that I might go back to the castle, though that I might march to the wars he much misdoubted. Among the archers I had the best of greetings, and all quarrels were laid by, for, as was said, we were to set forth to Orleans, where would be blows enough to stay the greediest stomach. For now the Maid had won all hearts, taking some with her piety, and others with her wit and knowledge, that confounded the doctors, how she, a simple wench, was so subtle in doctrine, which might not be but by inspiration. Others, again, were moved by her mirth and good-fellowship, for she would strike a man-at-arms on the shoulder like a comrade, and her horsemanship and deftness with sword and lance bewitched others, she seeming as valiant and fair as these lady crusaders of whom old romances tell. And others, again, she gained by bourdes and jests; others by her manners, the fairest and most courtly that might be, for she, a manant's daughter, bore herself as an equal before the blood of France, and was right dear to the young bride of the fair Duc d'Alencon. Yet was there about her such a grace of purity, as of one descended from the skies, that no man of them all was so hardy as to speak to her of love, or even so much as to think thereof in the secret of his heart.

So all reported of her, and she had let write a letter to the English at Orleans, bidding them yield to God and the Maid, and begone to their own country, lest a worse thing befall them. At this letter they mocked, swearing that they would burn her heralds who carried the message. But the King had named her chief of war, and given her a household, with a good esquire, Jean d'Aulon, to govern it, and all that beseems noble or royal blood. New armour had been made for her, all of steel and silver, and there was talk of a sword that she had come by in no common way, but through revelation of the saints. For she being in Tours had it revealed to her that a certain ancient sword, with five crosses on the blade, lay buried behind the altar of St. Catherine of Fierbois. An armourer of Tours was therefore sent thither, and after much labour and search they of St. Catherine's Church found that sword, very ancient, and much bestained with rust. Howbeit, they cleaned it and made for it a sheath of cloth of gold. Nevertheless, the Maid wore it in a leathern scabbard.

Andrew Lang

CHAPTER XI

HOW MADAME CATHERINE OF FIERBOIS WROUGHT A MIRACLE FOR A SCOT, AND HOW NORMAN RODE TO THE WARS

Now, in this place I cannot withhold me from telling of an adventure which at this very time befell, though it scarce belongs to my present chronicle. But it may be that, in time to come, faith will wax cold, and the very saints be misdoubted of men. It therefore behoves me not to hold back the truth which I know, and which this tale makes plain and undeniable even by Hussites, Lollards, and other miscreants. For he who reads must be constrained to own that there is no strait so terrible but the saints can bring safely forth therefrom such men as call upon them.

There came at this season to Chinon from Fierbois (where the Maid's sword was found by miracle) a Scottish archer, not aforetime of our company, though now he took service with us. He was named Michael Hamilton, and was a tall man and strong, grim of face, sudden in anger, heavy of hand, walked a little lame, and lacked one ear. That which follows he himself told to us and to our chaplain, Father Urquhart, and I myself have read it in the Book of the Miracles of Madame St. Catherine of Fierbois. {22}

You must know that Brittany, as at this time, held for the English, and Michael Hamilton had gone thither reiving and pillaging the country with a company of Scots men-at-arms. Hard by a place called Clisson they had seized a deserted tower and held it for some days. It so fell out that they took a burgess of the country, who was playing the spy on their quarters; him they put to the torture, and so learned that the English were coming against them with a great company of men-at-arms and of the country folk, on that very night. They therefore delayed no longer than to hang the spy from a sufficient bough of a tree, this Michael doing what was needful, and so were hurrying to horse, when, lo! the English were upon them. Not having opportunity to reach the stables and mount, Michael Hamilton fled on foot, with what speed he might, but sorely impeded by the weight of his armour. The country folk, therefore, being light of foot, easily overtook him, and after slaying one and wounding more, he was caught in a noose of rope thrown over him from behind. Now, even as he felt the noose tighten about his arms, he (though not commonly pious beyond the wont of men-at-arms) vowed in his heart to make a pilgrimage to Fierbois, and to the shrine of Madame St. Catherine, if she would but aid him. And, indeed, he was ever a worshipper of St. Catherine, she being the patroness of his own parish kirk, near Bothwell. None the less, he was overcome and bound, whereon he that had thrown the noose, and was son of the spy whom Michael had hanged, vowed that he would, with his own hands, hang Michael. No ransom would this manant take, nor would he suffer Michael, as a gentleman of blood and birth, to die by the sword. So hanged Michael was; doubt not but it was done in the best manner, and there he was left hanging.

Now, that night of Maundy Thursday the cure of Clisson was in his chamber and was about to go to bed. But as he made ready for bed he heard, from a corner of the chamber, a clear voice saying, "Go forth and cut down the Scots man-at-arms who was hanged, for he yet lives."

The cure, thinking that he must be half asleep and dreaming, paid no manner of regard to these commands. Thereon the voice, twice and thrice, spoke aloud, none save the cure being present, and said, "Go forth and cut down the Scots man-at-arms who was hanged, for he yet lives."

It often so chances that men in religion are more hard of heart to believe than laymen and the simple. The cure, therefore, having made all due search, and found none living who could have uttered that voice, went not forth himself, but at noon of Good Friday, his service being done, he sent his sexton, as one used not to fear the sight and company of dead men. The sexton set out, whistling for joy of the slaying of the Scot, but when he came back he was running as fast as he might, and scarce could speak for very fear. At the last they won from him that he had gone to the tree where the dead Scot was hanging, and first had heard a faint rustle of the boughs. Not affrighted, the sexton drew out a knife and slit one of Michael's bare toes, for they had stripped him before they hanged him. At the touch of the knife the blood came, and the foot gave a kick, whereon the sexton hastened back with these tidings to the cure. The holy man, therefore, sending for such clergy as he could muster, went at their head, in all his robes canonical, to the wild wood, where they cut Michael down and rubbed his body and poured wine into his throat, so that, at the end of half an hour, he sat up and said, "Pay Waiter Hay the two testers that I owe him."

Thereon most ran and hid themselves, as if from a spirit of the dead, but the manant, he whose father Michael had hanged, made at him with a sword, and dealt him a great blow, cutting off his ear. But others who had not fled, and chiefly the cure, held the manant till his hands were bound, that he might not slay one so favoured of Madame St. Catherine. Not that they knew of Michael's vow, but it was plain to the cure that the man was under the protection of Heaven. Michael then, being kindly nursed in a house of a certain Abbess, was wellnigh recovered, and his vow wholly forgotten, when lo! he being alone, one invisible smote his cheek, so that the room rang with the buffet, and a voice said to him, "Wilt thou never remember thy pilgrimage?" Moved, therefore, to repentance, he stole the cure's horse, and so, journeying by night till he reached France, he accomplished his vows, and was now returned to Chinon. This Michael Hamilton was hanged, not very long afterwards, by command of the Duc d'Alencon, for plundering a church at Jargeau.

The story I have thought it behoved me to tell in this place, because it shows how good and mild is Madame St. Catherine of Fierbois, also lest memory of it be lost in Scotland, where it cannot but be of great comfort to all gentlemen of Michael's kin and of the name and house of Hamilton. Again, I tell it because I heard it at this very season of my waiting to be recovered of my wound. Moreover, it is a tale of much edification to men-at-arms, as proving how ready are the saints to befriend us, even by speaking as it were with human voices to sinful men. Of this I myself, later, had good proof, as shall be told, wherefore I praise and thank the glorious virgin, Madame St. Catherine of Fierbois.

This tale was the common talk in Chinon, which I heard very gladly, taking pleasure in the strangeness of it. And in the good fortune of the Maid I was yet more joyful, both for her own sake and for Elliot's, to whom she was so dear. But, for my own part, the leeches gave me little comfort, saying that I might in no manner set forth with the rest, for that I could not endure to march on foot, but must die by the way.

Poor comfort was this for me, who must linger in garrison while the fortune of France was on the cast of the dice, and my own fortune was to be made now or never. So it chanced that one day I was loitering in the gateway, watching the soldiers, who were burnishing armour, sharpening swords, and all as merry and busy as bees in spring. Then to me comes my master, with a glad countenance, and glad was I, for these eight days or nine I had no tidings of him, and knew not if Elliot had returned from pilgrimage. I rose to greet him, and he took my hand, bidding me be of good cheer, for that he had good tidings. But what his news might be he would not tell me; I must come with him, he said, to his house.

All about his door there was much concourse of people, and among them two archers led a great black charger, fairly caparisoned, and covered with a rich silk hucque of colour cramoisie, adorned with lilies of silver. As I marvelled who the rider might be, conceiving that he was some great lord, the door of my master's house opened, and there, within, and plain to view, was Elliot embracing a young knight; and over his silver armour fell her yellow hair, covering gorget and rere-brace. Then my heart stood still, my lips opened but gave no cry, when, lo! the knight kissed her and came forth, all in shining armour, but unhelmeted. Then I saw that this was no knight, but the Maid herself, boden in effeir of war, {23} and so changed from what she had been that she seemed a thing divine. If St. Michael had stepped down from a church window, leaving the dragon slain, he would have looked no otherwise than she, all gleaming with steel, and with grey eyes full of promise of victory: the holy sword girdled about her, and a little battle-axe hanging from her saddle-girth. She sprang on her steed, from the mounting-stone beside the door, and so, waving her hand, she cried farewell to Elliot, that stood gazing after her with shining eyes. The people went after the Maid some way, shouting

Noel! and striving to kiss her stirrup, the archers laughing, meanwhile, and bidding them yield way. And so we came, humbly enough, into the house, where, her father being present and laughing and the door shut, Elliot threw her arms about me and wept and smiled on my breast.

"Ah, now I must lose you again," she said; whereat I was half glad that she prized me so; half sorry, for that I knew I might not go forth with the host. This ill news I gave them both, we now sitting quietly in the great chamber.

"Nay, thou shalt go," said Elliot. "Is it not so, father? For the Maid gave her promise ere she went to Poictiers, and now she is fulfilling it. For the gentle King has given her a household—pages, and a maitre d'hotel, a good esquire, and these two gentlemen who rode with her from Vaucouleurs, and an almoner, Brother Jean Pasquerel, an Augustine, that the Maid's mother sent with us from Puy, for we found her there. And the Maid has appointed you to go with her, for that you took her part when men reviled her. And money she has craved from the King; and Messire Aymar de Puiseux, that was your adversary, is to give you a good horse, for that you may not walk. And, above all, the Maid has declared to me that she will bring you back to us unscathed of sword, but, for herself, she shall be wounded by an arrow under Orleans, yet shall she not die, but be healed of that wound, and shall lead the King to his sacring at Rheims. So now, verily, for you I have no fear, but my heart is sore for the Maid's sake, and her wound."

None the less, she made as if she would dance for joy, and I could have done as much, not, indeed, that as then I put my faith in prophecies, but for gladness that I was to take my fortune in the wars. So the hours passed in great mirth and good cheer. Many things we spoke of, as concerning the mother of the Maid—how wise she was, yet in a kind of amazement, and not free from fear, wherefore she prayed constantly for her child.

Moreover Elliot told me that the jackanapes was now hers of right, for that the woman, its owner, had been at Puy, but without her man, and had sold it to her, as to a good mistress, yet with tears at parting. This news was none of the gladdest to me, for still I feared that tidings of us might come to Brother Thomas. Howbeit, at last, with a light heart, though I was leaving Elliot, I went back to the castle. There Aymar de Puiseux, meeting me, made me the best countenance, and gave me a right good horse, that I named Capdorat after him, by his good will. And for my armour, which must needs be light, they gave me a maillet—a coat of slender mail, which did not gall my old wound. So accoutred, I departed next day, in good company, to Blois, whence the Maid was to set forth to Orleans. Marvel it was to find the road so full of bestial—oxen, cows, sheep, and swine—all gathered, as if to some great market, for the victualling of Orleans. But how they were to be got through the English lines into the city men knew not. For the English, by this time, had girdled the city all about with great bastilles, each joined to other by sunken ways dug in the earth, wherein were streets, and marts, and chambers with fires and chimneys, as I have written in my Latin chronicle. {24} There false Frenchmen came, as to a fair, selling and buying, with store of food, wine, arms, and things of price, buying and selling in safety, for the cannon and couleuvrines in the town could not touch them. But a word ran through the host how the Maid knew, by inspiration of the saints, that no man should sally forth from among the English, but that we should all pass unharmed.

Meantime the town of Blois was in great turmoil—the cattle lowing in the streets, the churches full to the doors of men-at-arms, waiting their turn to be shrived, for the Maid had ordained that all who followed her must go clean of sin. And there was great wailing of light o' loves, and leaguer lasses that had followed the army, as is custom, for this custom the Maid did away, and drove these women forth, and whither they wandered I know not. Moreover, she made proclamation that all dice, and tabliers, and instruments of gambling must be burned, and myself saw the great pile yet smoking in the public place, for this was to be a holy war. So we lodged at Blois, where the Maid showed me the best countenance, speaking favourable words of Elliot and me, and bidding me keep near her banner in battle, which I needed no telling to make me resolve to do. So there, for that night, we rested.

Andrew Lang

CHAPTER XII

HOW THE MAID CAME TO ORLEANS, AND OF THE DOLOROUS STROKE THAT FIRST SHE STRUCK IN WAR

Concerning the ways of the saints, and their holy counsel, it is not for sinful men to debate, but verify their ways are not as our ways, as shall presently be shown, in the matter of the Maid's march to Orleans.

For the town of Blois, where now we lay, is, as all men know, on the right bank of the water of Loire, a great river, wider and deeper and stronger by far than our Tay or Tweed, and the town of Orleans, whither we were bound, is also on the same side, namely, the right side of the river. Now, Orleans was beleaguered in this manner: The great stone bridge had been guarded, on the left, or further side of the stream, first by a boulevard, or strong keep on the land, whence by a drawbridge men crossed to a yet stronger keep, called "Les Tourelles," builded on the last arches of the bridge. But early in the siege the English had taken from them of Orleans the boulevard and Les Tourelles, and an arch of the bridge had been broken, so that in nowise might men-at-arms of the party of France enter into Orleans by way of that bridge from the left bank through the country called Sologne.

Yet that keep, Les Tourelles, had not been a lucky prize to our enemies of England. For their great captain, the Lord Salisbury, had a custom to watch them of Orleans and their artillery from a window in that tower, and, to guard him from arrow-shots, he had a golden shield pierced with little holes to look through, that he held before his face. One day he came into this turret when they who worked the guns in Orleans were all at their meat. But it so chanced that two boys, playing truant from school, went into a niche of the wall, where was a cannon loaded and aimed at Les Tourelles. They, seeing the gleam of the golden shield at the window of the turret, set match to the touch-hole of the cannon, and, as Heaven would have it, the ball struck a splinter of stone from the side of the window, which, breaking through the golden shield, slew my Lord of Salisbury, a good knight. Thus plainly that tower was to be of little comfort to the English.

None the less, as they held Les Tourelles and the outer landward boulevard thereof, the English built but few works on the left side of the river, namely, Champ St. Prive, that guarded the road by the left bank from Blois; Les Augustins, that was a little inland from the boulevard of Les Tourelles, so that no enemy might pass between these two holds; and St. Jean le Blanc, that was higher up the river, and a hold of no great strength. On the Orleans side, to guard the road from Burgundy, the English had but one fort, St. Loup, for Burgundy and the north were of their part, and by this way they expected no enemy. But all about Orleans, on the right bank of the river, to keep the path from Blois on that hand, the English had builded many great bastilles, and had joined them by hollow ways, wherein, as I said, they lived at ease, as men in a secure city underground. And the skill of it was to stop convoys of food, and starve them of Orleans, for to take the town by open force the English might in nowise avail, they being but some four thousand men-at-arms.

Thus Matters stood, and it was the Maid's mind to march her men and all the cattle clean through and past the English bastilles on the right side of the river, and by inspiration she well knew that no man would come forth against us. Moreover, she saw not how, by the other way, and the left bank, the cattle might be ferried across, and the great company of men-at-arms, into Orleans town, under the artillery of the English. For the English held the pass of the broken bridge, as I said, and therefore all crossing of the water must be by boat.

Now, herein it was shown, as often again, that the ways of the saints are not as our ways. For the captains, namely, the Sieur de Rais (who afterwards came to the worst end a man might), and La Hire, and Ambroise de Lore, and De Gaucourt, in concert with the Bastard of Orleans, then commanding for the King in that town, gave the simple Maid to understand that Orleans was on the left bank of the river. This they did, because they were faithless and slow of belief, and feared that so great a company as ours might in nowise pass Meun and Beaugency, towns of the English, and convey so many cattle through the bastilles on the right bank. Therefore, with many priests going before, singing the Veni Creator, with holy banners as on a pilgrimage; with men-at-arms, archers, pages, and trains of carts; and with bullocks rowting beneath the goad, and swine that are very hard to drive, and slow-footed sheep, we all crossed the bridge of Blois on the morning of April 25th.

Now, had the holy saints deemed it wise and for our good to act as men do, verily they would have spoken to the Maid, telling her that we were all going clean contrary to her counsel. Nevertheless, the saints held their peace, and let us march on. Belike they designed that this should turn to the greater glory of the Maid and to the confusion of them that disbelieved, which presently befell, as I shall relate.

All one day of spring we rode, and slept beneath the stars, the Maid lying in her armour, so that as one later told me who knew, namely, Elliot, her body was sorely bruised with her harness. Early in the morning we mounted again, and so rode north, fetching a compass inland; after noontide we came to a height, and lo! beneath us lay the English bastilles and holds on the left bank, and, beyond the glittering river and the broken bridge, the towers and walls of Orleans. Then I saw the Maid in anger, for well she knew that she had been deceived by them who should have guided her. Between us and the town of Orleans lay the wide river, the broken bridge, and the camps of the English. On the further shore we beheld the people swarming on the walls and quays, labouring to launch boats with sails, and so purposing to ascend the river against the stream and meet us two leagues beyond the English lines. But this they might not do, for a strong wind was blowing down stream, and all their vessels were in disarray.

The Maid spurred to the front, where were De Rais, Lore, Kennedy, and La Hire. We could see her pointing with her staff, and hear speech high and angry, but the words we could not hear. The captains looked downcast, as children caught in a fault, and well they might, for we were now as far off victualling Orleans as ever we had been. The Maid pointed to the English keep at St. Jean le Blanc, on our side of the water, and, as it seems, was fain to attack it; but the English had drawn off their men to the stronger places on the bridge, and to hold St. Jean le Blanc against them, if we took it, we had no strength. So we even wended, from the height of Olivet, for six long miles, till we reached the stream opposite Checy, where was an island. A rowing-boat, with a knight in glittering arms, was pulled across the stream, and the Maid, in her eagerness, spurred her steed deep into the water to meet him. He was a young man, brown of visage, hardy and fierce, and on his shield bore the lilies of Orleans, crossed with a baton sinister. He bowed low to the Maid, who cried—

"Are you the Bastard of Orleans?"

"I am," he said, "and right glad of your coming."

"Was it you who gave counsel that I should come by this bank, and not by the other side, and so straight against Talbot and the English?"

She spoke as a master to a faulty groom, fierce and high, and to hear her was marvel.

"I, and wiser men than I, gave that counsel," said he, "deeming this course the surer."

"Nom Dieu!" she cried. "The council of Messire is safer and wiser than yours." She pointed to the rude stream, running rough and strong, a great gale following with it, so that no sailing-boats might come from the town. "You thought to beguile me, and are yourselves beguiled, for I bring you better succour than ever came to knight or town—the help of the King of Heaven."

Then, even as she spoke, and as by miracle, that fierce wind went right about, and blew straight up the stream, and the sails of the vessels filled.

"This is the work of our Lord," said the Bastard of Orleans, crossing himself: and the anger passed from the eyes of the Maid.

Then he and Nicole de Giresme prayed her to pass the stream with them, and to let her host march back to Blois and so come to Orleans, crossing by the bridge of Blois. To this she said nay, that she could not leave her men out of her sight, lest they fell to sin again, and all her pains were lost. But, with many prayers, her confessor Pasquerel joining in them, she was brought to consent. So the host, with priests and banners, must set forth again to Blois, while the Maid, and we that were of her company, crossed the river in boats, and so rode towards the town. On this way (the same is a road of the old Romans) the English held a strong fort, called St. Loup, and well might they have sallied forth against us. But the people of Orleans, who ever bore themselves more hardily than any townsfolk whom I have known, made an onfall against St. Loup, that the English within might not sally out against us, where was fierce fighting, and they took a standard from the English.

So, at nightfall, the Maid, with the Bastard and other captains at her side, rode into the town, all the people welcoming her with torches in hand, shouting Noel! as to a king, throwing flowers before her horse's feet, and pressing to touch her, or even the harness of her horse, which leaped and plunged, for the fire of a torch caught the fringe of her banner. Lightly she spurred and turned him, and lightly she caught at the flame with her hand and quenched it, while all men marvelled at her grace and goodly bearing.

Never saw I more joy of heart, for whereas all had feared to fall into the hands of the English, now there was such courage in them, as if Monseigneur St. Michael himself, or Monseigneur St Aignan, had come down from heaven to help his good town. If they were hardy before, as indeed they were, now plainly they were full of such might and fury that man might not stand against them. And soon it was plain that no less fear had fallen on the English. But the Maid, with us who followed her, was led right through the great street of Orleans, from the Burgundy gate to the gate Regnart, whereby the fighting was ever most fell, and there we lodged in the house of the Treasurer of the Duke of Orleans, Jacquet Boucher. Never was sleep sweeter to me, after the two weary marches, and the sounds of music and revelry in the street did not hum a moment in my ears, before I had passed into that blessed world of slumber without a dream.

But my waking next day brought instantly the thought of my brother Robin, concerning whom I had ever feared that he fell with the flower of Scotland, when the Comte de Clermont deserted us so shamefully on the day of the Battle of the Herrings. No sooner did this doubt come into my mind, than I leaped from my bed, attired myself, and went forth to the quarters of the Scots under Sir Christian Chambers. Little need I had to tell my errand, for they that met me guessed who I was, because, indeed, Robin and I favoured each other greatly in face and bodily presence.

It was even as I had deemed: my dear brother and friend and tutor of old days had died, charging back upon the English who pursued us, and fighting by the side of Pothon de Xaintrailles. All that day, and in the week which followed, my thought was ever upon him; a look in a stranger's face, a word on another's lips, by some magic of the mind would bring my brother almost visibly before me, ay, among the noise of swords on mail, and the screaming of arrows, and of great cannon-balls.

If I heard ill news, it was no more than I looked for; but better news, as it seemed, I also heard, though, in my sorrow, I marked it little. For the soldiers were lamenting the loss of their famed gunner, not John the Lorrainer, but one who had come to them, they said, now some weeks agone, in the guise of a cordelier, though he did not fight in that garb, but in common attire, and ever wore his vizor down, which men deemed strange. Whither he had gone, or how disappeared, they knew not, for he had not been with those who yesterday attacked St. Loup.

"He could never thole the thought of the Blessed Maid," said Allan Rutherford, "but would tell all that listened how she was a brain-sick wench, or a witch, and under her standard he would never fight. He even avowed to us that she had been a chamber-wench of an inn in Neufchateau, and there had learned to back a horse, and many a worse trick," which was a lie devised by the English and them of Burgundy. But, go where he would, or how he would, I deemed it well that Brother Thomas and I (for of a surety it was Brother Thomas) were not to meet in Orleans.

Concerning the English in this wonderful adventure of the siege, I have never comprehended, nor do I now know, wherefore they bore them as they did. That they sallied not out on the trains which the Maid led and brought into the town, a man might set down to mere cowardice and faint heart—they fearing to fight against a witch, as they deemed her. In later battles, when she had won so many a victory, they may well have feared her. But, as now, they showed no dread where honour was to be won, but rather pride and disdain. On this very Saturday, the morrow of our arrival, La Hire, with Florent d'Illiers and many other knights, pushed forth a matter of two bowshots from the city walls, and took a keep that they thought to have burned. They were very hardy men, and being comforted by the Maid's coming, were full of courage and goodwill; yet the English rallied and drove them back, with much firing of guns, and now first I heard the din of war and saw the great stone balls fly, scattering, as they fell, into splinters that screamed in the air, with a very terrible sound. Truly the English had the better of that fray, and were no whit adread, for at sunset the Maid sent them two heralds, bidding them begone; yet they answered only that they would burn her for a witch, and called her a ribaulde, or loose wench, and bade her go back and keep her kine.

I was with her when this message came, and her brows met and her eyes flashed with anger. Telling us of her company to follow, she went to the Fair Cross on the bridge, where now her image stands, fashioned in bronze, kneeling before the Cross, with the King kneeling opposite. There she stood and cried aloud to the English, who were in the fort on the other side of the bridge that is called Les Tourelles, and her voice rang across the water like a trumpet, so that it was marvel. Then came out on to the bridge a great knight and a tall, Sir William Glasdale; no bigger man have I seen, and I bethought me of Goliath in Holy Scripture. He spoke in a loud, north-country voice, and, whereas she addressed him courteously, as she did all men, he called her by the worst of names, mocking at her for a ribaulde. She made answer that he lied, and that he should die in four days' time or five, without stroke of sword; and so, waving her hand haughtily, turned and went back. But I, who walked close by her, noted that she wept like any girl at his evil and lying accusations.

Next day was Sunday, and no stroke was struck, but the Bastard of Orleans set forth to bring back the army from Blois. And on Monday the Maid rode out and under the very walls of the English keeps, the townsfolk running by her rein, as if secure in her company; yet no man came forth against them, which was marvel. And on the Wednesday, the Maid, with many knights, rode forth two leagues, and met the Bastard of Orleans and all the array from Blois, and all the flocks and herds that were sent to Orleans by the good towns. Right beneath the forts of the English they rode and marched, with chanting of hymns, priests leading the way, but none dared meddle with them. Yet a child might have seen that now or never was the chance: howbeit Talbot and Glasdale and Scales, men well learned in war, let fire not even a single cannon. It may be that they feared an attack of the Orleans folk on their bastilles, if they drew out their men. For, to tell the plain truth, the English had not men-at-arms enough for the task they took in hand; but they oft achieve much with but little force, and so presume the more, sometimes to their undoing. And, till the Maid came, ten of them could chase a hundred of the French.

So the Maid returned, leading the army, and then, being very weary, she went into her chamber, and lay down on a couch to sleep, her esquire, D'Aulon, also resting in the room, where were the lady and a daughter of the house, one Charlotte Boucher. There was I, devising idly with her page, Louis de Coutes, a boy half Scots by birth, and good-brother to Messire Florent d'Illiers, who had married his sister. But alas! he was more French than Scots, and later he left the Maid. But then we were playing ourselves at the door of the house, and all was still, the men-at-arms reposing, as we deemed, after their march. Then suddenly the Maid ran forth to us, her face white and her eyes shining, and cried to Louis de Coutes, in great anger—

"Wretched boy, the blood of France is being shed, and you told me no word of it!"

"Demoiselle," said he, trembling, "I wotted not of it. What mean you?"

And I also stood in amaze, for we had heard no sound of arms.

"Go, fetch my horse," she said, and was gone.

I went with him, and we saddled and bridled a fresh courser speedily; but when we reached the door, she stood there already armed, and sprang on the horse, crying for her banner, that De Coutes gave her out of the upper window.

Then her spurs were in her horse's side, and the sparks flying from beneath his hoofs, as she galloped towards St. Loup, the English fort on the Burgundy road. Thither we followed her, with what speed we might, yet over tardily; and when we came through crowds of people, many bearing the wounded on litters, there was she, under the wall of that fort, in a rain of arrows, holding up her banner, and crying on the French and Scots to the charge. They answered with a cry, and went on, De Coutes and I pressing forward to be with them; but ere ever we could gain the fosse, the English had been overwhelmed, and, for the more part, slain. For, as we found, the French captains had commanded an attack on St. Loup, and had told the Maid no word of it, whether as desiring to win honour without her, or to spare her from the peril of the onslaught, I know not. But their men were giving ground, when by the monition of the saints, as I have shown, she came to them and turned the fray.

Of the English, as I said, most were slain, natheless certain men in priests' raiment came forth from the Church of St. Loup, and very humbly begged their lives of the Maid, who, turning to D'Aulon, her esquire, bade him, with De Coutes and me, and such men as we could gather, to have charge of them and be answerable for them.

So, while the French were plundering, we mustered these priests orderly together, they trembling and telling their beads, and we stood before them for their guard. False priests, I doubt, many of them were, Englishmen who had hastily done on such holy robes as they found in the church of St Loup. Now Louis de Coutes, being but a boy, and of a mad humour, cried—

"'Cucullus non facit monachum!' Good sirs, let us see your reverend tonsures."

With that he twitched the hood from the head of a tall cordelier, who, without more ado, felled him to the earth with his fist.

The hood was off but for a flash of time, yet I saw well the shining wolf's eyes and the long dark face of Brother Thomas. So, in the pictures of the romance of Renard Fox, have I seen Isengrim the wolf in the friar's hood.

"Felon and traitor!" I cried, and drawing my sword, was about to run him through the body, when my hand was stunned by a stroke, and the sword dropped from it. I turned, in great anger, and saw the Maid, her sword in her hand, wherewith she had smitten me flatlings, and not with the edge.

"Knave of a Scot," she cried, "wouldst thou strike a holy man and my prisoner? Verily they say well that the Scots are all savages. Begone home, till I speak with the captains about thy case! And for these holy men," she said to D'Aulon, in a soft voice, "see that they are safely housed and ministered to in the Church of Monseigneur St. Aignan."

With that I shrank back like a beaten hound, and saw the Maid no more that night, as fearing her wrath. So was I adread and out of all comfort. But, when first I might, I sought D'Aulon and told him all the tale of Brother Thomas, and all the evil I knew of him, as well as I could, and I showed him wherefore I had sought to slay the man, as forsworn and a traitor, who had manifestly fled to the English, being by his doggish nature the enemy of the Maid. I so wrought with him, though he was weary, and would scarce listen to my tale, that he promised to speak for me to the Maid, without whom I was a man lost. Moreover, he swore that, as early as might be, he would visit the Church of St. Aignan, and there examine into the matter of this cordelier, whom some knew, and could testify against, if he was my man.

No more could I do that night, but next morning D'Aulon awoke me a little after dawn.

"It is a true tale," he said, "and worse than I deemed, for your bird has flown! Last night he so spoke with me in the church when I lodged him there, that I reckoned him a simple man and a pious. But he has vanished from among his brethren, none knows how or whither."

"The devil, his master, knows," I said. "Faith, he has a shrewd care of his own. But this, I misdoubt me, is the beginning of evil to us and to the Maid."

"A knave more or less is of little count in the world," said he; "but now I must make your peace with the Maid, for she speaks of no less than sending you forth from her household."

His promise he kept so well—for he was a very honourable man, as any in France—that the Maid sent for me and showed me the best countenance, even begging my pardon with all sweetness, and in so fair a manner that I could have wept.

"It was my first blow in war," she said, smiling kindly, as was her manner, "and I hope to strike no more as with my own hand, wherefore I carry my banner to avoid the slaying of men. But verily I deemed that you were about stabbing my prisoner, and him a priest. Belike we shall hear no more of him, and I misdoubt that he is no true son of Holy Church. To-day let me see you bear yourself as boldly against armed men, that I may report well of you to your lady and my friend."

Therewith she held out her hands and took mine, as frankly as does one brother in arms with another. And I kissed her hand, and kept my tears in my own heart. But no deadlier blow for France and for herself was ever dealt than when the Maid struck down my sword, that was thirsting for the blood of Brother Thomas, and was within an inch of his throat. Often have I marvelled how the saints, who, as then, guarded her, gave her no warning, as they did of the onslaught on St. Loup; but it might not be, or it was not their will, to which we must humbly submit ourselves. And now I think I see that wolf's face, under the hood, with anger and fear in the ominous eyes. In the Church of St. Loup we found him, and he was a wolf of the holy places. None the less, the words of the Maid brought more keenly to my mind the thought of Elliot, whom in these crowded hours, between my sorrow and anger, and fear of the Maid's wrath, I had to some degree forgotten. They were now ordering an onslaught on a post of the English beyond the river, and there came into my heart that verse of the "Book of a Hundred Ballades": how a lover must press into breach, and mine, and escalade to win advancement and his lady's favour; and I swore within myself that to-day I would be among the foremost.

Andrew Lang

CHAPTER XIII

OF THE FIGHTING AT LES AUGUSTINS
AND THE PROPHECY OF THE MAID

Just above the broken bridge of Orleans there is a broad island, lying very near the opposite shore, with a narrow, swift passage of water between bank and island. Some two furlongs higher up the river, and on the further bank, the English had built a small fort, named St. Jean le Blanc, to guard the road, and thither they sent men from Les Augustins. The plan of our captains was to cross by boats on to the island, and thence by a bridge of planks laid on boats to win over the narrow channel, and so make an onslaught on St. Jean le Blanc. For this onslaught the Maid had now been armed by her women, and with all her company, and many knights, was making ready to cross. But before she, or we with her, could attain the shore, horses being ill beasts in a boat ferry, the light-armed townsfolk had crossed over against St. Jean le Blanc to spy on it, and had found the keep empty, for the English had drawn back their men to the Bastille of Les Augustins.

Thus there was no more to do, for the captains deemed not that we were of any avail to attack Les Augustins. They were retreating then to the bridge of boats, and Messires de Gaucourt, De Villars, and other good knights were guarding the retreat, all orderly, lest the English might sally out from Les Augustins, and, taking us in the rear, might slay many in the confusion of crossing the boat-bridge, when the Maid and La Hire, by great dint of toil, passed their horses in a ferry-boat on to the further bank. At this moment the English sallied forth, with loud cries, from Les Augustins, and were falling on our men, who, fearing to be cut off, began to flee disorderly, while the English called out ill words, as "cowards" and "ribaulds," and were blaspheming God that He should damn all Frenchmen.

Hereon the Maid, with her banner, and La Hire, with lance in rest, they two alone, spurred into the press, and now her banner was tossing like the flag of a ship in the breakers, and methought there was great jeopardy lest they should be taken. But the other French and Scots, perceiving the banner in such a peril, turned again from their flight, and men who once turn back to blows again are ill to deal with. Striking, then, and crying, Montjoie! St. Denis! and St. Andrew for Scotland! they made the English give ground, till they were within the palisade of Les Augustins, where they deemed them safe enough. Now I had struggled through the throng on the island, some flying, some advancing, as each man's heart bade him, till I leaped into the water up to my waist and won the land. There I was running to the front of the fight when D'Aulon would have stopped me, for he had a command to hold a certain narrow way, lest the English should drive us to the water again.

All this was rightly done, but I, hearing the cry of St. Andrew, was as one possessed, and paying no heed to D'Aulon, was for thrusting me forward, when a certain Spaniard, Alphonse de Partada, caught me by the arm, and told me, with an oath, that I might well bide where better men than I were content to be. At this I made answer that my place was with the Maid, and, as for better men, bigger he might well be, but I, for one, was not content to look on idly where blows were being dealt. He answered in such terms that I bade him follow me, and see which of us would fare furthest into the press.

"And for that you may be swifter of foot than I, as you have longer legs," I cried, "clasp hands on this bargain, and let us reach the palisades with the same step."

To this he agreed, and D'Aulon not refusing permission (for he loved to look on a vaillance), we, clasping hands, ran together swiftly, and struck our swords in the same moment against the wooden fence. A little opening there was, not yet closed, or he that kept it deemed he might win more honour by holding it with his body. He was a great knight and tall, well armed, the red cross of St. George on his breast, and he fought with a mighty sword. Together, then, we made at him, two to one, as needs must be, for this was no gentle passage of arms, but open battle. One sweep of his sword I made shift to avoid, but the next lighting on my salade, drove me staggering back for more yards than two or three, and I reeled and fell on my hands. When I rose, Alphonse de Partada was falling beneath a sword-stroke, and I was for running forward again; but lo! the great English knight leaped in the air, and so, turning, fell on his face, his hands grasping at the ground and his feet kicking.

Later I heard from D'Aulon that he had bidden John the Lorrainer mark the man with his couleuvrine, for that he did overmuch mischief. But, thinking of nought save to be foremost in the breach, I ran in, stumbling over the dead man's body, and shouldered at the same time by Alphonse, who warded off a stab of a pike that was dealt at me. Then it was a fair mellay, our men pressing after us through the gap, and driving us forward by mere weight of onset, they coming with all speed against our enemies that ran together from all parts of the keep, and so left bare the further wall. It was body to body, weight against weight, short strokes at close quarters, and, over our heads, bills striking and foining at the English. Each man smote where he could; we wavered and swayed, now off our feet in the press, now making some yard of ground, and evil was the smell and thick the dust that arose. Meanwhile came the sound of the riving of planks from the other side of the palisade; above the steel points and the dust I saw the Maid's pennon advancing with the face of my lady painted thereon, and I pressed towards it, crying "St. Andrew" with such breath as was in me. Then rang out the Maid's voice, like a clarion, "St. Denis!" and so, stroke echoing stroke, and daggers going at close quarters, beaten on and blinded, deaf and breathless, now up, now down, we staggered forward, till I and the Maid stood side by side, and the English broke, some falling, some flying to the out-gate.

And, when all was done, there was I, knowing little enough of what had come and gone, dazed, with my sword bloody and bent, my head humming, and my foot on the breast of an English knight, one Robert Heron. Him I took to prisoner, rescue or no rescue, and so sat we down, very weary, in the midst of blood and broken arms, for many had been slain and a few taken, though the more part had fled into the boulevard of Les Tourelles. And here, with a joyous face, and the vizor of her helm raised, stood the Maid, her sword sheathed, waving her banner in the sight of the English that were on the bridge fort.

Natheless, her joy was but for a moment, and soon was she seated lowly on the ground, holding in her arms the head of an English knight, sore wounded, for whom her confessor, Father Pasquerel, was doing the offices of religion. Tears were running down her cheeks, even as if he had been one of her own people; and so, comforting and helping the wounded as she might, she abode till the darkness came, and the

Andrew Lang

captains had made shift to repair the fortress and had set guards all orderly. And all the river was dark with boats coming and going, their lanterns glittering on the stream, and they were laden with food and munitions of war. In one of these boats did the Maid cross the river, taking with her us of her company, and speaking to me, above others, in the most gracious manner, for that I had been the first, with that Spanish gentleman, to pass within the English palisade. And now my heart was light, though my flesh was very weary, for that I had done my devoir, and taken the firstfruits of Elliot's wedding portion. No heavy ransom I put on that knight, Sir Robert Heron, and it was honourably paid in no long time, though he ill liked yielding him to one that had not gained his spurs. But it was fortune of war. So, half in a dream, we reached our house, and there was the greatest concourse of townsfolk clamouring in the praise of the Maid, who showed herself to them from the window, and promised that to-morrow they should take Les Tourelles. That night was Friday, yet, so worn were we all that the Maid bade us sup, and herself took some meat and a little wine in her water, though commonly she fasted on Friday. And now we were about to boun us for bed, and the Maid had risen, and was standing with her arms passed about the neck of the daughter of the house, a fair lass and merry, called Charlotte Boucher, who always lay with her (for she had great joy to be with girls of her own age), when there came the sound of a dagger-hilt beating at the door. We opened, and there stood a tall knight, who louted low to the Maid, cap in hand, and she bade him drink to the taking of Les Tourelles that should be to-morrow.

But he, with the flagon full in his hands, and withal a thirsty look upon his face, shook his head.

"To another pledge, Maiden, I will gladly drink, namely, to the bravest damsel under the sky."

And therewith he drank deep.

"But now I am sent from Gaucourt, and the Bastard, for all the captains are in counsel again. And they bid me tell you that enough hath been done, and they are right well content. But we are few against so great a host, in a place so strong that men may not avail to master it by main force. The city is now well seen in all manner of victual; moreover, we can now come and go by Sologne and the left bank. The skill is therefore to hold the city till the English wax weary and depart, or till we have succour anew from the King. Therefore to-morrow the men-at-arms shall take rest, having great need thereof; and therefore, gentle Maid, pardon me that I drank not to the pledge which a lady called."

Then he drained the flagon.

The Maid, holding the girl Charlotte yet closer to her, smote her right hand on the table, so that it dirled, and the cups and dishes leaped.

"You have been with your counsel," she cried, "and I have been with mine! The counsel of Messire will stand fast and prevail, and yours shall perish, for it is of men. Go back, and bear my words to the captains," quoth she; and then, turning to us, who looked on her in amazement, she said—

"Do ye all rise right early, and more than ye have done to-day shall ye do. Keep ever close by me in the mellay, for to-morrow I shall have much to do, and more than ever yet I did. And to-morrow shall my blood leap from my body, above my breast, for an arrow shall smite here!" and she struck the place with her hand.

Thereon the knight, seeing that she was not to be moved, made his obeisance, and went back to them that sent him, and all we lay down to sleep while we might.

These words of the Maid I, Norman Leslie, heard, and bear record that they are true.

CHAPTER XIV

OF THE FIGHTING AT THE BRIDGE, AND OF THE PRIZE WON BY NORMAN LESLIE FROM THE RIVER

On that night I slept soft, and woke oft, being utterly foredone. In the grey dawn I awoke, and gave a little cough, when, lo! there came a hot sweet gush into my mouth, and going to the window, I saw that I was spitting of blood, belike from my old wound. It is a strange thing that, therewith, a sickness came over me, and a cold fit as of fear, though fear I had felt none where men met in heat of arms. None the less, seeing that to-day, or never, I was to be made or marred, I spoke of the matter neither to man nor woman, but drinking a long draught of very cold water, I spat some deal more, and then it stanched, and I armed me and sat down on my bed.

My thoughts, as I waited for the first stir in the house, were not glad. Birds were singing in the garden trees; all else was quiet, as if men were not waking to slay each other and pass unconfessed to their account. There came on me a great sickness of war. Yesterday the boulevard of Les Augustins, when the fight was over, had been a shambles; white bodies that had been stripped of their armour lay here and there like sheep on a hillside, and were now smirched with dust, a

Andrew Lang

thing unseemly. I put it to myself that I was engaged, if ever man was, in a righteous quarrel, fighting against cruel oppression; and I was under the protection of one sent, as I verily believed, by Heaven.

But blood runs tardy in the cold dawn; my thoughts were chilled, and I deemed, to speak sooth, that I carried my death within me, from my old wound, and, even if unhurt, could scarce escape out of that day's labour and live. I said farewell to life and the sun, in my own mind, and to Elliot, thinking of whom, with what tenderness she had nursed me, and of her mirth and pitiful heart, I could scarce forbear from weeping. Of my brother also I thought, and in death it seemed to me that we could scarcely be divided. Then my thought went back to old days of childhood at Pitcullo, old wanderings by Eden banks, old kindness and old quarrels, and I seemed to see a vision of a great tree, growing alone out of a little mound, by my father's door, where Robin and I would play "Willie Wastle in his castle," for that was our first manner of holding a siege. A man-at-arms has little to make with such fancies, and well I wot that Randal Rutherford troubled himself therewith in no manner. But now there came an iron footstep on the stairs, and the Maid's voice rang clear, and presently there arose the sound of hammers on rivets, and all the din of men saddling horses and sharpening swords, so I went forth to join my company.

Stiff and sore was I, and felt as if I could scarce raise my sword-arm; but the sight of the Maid, all gleaming in her harness, and clear of voice, and swift of deed, like St. Michael when he marshalled his angels against the enemies of heaven, drove my brooding thoughts clean out of mind. The sun shone yellow and slanting down the streets; out of the shadow of the minster came the bells, ringing for war. The armed townsfolk thronged the ways, and one man, old and ill-clad, brought to the Maid a great fish which he had caught overnight in the Loire. Our host prayed her to wait till it should be cooked, that she might breakfast well, for she had much to do. Yet she, who scarce seemed to live by earthly meat, but by the will of God, took only a sop of bread dipped in wine, and gaily leaping to her selle and gathering the reins, as a lady bound for a hunting where no fear was, she cried, "Keep the fish for supper, when I will bring back a goddon {25} prisoner to eat his part. And to-night, gentle sir, my host, I will return by the bridge!"—which, as we deemed, might in no manner be, for an arch of the bridge was broken. Thereon we all mounted, and rode down to the Burgundy gate, the women watching us, and casting flowers before the Maiden. But when we won the gate, behold, it was locked, and two ranks of men-at-arms, with lances levelled, wearing the colours of the Sieur de Gaucourt, were drawn up before it. That lord himself, in harness, but bareheaded, stood before his men, and cried, "Hereby is no passage. To-day the captains give command that no force stir from the town."

"To-day," quoth the Maid, "shall we take Les Tourelles, and to-morrow not a goddon, save prisoners and slain men, shall be within three leagues of Orleans. Gentle sir, bid open the gate, for to-day have I work to do."

Thereat Gaucourt shook his head, and from the multitude of townsfolk rose one great angry shout. They would burn the gate, they cried; they would fire the town, but they would follow the Maid and the guidance of the saints.

Thereon stones began to fly, and arbalests were bended, till the Maid turned, and, facing the throng, her banner lifted as in anger—

"Back, my good friends and people of Orleans," she said, "back and open the postern door in the great tower on the river wall. By one way or another shall I meet the English this day, nor shall might of man prevent me."

Then many ran back, and soon came the cry that the postern was opened, and thither streamed the throng. Therefore Gaucourt saw well that an onslaught would verily be made; moreover, as a man wise in war, he knew that the townsfolk, that day, would be hard to hold, and would go far. So he even yielded, not ungraciously, and sending a messenger to the Bastard and the captains, he rode forth from the Burgundy Gate by the side of the Maid. He was, indeed, little minded to miss his part of the honour; nor were the other captains more backward, for scarce had we taken boat and reached the farther bank, when we saw the banners of the Bastard and La Hire, Florent d'Illiers and Xaintrailles, Chambers and Kennedy, above the heads of the armed men who streamed forth by the gate of Burgundy. Less orderly was no fight ever begun, but the saints were of our party. It was the wise manner of the Maid to strike swift, blow upon blow, each stroke finding less resistance among the enemy, that had been used to a laggard war, for then it was the manner of captains to dally for weeks or months round a town, castle, or other keep, and the skill was to starve the enemy. But the manner of the Maid was ever to send cloud upon cloud of men to make escalade by ladders, their comrades aiding them from under cover with fire of couleuvrines and bows. Even so fought that famed Knight of Brittany, Sir Bertrand du Guesclin. But he was long dead, and whether the Maid (who honoured his memory greatly) fought as she did through his example, or by direct teaching of the saints, I know not.

If disorderly we began, the fault was soon amended; they who had beleaguered the boulevard all night were set in the rear, to rest out of shot; the fresh men were arrayed under their banners, in vineyards and under the walls of fields, so that if one company was driven back another was ready to come on, that the English might have no repose from battle.

Now, the manner of the boulevard was this: first, there was a strong palisade, and many men mustered within it; then came a wide, deep, dry fosse; then a strong wall of earth, bound in with withes and palisaded, and within it the gate of the boulevard. When that was won, and the boulevard taken, men defending it might flee across a drawbridge, over a stream, narrow and deep and swift, into Les Tourelles itself. Here they were safe from them on the side of Orleans, by reason of the broken arch of the bridge. So strong was this tower, that Monseigneur the Duc d'Alencon, visiting it later, said he could have staked his duchy on his skill to hold it for a week at least, with but few men, against all the forces in France. The captain of the English was that Glasdale who had reviled the Maid, and concerning whom she had prophesied that he should die without stroke of sword. There was no fiercer squire in England, and his men were like himself, being picked and chosen for that post; moreover their backs were at the wall, for the French and Scots once within the boulevard, it was in nowise easy for Talbot to bring the English a rescue, as was seen.

The battle began with shooting of couleuvrines at the palisade, to weaken it, and it was marvel to see how the Maid herself laid the guns, as cunningly as her own countryman, the famed Lorrainer. Now, when there was a breach in the palisade, Xaintrailles led on his company, splendid in armour, for he was a very brave young knight. We saw the pales fall with a crash, and the men go in, and heard the cry of battle; but slowly, one by one, they staggered back, some falling, some reeling wounded, and rolling their bodies out of arrow-shot. And there, in the breach, shone the back-plate of Xaintrailles, his axe falling and rising, and not one foot he budged, till the men of La Hire, with a cry, broke in to back him, and after a little space, swords fell and rose no more, but we saw the banners waving of Xaintrailles and La Hire. Soon the side of the palisade towards us was all down, as if one had swept it flat with his hand, but there stood the earthen wall of the boulevard, beyond the fosse. Then, all orderly, marched forth a band of men in the colours of Florent d'Illiers, bearing scaling-ladders, and so began the escalade, their friends backing them by shooting of arbalests from behind the remnant of the palisade. A ladder would be set against the wall, and we could see men with shields, or doors, or squares of wood on their heads to fend off stones, swarm up it, and axes flashing on the crest of the wall, and arrows flying, and smoke of guns: but the smoke cleared, and lo! the ladder was gone, and the three libbards grinned on the flag of England. So went the war, company after company staggering thinned from the fosse, and re-forming behind the cover of the vineyards; company after company marching forth, fresh and glorious, to fare as their friends had fared. And ever, with each company, went the Maid at their head, and D'Aulon, she crying that the place was theirs and now was the hour! But the day went by, till the sun turned in heaven towards evening, and no more was done. The English, in sooth, showed no fear nor faint heart; with axe, and sword, and mace, and with their very hands they smote and grappled with the climbers, and I saw a tall man, his sword being broken, strike down a French knight with his mailed fist, and drag another from a ladder and take him captive. Boldly they showed themselves on the crest, running all risk of our arrows, as our men did of theirs.

Now came the Scots, under Kennedy. A gallant sight it was to see them advance, shoulder to shoulder—Scots of the Marches and the Lennox, Fife, Argyll, and the Isles, all gentlemen born.

"Come on!" cried Randal Rutherford. "Come on, men of the

Marches, Scots of the Forest, Elliots, Rutherfords, Armstrongs, and deem that, wheresoever a Southron slinks behind a stone, there is Carlisle wall!"

The Rough Clan roared "Bellenden!" the Buchanans cried "Clare Innis," a rag of a hairy Highlander from the Lennox blew a wild skirl on the war-pipes, and hearing the Border slogan shouted in a strange country, nom Dieu! my blood burned, as that of any Scotsman would. Contrary to the Maid's desire, for she had noted that I was wan and weary, and had commanded me to bide in cover, I cried "A Leslie! a Leslie!" and went forward with my own folk, sword in hand and buckler lifted.

Beside good Randal Rutherford I ran, and we both leaped together into the ditch. There was a forest of ladders set against the wall, and I had my foot on a rung, when the Maid ran up and cried, "Nom Dieu! what make you here? Let me lead my Scots"; and so, pennon and axe in her left hand, she lightly leaped on the ladder, and arrows ringing on her mail, and a great stone glancing harmless from her salade, she so climbed that my lady's face on the pennon above her looked down into the English keep.

But, even then, I saw a face at an archere, an ill face and fell, the wolf's eyes of Brother Thomas glancing along the stock of an arbalest.

"Gardez-vous, Pucelle, gardez-vous!" I cried in her ear, for I was next her on the ladder; but a bolt whistled and smote her full, and reeling, she fell into my arms.

I turned my back to guard her, and felt a bolt strike my back-piece; then we were in the fosse, and all the Scots that might be were between her and harm. Swiftly they bore her out of the fray, into a little green vineyard, where was a soft grassy ditch. But the English so cried their hurrah, that it was marvel, and our men gave back in fear; and had not the Bastard come up with a fresh company, verify we might well have been swept into the Loire.

Some while I remained with Rutherford, Kennedy, and many others, for what could we avail to help the Maid? and to run has an ill look, and gives great heart to an enemy. Moreover, that saying of the Maid came into my mind, that she should be smitten of a bolt, but not unto death. So I even abode by the fosse, and having found an arbalest, my desire was to win a chance of slaying Brother Thomas, wherefore I kept my eyes on that archere whence he had shot. But no arbalest was pointed thence, and the fight flagged. On both sides men were weary, and they took some meat as they might, no ladders being now set on the wall.

Then I deemed it no harm to slip back to the vineyard where the Maid lay, and there I met the good Father Pasquerel, that was her confessor. He told me that now she was quiet, either praying or asleep, for he had left her as still as a babe in its cradle, her page watching her. The bolt had sped by a rivet of her breast-piece, clean through her breast hard below the shoulder, and it stood a hand-breadth out beyond. Then she had wept and trembled, seeing her own blood; but presently, with such might and courage as was marvel, she had dragged out the bolt with her own hands. Then they had laid on the wound cotton steeped with olive oil, for she would not abide that they should steep the bolt with weapon salve and charm the hurt with a song, as the soldiers desired. Then she had confessed herself to Pasquerel, and so had lain down among the grass and the flowers. But it was Pasquerel's desire to let ferry her across secretly to Orleans. This was an ill hearing for me, yet it was put about in the army that the Maid had but taken a slight scratch, and again would lead us on, a thing which I well deemed to be impossible. So the day waxed late, and few onslaughts were made, and these with no great heart, the English standing on the walls and openly mocking us.

They asked how it went with the Maid, and whether she would not fain be at home among her kine, or in the greasy kitchen? We would cry back, and for my own part I bade them seek the kitchen as pock-puddings and belly-gods, and that I cried in their own tongue, while they, to my great amaze, called me "prentice boy" and "jackanapes." Herein I saw the craft and devilish enmity of Brother Thomas, and well I guessed that he had gotten sight of me; but his face I saw not.

Ill names break no bones, and arrows from under cover wrought slight scathe; so one last charge the Bastard commanded, and led himself, and a sore tussle there was that time on the wall-crest, one or two of our men leaping into the fort, whence they came back no more.

Now it was eight hours of the evening, the sky grey, the men out-worn and out of all heart, and the captains were gathered in council. Of this I conceived the worst hope, for after a counsel men seldom fight. So I watched the fort right sullenly, and the town of Orleans looking black against a red, lowering sky in the west. Some concourse of townsfolk I saw on the bridge, beside the broken arch, and by the Boulevard Belle Croix; but I deemed that they had only come to see the fray as near as might be. Others were busy under the river wall with a great black boat, belike to ferry over the horses from our side.

All seemed ended, and I misdoubted that we would scarce charge again so briskly in the morning, nay, we might well have to guard our own gates.

As I sat thus, pondering by the vineyard ditch, the Maid

stood by me suddenly. Her helmet was off, her face deadly white, her eyes like two stars.

"Bring me my horse," she said, so sternly that I crushed the answer on my lips, and the prayer that she would risk herself no more.

Her horse, that had been cropping the grass near him happily enough, I found, and brought to her, and so, with some ado, she mounted and rode at a foot's pace to the little crowd of captains.

"Maiden, ma mie," said the Bastard. "Glad I am to see you able to mount. We have taken counsel to withdraw for this night. Martin," he said to his trumpeter, "sound the recall."

"I pray you, sir," she said very humbly, "grant me but a little while"; and so saying, she withdrew alone from the throng of men into the vineyard.

What passed therein I know not and no man knows; but in a quarter of an hour's space she came forth, like another woman, her face bright and smiling, her cheeks like the dawn, and so beautiful that we marvelled on her with reverence, as if we had seen an angel.

"The place is ours!" she cried again, and spurred towards the fosse. Thence her banner had never gone back, for D'Aulon held it there, to be a terror to the English. Even at that moment he had given it to a certain Basque, a very brave man, for he himself was out-worn with its weight. And he had challenged the Basque to do a vaillance, or boastful deed of arms, as yesterday I and the Spaniard had done. So D'Aulon leaped into the fosse, his shield up, defying the English; but the Basque did not follow, for the Maid, seeing her banner in the hands of a man whom she knew not, laid hold of it, crying, "Ha, mon estandart! mon estandart!"

There, as they struggled for it, the Basque being minded to follow D'Aulon to the wall foot, the banner wildly waved, and all men saw it, and rallied, and flocked amain to the rescue.

"Charge!" cried the Maid. "Forward, French and Scots; the place is yours, when once my banner fringe touches the wall!"

With that word the wind blew out the banner fringe, and so suddenly that, though I saw the matter, I scarce knew how it was done, the whole host swarmed up and on, ladders, lifted, and so furiously went they, that they won the wall crest and leaped within the fort. Then the more part of the English, adread, as I think, at the sight of the Maid whom they had deemed slain, fled madly over the drawbridge into Les Tourelles.

Then standing on the wall crest, whither I had climbed, I beheld strange sights. First, through the dimness of the dusk, I saw a man armed, walking as does a rope-dancer, balancing himself with his spear, across the empty air, for so it seemed, above the broken arch of the bridge. This appeared, in very sooth, to be a miracle; but, gazing longer, I saw that a great beam had been laid by them of Orleans to span the gap, and now other beams were being set, and many men, bearing torches, were following that good knight, Nicole Giresme, who first showed the way over such a bridge of dread. So now were the English in Les Tourelles between two fires.

Another strange sight I saw, for in that swift and narrow stream which the drawbridge spanned whereby the English fled was moored a great black barge, its stem and stern showing on either side of the bridge. Boats were being swiftly pulled forth from it into the stream, and as I gazed, there leaped up through the dark one long tongue of fire. Then I saw the skill of it, namely, to burn down the drawbridge, and so cut the English off from all succour. Fed with pitch and pine the flame soared lustily, and now it shone between the planks of the drawbridge. On the stone platform of the boulevard, wherein the drawbridge was laid, stood a few English, and above them shone the axe of a tall squire, Glasdale, as it fell on shield and helm of the French. Others held us at bay with long lances, and never saw I any knight do his devoir more fiercely than he who had reviled the Maid. For on his head lay all the blame of the taking of the boulevard. To rear of him rang the shouts of them of Orleans, who had crossed the broken arch by the beam; but he never turned about, and our men reeled back before him. Then there shone behind him the flames from the blazing barge; and so, black against that blaze, he smote and slew, not knowing that the drawbridge began to burn.

On this the Maid ran forth, and cried to him—

"Rends-toi, rends-toi! Yield thee, Glacidas; yield thee, for I stand in much sorrow for thy soul's sake."

Then, falling on her knees, her face shining transfigured in that fierce light, she prayed him thus—

"Ah! Glacidas, thou didst call me ribaulde, but I have sorrow for thy soul. Ah! yield thee, yield thee to ransom"; and the tears ran down her cheeks, as if a saint were praying for a soul in peril.

Not one word spoke Glasdale: he neither saw nor heard. But the levelled spears at his side flew up, a flame caught his crest, making a plume of fire, and with a curse he cast his axe among the throng, and the man who stood in front of it got his death. Glasdale turned about as he threw; he leaped upon the burning drawbridge, where the last of his men were huddled in flight, and lo! beneath his feet it crashed; down he plunged through smoke and flame, and the stream below surged up as bridge and flying men went under in one ruin.

The Maid gave a cry that rang above the roar of fire and water.

"Saints! will no man save him?" she shrieked, looking all around her on the faces of the French.

A mad thought leaped up in my mind.

"Unharness me!" I cried; and one who stood by me undid the clasps of my light jaseran. I saw a head unhelmeted, I saw a hand that clutched at a floating beam. I thought of the Maid's desire, and of the ransom of so great a squire as Glasdale, and then I threw my hands up to dive, and leaped head foremost into the water.

Deep down I plunged, and swam far under water, to avoid a stroke from floating timber, and then I rose and glanced up-stream. All the air was fiercely lit with the blaze of the burning barge; a hand and arm would rise, and fall ere I could seize it. A hand was thrown up before me, the glinting fingers gripping at empty air. I caught the hand, swimming strongly with the current, for so the man could not clutch at me, and if a drowning man can be held apart, it is no great skill to save him. In this art I was not unlearned, and once had even saved two men from a wrecked barque in the long surf of St. Andrews Bay. Save for a blow from some great floating timber, I deemed that I had little to fear; nay, now I felt sure of the Maid's praise and of a rich ransom.

A horn of bank with alder bushes ran out into the stream, a

smooth eddy or backwater curling within. I caught a bough of alder, and, though nigh carried down by the drowning man's weight, I found bottom, yet hardly, and drew my man within the backwater. He lay like a log, his face in the stream. Pushing him before me, I rounded the horn, and, with much ado, dragged him up to a sloping gravelly beach, where I got his head on dry land, his legs being still in the water. I turned him over and looked eagerly. Lo! it was no Glasdale, but the drowned face of Brother Thomas!

Then something seemed to break in my breast; blood gushed from my mouth, and I fell on the sand and gravel. Footsteps I heard of men running to us. I lifted my hand faintly and waved it, and then I felt a hand on my face.

CHAPTER XV

HOW NORMAN LESLIE WAS
ABSOLVED BY BROTHER THOMAS

Certain Scots that found me, weak and bleeding, by the riverside, were sent by the Maid, in hopes that I had saved Glasdale, whereas it was the accursed cordelier I had won from the water. What they did with him I knew not then, but me they laid on a litter, and so bore me to a boat, wherein they were ferrying our wounded men across to Orleans. The Maid herself, as she had foretold, returned by way of the bridge, that was all bright with moving torches, as our groaning company were rowed across the black water to a quay. Thence I was carried in a litter to our lodgings, and so got to bed, a physician doing what he might for me. A noisy night we passed, for I verily believe that no man slept, but all, after service held in the Church of St. Aignan, went revelling and drinking from house to house, and singing through the streets, as folk saved from utter destruction.

With daybreak fell a short silence; short or long, it seemed brief to me, who was now asleep at last, and I was rueful enough when a sound aroused me, and I found the Maid herself standing by my bedside, with one in the shadow behind her. The chamber was all darkling, lit only by a thread of light that came through the closed shutters of wood, and fell on her pale face. She was clad in a light jaseran of mail, because of her wound, and was plainly eager to be gone and about her business, that is, to meet the English in open field.

"Leslie, my friend," she said, in her sweet voice, "there were many brave men in the fight yesterday, but, in God's name, none did a braver deed than thou! Nay, speak not," she said, as I opened my lips to thank her, "for the leech that tended thee last night forbids it, on peril of thy very life. So I have brought thee here a sheet of fair paper, and a pen and horn of ink, that thou, being a clerk, mayst write what thou hast to say. Alas! such converse is not for me, who know not A from his brother B. But the saints who helped thee have rewarded thee beyond all expectation. Thou didst not save that unhappy Glacidas, whom God in His mercy forgive! but thou hast taken a goodlier prize—this holy man, that had been prisoner in the hands of the English."

Here she stood a little aside, and the thread of light shone on the fell face of Brother Thomas, lowering beneath his hood.

Then I would have spoken, leech or no leech, to denounce him, for the Maid had no memory of his face, and knew him not for the false friar taken at St. Loup. But she laid her mailed finger gently on my lips.

"Silence! Thou art my man-at-arms and must obey thy captain. This worthy friar hath been long in the holy company of the blessed Colette, and hath promised to bring me acquainted with that daughter of God. Ay, and he hath given to me, unworthy as I am, a kerchief which has touched her wonder-working hands. Almost I believe that it will heal thee by miracle, if the saints are pleased to grant it."

Herewith she drew a kerchief across my lips, and I began,

being most eager to instruct her innocence as to this accursed man—

"Lady—" but alas! no miracle was wrought for a sinner like me. Howbeit I am inclined to believe that the kerchief was no saintly thing, and had never come near the body of the blessed Colette, but rather was a gift from one of the cordelier's light-o'-loves. Assuredly it was stained red with blood from my lungs ere I could utter two words.

The Maid stanched the blood, saying—

"Did I not bid thee to be silent? The saints forgive my lack of faith, whereby this blessed thing has failed to heal thee! And now I must be gone, to face the English in the field, if they dare to meet us, which, methinks, they will not do, but rather withdraw as speedily as they may. So now I leave thee with this holy man to be thy nurse-tender, and thou canst write to him concerning thy needs, for doubtless he is a clerk. Farewell!"

With that she was gone, and this was the last I saw of her for many a day.

Never have I known such a horror of fear as fell on me now, helpless and dumb, a sheep given over to the slaughter, in that dark chamber, which was wondrous lown, {26} alone with my deadly foe.

Never had any man more cause for dread, for I was weak, and to resist him was death. I was speechless, and could utter no voice that the people in the house might hear. As for mine enemy, he had always loathed and scorned me; he had a long account of vengeance to settle with me; and if—which was not to be thought of—he was minded to spare one that had saved his life, yet, for his own safety, he dared not. He had beguiled the Maid with his false tongue, and his face, not seen by her in the taking of St. Loup, she knew not. But he knew that I would disclose all the truth so soon as the Maid returned, wherefore he was bound to destroy me, which he would assuredly do with every mockery, cruelty, and torture of body and mind. Merely to think of him when he was absent was wont to make my flesh creep, so entirely evil beyond the nature of sinful mankind was this monster, and so set on working all kinds of mischief with greediness. Whether he had suffered some grievous wrong in his youth, which he spent his life in avenging on all folk, or whether, as I deem likely, he was the actual emissary of Satan, as the Maid was of the saints, I know not, and, as I lay there, had no wits left to consider of it. Only I knew that no more unavailing victim than I was ever so utterly in the power of a foe so deadly and terrible.

The Maid had gone, and all hope had gone with her. For a time that seemed unending mine enemy neither spoke nor moved, standing still in the chink of light, a devil where an angel had been.

There was silence, and I heard the Maid's iron tread pass down the creaking wooden stairs, and soon I heard the sound of singing birds, for my window looked out on the garden.

The steps ceased, and then there was a low grating laughter in the dark room, as if the devil laughed.

Brother Thomas moved stealthily to the door, and thrust in the wooden bolt. Then he sat him heavily down on my bed, and put his fiend's face close to mine, his eyes stabbing into my eyes. But I bit my lip, and stared right back into his yellow wolf's eyes, that shone like flames of the pit with evil and cruel thoughts.

So I lay, with that yellow light on me; and strength came strangely to me, and I prayed that, since die I must, I might at least gladden him with no sign of fear. When he found that he could not daunton me, he laughed again.

"Our chick of Pitcullo has picked up a spirit in the wars," he said; and turning his back on me, he leaned his face on his hand, and so sat thinking.

The birds of May sang in the garden; there was a faint shining of silver and green, from the apple-boughs and buds without, in the little chamber; and the hooded back of the cordelier was before me on my bed, like the shape of Death beside the Sick Man, in a picture. Now I did not even pray, I waited.

Doubtless he knew that no cruel thing which the devil could devise was more cruel than this suspense.

Then he turned about and faced me, grinning like a dog.

"These are good words," said he, "in that foolish old book they read to the faithful in the churches, 'Vengeance is Mine, saith the Lord.' Ay, it is even too sweet a morsel for us poor Christian men, such as the lowly Brother Thomas of the Order of St. Francis. Nevertheless, I am minded to put my teeth in it"; and he bared his yellow dog's fangs at me, smiling like a hungry hound. "My sick brother," he went on, "both as one that has some science of leech-craft and as thy ghostly counsellor, it is my duty to warn thee that thou art now very near thine end. Nay, let me feel thy pulse"; and seizing my left wrist, he grasped it lightly in his iron fingers. "Now, ere I administer to thee thy due, as a Christian man, let me hear thy parting confession. But, alas! as the blessed Maid too truly warned thee, thou must not open thy poor lips in speech. There is death in a word! Write, then, write the story of thy sinful life, that I may give thee absolution."

So saying, he opened the shutter, and carefully set the paper and inkhorn before me, putting the pen in my fingers.

"Now, write what I shall tell thee"; and here he so pressed and wrung my wrist that his fingers entered into my living flesh with a fiery pang. I writhed, but I did not cry.

"Write—"

"I, Norman Leslie of Pitcullo—" and, to escape that agony, I wrote as he bade me.

"—being now in the article of death—"

And I wrote.

"—do attest on my hope of salvation—" And I wrote.

"—and do especially desire Madame Jeanne, La Pucelle, and all Frenchmen and Scots loyal to our Sovereign Lord the Dauphin, to accept my witness, that Brother Thomas, of the Order of St. Francis, called Noiroufle while of the world, has been most falsely and treacherously accused by me—"

I wrote, but I wrote not his false words, putting my own in their place—"has been most truly and righteously accused by me—"

"—of divers deeds of black treason, and dealing with our enemies of England, against our Lord the Dauphin, and the Maid, the Sister of the Saints, and of this I heartily repent me,—"

But I wrote, "All which I maintain—"

"—as may God pardon my sins, on the faith of a sinful and dying man."

"Now sign thy name, and that of thy worshipful cabbage-garden and dunghill in filthy Scotland." So I signed, "Norman Leslie, the younger, of Pitcullo," and added the place, Orleans, with the date of day and year of our Lord, namely, May the eighth, fourteen hundred and twenty-nine.

"A very laudable confession," quoth Brother Thomas; "would that all the sinners whom I have absolved, as I am about to absolve thee, had cleansed and purged their sinful souls as freely. And now, my brother, read aloud to me this scroll; nay, methinks it is ill for thy health to speak or read. A sad matter is this, for, in faith, I have forgotten my clergy myself, and thou mayst have beguiled me by inditing other matter than I have put into thy lying mouth. Still, where the safety of a soul is concerned, a few hours more or less of this vain, perishable life weigh but as dust in the balance."

Here he took from about his hairy neck a heavy Italian crucifix of black wood, whereon was a figure of our Lord, wrought in white enamel, with golden nails, and a golden crown of thorns.

"Now read," he whispered, heaving up the crucifix above me. And as he lifted it, a bright blade, strong, narrow, and sharp, leaped out from beneath the feet of our Lord, and glittered within an inch of my throat. An emblem of this false friar it was, the outside of whom was as that of a holy man, while within he was a murdering sword.

"Read!" he whispered again, pricking my throat with the dagger's point.

Then I read aloud, and as I read I was half choked with my

blood, and now and then was stopped; but still he cried—

"Read, and if one word is wrong, thine absolution shall come all the swifter."

So I read, and, may I be forgiven if I sinned in deceiving one so vile! I uttered not what I had written, but what he had bidden me to write.

"I, Norman Leslie of Pitcullo, being now in the article of death, do attest on my hope of salvation, and do especially desire Madame Jeanne, La Pucelle, and all Frenchmen and Scots loyal to our Sovereign Lord the Dauphin, to accept my witness that Brother Thomas, of the Order of St. Francis, called Noiroufle while of the world, has been most falsely and treacherously accused by me of divers deeds of black treason, and dealing with our enemies of England, against our Lord the Dauphin, and the Maid, the Sister of the Saints, and of this I heartily repent me, as may God pardon my sins, on the faith of a sinful and dying man. Signed, at Orleans, Norman Leslie, the younger, of Pitcullo, this eighth of May, in the year of our Lord fourteen hundred and twenty-nine."

When I had ended, he took away his blasphemous dagger-point from my throat.

"Very clerkly read," he spake, "and all runs smooth; methinks myself had been no poor scribe, were I but a clerk. Hadst thou written other matter, to betray my innocence, thou couldst not remember what I said, even word for word," he added gleefully. "Now I might strangle thee slowly"; and he set his fingers about my throat, I being too weak to do more than clutch at his hand, with a grasp like a babe's. "But that leaves black finger-marks, another kind of witness than thine in my favour. Or I might give thee the blade of this blessed crucifix; yet dagger wounds are like lips and have a voice, and blood cries from the ground, says Holy Writ. Pardon my tardiness, my poor brother, but this demands deep thought, and holy offices must not be hurried unseemly." He sat now with his back to me, his hand still on my throat, so deep in thought that he heard not, as did my sharpened ears, a door shut softly, and foot-falls echoing in the house below. If I could only cry aloud! but he would stifle me ere the cry reached my throat!

"This will serve," he said. "Thou wilt have died of thy malady, and I will go softly forth, and with hushed voice will tell how the brave young Scot passed quietly to the saints. Yet, after all, I know not. Thou hast been sent by Heaven to my aid; clearly thou art an instrument of God to succour the unworthy Brother Thomas. Once and twice thou hast been a boat to carry me on my way, and to save my useful life. A third time thou mightst well be serviceable, not by thy will, alas! but by God's, my poor brother"; and he mockingly caressed my face with his abhorred hand. "Still, this must even serve, though I would fain find for thee a more bitter way to death"; and he gently and carefully drew the pillow from beneath my head. "This leaves no marks and tells no tales, and permits no dying cry."

He was looking at me, the pillow in his hands, his gesture that of a tender nurse, when a light tap sounded on the door. He paused, then came a louder knock, one pushed, and knocked again.

"Open, in the name of the Dauphin!" came a voice I knew well, the voice of D'Aulon.

"The rope of Judas strangle thee!" said Brother Thomas, dropping the pillow and turning to the casement. But it was heavily barred with stanchions of iron, as the manner is, and thereby he might not flee.

Then came fiercer knocking with a dagger hilt, and the cry, "Open, in the name of the Dauphin, or we burst the door!"

Brother Thomas hastily closed the wooden shutter, to darken the chamber as much as might be. "Gently, gently," he said. "Disturb not my penitent, who is newly shrived, and about to pass"; and so speaking, he withdrew the bolt.

D'Aulon strode in, dagger in hand, followed by the physician.

"What make you here with doors barred, false priest?" he said, laying his hand on the frock of Noiroufle.

"And what make you here, fair squire, with arms in a sick man's chamber, and loud words to disturb the dying? And wherefore callest thou me 'false priest'? But an hour agone, the blessed Maid herself brought me hither, to comfort and absolve her follower, to tend him, if he lived and, if he must die, to give him his dues as a Christian man. And the door was bolted that the penitent might be private with his confessor, for he has a heavy weight to unburden his sinful soul withal."

"Ay, the Maid sent thee, not knowing who thou wert, the traitor friar taken at St. Loup, and thou hast a tongue that beguiled her simplicity. But one that knew thee saw thy wolfs face in her company, and told me, and I told the Maid, who sent me straightway back from the gate, that justice might be done on thee. Thou art he whom this Scot charged with treason, and would have slain for a spy, some nights agone."

Brother Thomas cast up his eyes to heaven.

"Forgive us our trespasses," said he, "as we forgive them that trespass against us. Verily and indeed I am that poor friar who tends the wounded, and verify I am he against whom this young Scot, as, I fear, is the manner of all his benighted people, brought a slanderous accusation falsely. All the more reason was there that I should hear his last confession, and forgive him freely, as may I also be forgiven."

"Thou liest in thy throat," said D'Aulon. "This is a brave man-at-arms, and a loyal."

"Would that thou wert not beguiled, fair sir, for I have no pleasure in the sin of any man. But, if thou wilt believe him rather than me, even keep thy belief, and read this written confession of his falsehood. Of free will, with his own hand, my penitent hereby absolves me from all his slanders. As Holy Church enjoins, in the grace of repentance he also makes restitution of what he had stolen, namely, all my wealth in this world, the good name of a poor and lowly follower of the blessed Francis. Here is the scroll."

With these words, uttered in a voice of sorrowing and humble honesty, the friar stretched out the written sheet of paper to D'Aulon.

"Had I been a false traitor," he said, "would not her brethren of heaven have warned the blessed Maid against me? And I have also a written safe-conduct from the holy sister Colette."

Then I knew that he had fallen into my trap, and, weak as I was, I could have laughed to think of his face, when the words I had written came out in place of the words he had bidden me write. For a clerk hath great power beyond the simple and unlettered of the world, be they as cunning even as Brother Thomas.

"Nom Dieu! this is another story," said D'Aulon, turning the paper about in his hands and looking doubtfully at me. But I smiled upon him, whereby he was the more perplexed. "The ink is hardly dry, and in some places has run and puddled, so that, poor clerk as I am, I can make little of it"; and he pored on it in a perplexed sort. "Tush, it is beyond my clerkhood," he said at last. "You, Messire Saint-Mesmin,"—turning to the physician—"must interpret this."

"Willingly, fair sir," said the physician, moving round to the shutter, which he opened, while the cordelier's eyes glittered, for now there was one man less between him and the half-open door. I nodded to D'Aulon that he should shut it, but he marked me not, being wholly in amaze at the written scroll of my confession.

The physician himself was no great clerk, and he read the paper slowly, stumbling over the words, as it were, while Brother Thomas, clasping his crucifix to his breast, listened in triumph as he heard what he himself had bidden me write.

"I, Norman Leslie, of—of Peet—What name is this? Peet—I cannot utter it."

"Passez outre," quoth D'Aulon.

"I, Norman Leslie, being now in the article of death"—here the leech glanced at me, shaking his head mournfully—"do attest on my hope of salvation, and do especially desire Madame Jeanne La Pucelle, and all Frenchmen and Scots loyal to our Sovereign Lord the Dauphin, to accept my witness that Brother Thomas, of the Order of St. Francis, called Noiroufle while of the world, has been most truly and righteously accused by me of divers deeds of black treason."

At these words the cordelier's hand leaped up from his

breast, his crucifix dagger glittered bright, he tore his frock from D'Aulon's grip, leaving a rag of it in his hand, and smote, aiming at the squire where the gorget joins the vambrace. Though he missed by an inch, yet so terrible was the blow that D'Aulon reeled against the wall, while the broken blade jingled on the stone floor. Then the frock of the friar whisked through the open door of the chamber; we heard the stairs cleared in two leaps, and D'Aulon, recovering his feet, rushed after the false priest. But he was in heavy armour, the cordelier's bare legs were doubtless the nimbler, and the physician, crossing himself, could only gape and stare on the paper in his hand. As he gazed with his mouth open his eyes fell on me, white as my sheets, that were dabbled with the blood from my mouth.

"Nom Dieu!" he stammered, "Nom Dieu! here is business more to my mind and my trade than chasing after mad cordeliers that stab with crucifixes!"

Then, coming to my side, he brought water, bathed my face, and did what his art might do for a man in such deadly extremity as was mine. In which care he was still busy when D'Aulon returned, panting, having sent a dozen of townsfolk to hunt the friar, who had made good his flight over garden walls, and was now skulking none knew where. D'Aulon would fain have asked me concerning the mystery of the confession in which Brother Thomas had placed his hope so unhappily, but the physician forbade him to inquire, or me to answer, saying that it was more than my life was worth. But on D'Aulon's battered armour there was no deeper dint than that dealt by the murderous crucifix.

Thus this second time did Brother Thomas make his way out of our hands, the devil aiding him, as always; for it seemed that ropes could not bind or water drown him.

But, for my part, I lay long in another bout of sore fever, sick here at Orleans, where I was very kindly entreated by the people of the house, and notably by the daughter thereof, a fair maid and gentle. To her care the Maid had commanded me when she left Orleans, the English refusing battle, as later I heard, and withdrawing to Jargeau and Paris. But of the rejoicings in Orleans I knew little or nothing, and had no great desire for news, or meat, or drink, but only for sleep and peace, as is the wont of sick men. Now as touches sickness and fever, I have written more than sufficient, as Heaven knows I have had cause enow. A luckless life was mine, save for the love of Elliot; danger and wounds, and malady and escape, where hope seemed lost, were and were yet to be my portion, since I sailed forth out of Eden-mouth. And so hard pressed of sickness was I, that not even my outwitting of Brother Thomas was a cause of comfort to me, though to this day I cannot think of it without some mirthful triumph.

CHAPTER XVI

HOW SORROW CAME ON NORMAN LESLIE,
AND JOY THEREAFTER

It little concerns any man to know how I slowly recovered my health after certain failings back into the shadow of death. Therefore I need not tell how I was physicked, and bled, and how I drew on from a diet of milk to one of fish, and so to a meal of chicken's flesh, till at last I could sit, wrapped up in many cloaks, on a seat in the garden, below a great mulberry tree. In all this weary time I knew little, and for long cared less, as to what went on in the world and the wars. But so soon as I could speak it was of Elliot that I devised, with my kind nurse, Charlotte Boucher, the young daughter of Jacques Boucher, the Duke's treasurer, in whose house I lay. She was a fair lass, and merry of mood, and greatly hove up my heart to fight with my disease. It chanced that, as she tended me, when I was at my worst, she marked, hanging on a silken string about my neck, a little case of silver artfully wrought, wherein was that portrait of my mistress, painted by me before I left Chinon. Being curious, like all girls, and deeming that the case held some relic, she opened it, I knowing nothing then of what she did. But when I was well enough to lie abed and devise with her, it chanced that I was playing idly with my fingers about the silver case.

"Belike," said Charlotte, "that is some holy relic, to which, maybe, you owe your present recovery. Surely, when you are whole again, you have vowed a pilgrimage to the shrine of the saint, your friend?" Here she smiled at me gaily, for she was a right merry damsel, and a goodly.

"Nay," she said, "I have done more for you than your physician, seeing that I, or the saint you serve, have now brought the red colour into these wan cheeks of yours. Is she a Scottish saint, then? perchance St. Margaret, of whom I have read? Will you not let me look at the sacred thing?"

"Nay," said I. "Methinks, from your smiling, that you have taken opportunity to see my treasure before to-day, being a daughter of our mother Eve."

"She is very beautiful," said Charlotte; "nay, show her to me again!"

With that I pressed the spring and opened the case, for there is no lover but longs to hear his lady commended, and to converse about her. Yet I had spoken no word, for my part, about her beauty, having heard say that he who would be well with one woman does ill to praise another in her presence.

"Beautiful, indeed, she is," said Charlotte. "Never have I seen such eyes, and hair like gold, and a look so gracious! And for thy pilgrimage to the shrine of this fair saint, where does she dwell?"

I told her at Chinon, or at Tours, or commonly wheresoever the Court might be, for that her father was the King's painter.

"And you love her very dearly?"

"More than my life," I said. "And may the saints send you, demoiselle, as faithful a lover, to as fair a lady."

"Nay," she said, reddening. "This is high treason, and well you wot that you hold no lady half so fair as your own. Are you Scots so smooth-spoken? You have not that repute. Now, what would you give to see that lady?"

"All that I have, which is little but my service and goodwill. But she knows not where I am, nor know I how she fares, which irks me more than all my misfortunes. Would that I could send a letter to her father, and tell him how I do, and ask of their tidings."

"The Dauphin is at Tours," she said, "and there is much coming and going between Tours and this town. For the Maid is instant with the Dauphin to ride forthwith to Reims, and there be sacred and crowned; but now he listens and believes, and anon his counsellors tell him that this is foolhardy, and a thing impossible."

"O they of little faith!" I said, sighing.

"None the less, word has come that the Maid has been in her oratory at prayers, and a Voice from heaven has called to her, saying, 'Fille de Dieu, va, va, va! Je serai en ton aide. Va!' {27} The Dauphin is much confirmed in his faith by this sign, and has vowed that he will indeed march with the Maid to Reims, though his enemies hold all that country which lies between. But first she must take the towns which the English hold on Loire side, such as Jargeau. Now on Jargeau, while you lay knowing nothing, the Bastard of Orleans, and Xaintrailles, and other good knights, made an onslaught, and won nothing but loss for their pains, though they slew Messire Henry Bisset, the captain of the town. But if the Maid takes Jargeau, the Dauphin will indeed believe in her and follow her."

"He is hard of heart to believe, and would that I were where he should be—under her holy pennon, for thereon, at least, I should see the face painted of my lady. But how does all this bring me nearer the hope of hearing about her, and how she fares?"

"There are many messengers coming and going to Tours, for the Dauphin is gathering force under the Maid, and has set the fair Duc d'Alencon to be her lieutenant, with the Bastard, and La Hire, and Messire Florent d'Illiers. And all are to be here in Orleans within few days; wherefore now write to the father of thy lady, and I will myself write to her." With that she gave me paper and pen, and I indited a letter to my master, telling him how I had lain near to death of my old wound, in Orleans, and that I prayed him of his goodness to let me know how he did, and to lay me at the feet of my lady. Then Charlotte showed me her letter, wherein she bade Elliot know that I had hardly recovered, after winning much fame (for so she said) and a ransom of gold from an English prisoner, which now lay in the hands of her father, the Duke's treasurer. Then she said that a word from Elliot, not to say the sight of her face, the fairest in the world (a thing beyond hope), would be of more avail for my healing than all the Pharaoh powders of the apothecaries. These, in truth, I had never taken, but put them away secretly, as doubting whether such medicaments, the very dust of the persecuting Egyptian and idolatrous race, were fit for a Christian to swallow, with any hope of a blessing. Thus my kind nurse ended, calling herself my lady's sister in the love of France and of the Maid, and bidding my lady be mindful of so true a lover, who lay sick for a token at her hands. These letters she sealed, and intrusted to Colet de Vienne, the royal messenger, the same who rode from Vaucouleurs to Chinon, in the beginning of the Maid's mission, and who, as then, was faring to Tours with letters from Orleans.

Meanwhile all the town was full of joy, in early June, because the Maid was to visit the city, with D'Alencon and the Bastard, on her way to besiege Jargeau. It was June the ninth, in the year of our Lord fourteen hundred and twenty-nine, the sun shining warm in a clear blue sky, and all the bells of Orleans a-ringing, to welcome back the Maiden. I myself sat in the window, over the doorway, alone with Charlotte sitting by my side, for her father had gone to the Hotel de Ville, with her mother, to welcome the captains. Below us were hangings of rich carpets, to make the house look gay, for every house was adorned in the best manner, and flags floated in the long street, and flowers strewed the road, to do honour to our deliverer. Thus we waited, and presently the sound of music filled the air, with fragrance of incense, for the priests were walking in front, swinging censers and chanting the Te Deum laudamus. And then came a company of girls strewing flowers, and fair boys blowing on trumpets, and next, on a black horse, in white armour, with a hucque of scarlet broidered with gold, the blessed Maid herself, unhelmeted, glancing every way with her happy eyes, while the women ran to touch her armour with their rings, as to a saint, and the men kissed her mailed feet.

To be alive, and to feel my life returning in a flood of strength and joy in that sweet air, with the gladness of the multitude pulsing through it as a man's heart beats in his body, seemed to me like Paradise. But out of Paradise our first parents were driven long ago, as anon I was to be from mine. For, as the Maid passed, I doffed my cap and waved it, since to shout "Noel" with the rest, I dared not, because of my infirmity. Now, it so fell that, glancing around, she saw and knew me, and bowed to me, with a gesture of her hand, as queenly as if she, a manant's child, had been a daughter of France. At that moment, noting the Maid's courtesy towards me, Charlotte stood up from beside me, with a handful of red roses, which she threw towards her. As it chanced, belike because she was proud to be with one whom the Maid honoured, or to steady herself as she threw, she laid her left hand about my neck, and so standing, cast her flowers, and then looked laughing back into my eyes, with a happy face. The roses missed the Maid, whose horse caracoled at that moment as she went by, but they lit in the lap of a damsel that rode at her rein, on a lyart {28} palfrey, and she looking up, I saw the face of Elliot, and Elliot saw me, and saw Charlotte leaning on me and laughing. Then Elliot's face grew deadly pale, her lower lip stiff, as when she was angered with me at Chinon, and so, wrying her neck suddenly to the left, she rode on her way, nor ever looked towards us again.

"Who may that proud damsel be, and what ails her at my roses?" quoth Charlotte, sitting herself down again and still following them with her eyes. "Methinks I have seen her face before; and what ails you?" she asked, looking earnestly on me, "for you are as white as the last snow ere it melts in spring."

I had good reason to be pale, for I very well guessed that Elliot, having ridden in the Maiden's company to see me, and to surprise me with the unlooked-for gladness of her coming, had marked Charlotte as she so innocently leaned on me and laughed to me, and had conceived anger against us both, for of a truth Charlotte was very fair and of a joyous aspect. Yet, taken so suddenly as I was, between the extreme of delight in looking on my lady beyond hope, and the very deep of sorrow that she had so bitterly slighted me, I was yet wary of betraying myself. For the girl beside me had, in all honest and maidenly service that woman may do for man, been kinder to me than a sister, and no thought or word of earthly love had ever passed between us. That she should wot of

Elliot's anger, and of its cause, and so hold my lady lightly, ay, and triumph over her in her heart (as is the nature of a woman, her ministry being thus churlishly repaid), was more than I could endure. So, may the saints forgive me! I lied, and it is a strange thing, but true, that howsoever a gentleman may hate the very thought of a lie, yet often he finds it hard to tell the truth to a woman.

"Do I look white?" I said. "Then it is because I have a sudden pang of sorrow. For one moment I deemed that proud damsel was the lady of my love, whom, in verity, she most strangely favours, so that you might think them sisters. But alas! she is but the daughter of a good Scots knight at Chinon, whom I have seen there before to-day, and marvelled how much she and my lady favour each other. Therefore am I pale, because that hope of mine is broken. And you know her face, belike, from my poor picture of my lady."

Charlotte looked at me steadily, and flushed red; but even then, one who rode by among the men-at-arms noted me, and, waving his arm towards me, cried in a loud voice—

"Hail, fair son, soon will I be with thee!" and so, turning in his saddle to watch me, he laughed a loud laugh and rode onwards. He was my master, and as my eyes followed him, Charlotte spoke.

"And who is that great Scot, with his Scots twang of the tongue, who called you 'son'? By the Mass, she was your lady, and yonder wight is her father, of whom you have spoken to me more than once"; for, indeed, I had told her all the story of my loves.

Then I was confused, for I could no longer deny the truth, and not having one word to say, I sighed from my heart.

"O faint-spirited man-at-arms!" cried Charlotte, blushing, and laughing as if some exquisite jest were abroad. "Do you so terribly dread your mistress's anger? Nay, be of good cheer! Me she will never forgive while the world stands; for have I not been your nurse, and won you back to life and to her service? And has she not seen us twain together in one place, and happy, because of the coming of the Maid? She will pardon me never, because, also for my sake, she has been wroth with you, and shown you her wrath, and all without a cause. Therefore she will be ashamed, and all the more cruel. Nay, nor would I forgive her, in the same case, if it befell me, for we women are all alike, hearts of wolves when we love! Hast thou never marked a cat that had kittens, or a brachet that had whelps, how they will fly at man or horse that draws near their brood, even unwittingly. And so, when we love, are we all, and the best of us are then the worst. Verily the friendship of you and me is over and done; but for your part be glad, not sorry, for with all her heart and soul she loves you. Else she had not been angered."

"You must not speak, nor I hear, such words of my lady," I said; "it is not seemly."

"Such words of your lady, and of Aymeric's lady, and of Giles's lady, and of myself were I any man's lady, as I am no man's lady, I will think and speak," said Charlotte, "for my words are true, and we maids are, at best, pretty fools, and God willed us to be so for a while, and then to be wiser than the rest of you. For, were we not pretty, would you wed us? and were we not fools, would we wed you? and where would God's world be then? But now you have heard enough of my wisdom: for I love no man, being very wise; or you have heard enough of my folly that my mirth bids me speak, as you shall deem it. And now, we must consider how this great feud may be closed, and the foes set at one again."

"Shall I find out her lodgings, and be carried thither straightway in a litter? Her heart may be softened when she sees that I cannot walk or mount a horse?"

"Now, let me think what I should deem, if I had ridden by, unlooked for, and spied my lover with a maid, not unfriendly, or perchance uncomely, sitting smiling in a gallant balcony. Would I be appeased when he came straight to seek me, borne in a litter? Would I—?" And she mused, her finger at her mouth, and her brow puckered, but with a smile on her lips and in her eyes.

Then I, seeing her so fair, yet by me so undesired; and beholding her so merry, while my heart was amazed with the worst sorrow, and considering, too, that but for her all this would never have been, but I sitting happy by my lady's side,—thinking on all this, I say, I turned from her angrily, as if I would leave the balcony.

"Nay, wait," she cried, "for I must see all the show out, and here come the Scots Guard, thy friends, and I need time to take counsel with my wisdom on this weighty matter. See, they know you"; and, indeed, many a man in that gallant array waved his hand to me merrily, as they filed past under their banners—the Douglas's bloody heart, the Crescent moon of Harden, the Napier's sheaf of spears, the blazons of Lindsays and Leslies, Homes, and Hepburns, and Stuarts. It was a sight to put life into the dying breast of a Scot in a strange country, and all were strong men and young, ruddy and brown of cheek, high of heart and heavy of hand. And most beckoned to me, and pointed onwards to that way whither they were bound, in chase of fame and fortune. All this might have made a sick man whole, but my spirit was dead within me, so that I could scarce beckon back to them, or even remember their faces.

"Would I forgive you," said Charlotte, after she had thrown the remnant of her roses to her friends among the Scots, "if you hurried to me, pale, and borne in a litter? Nay, methinks not, or not for long; and then I should lay it on you never to see her face again;—she is I, you know, for the nonce. But if you waited and did not come, then my pride might yield at length, and I send for you. But then, if so, methinks I would hate her (that is, me) more than ever. Oh, it is a hard case when maids are angry!"

"You speak of yourself, how you would do this or that; but my lady is other than you, and pitiful. Did she not come all these leagues at a word from me, hearing that I was sick?"

"At a word from you, good youth! Nay, at a word from me! Did you speak of me in your letter to her father?"

"Nay!" said I.

"You did well. And therefore it was that I wrote, for I knew she would move heaven and earth and the Maid or she would come when she heard of another lass being in your company. Nay, trust me, we women understand each other, and she would ask the Maid, who lodged here with us, what manner of lass I was to look upon, and the Maid's answer would bring her."

"You have been kind," I said. "And to you and the saints I owe it that I yet live to carry a sore heart and be tormented with your ill tongue."

"And had you heard that a fair young knight, and renowned in arms, lay sick at your lady's house, she nursing him, would you not have cast about for ways of coming to her?"

To this I answered nothing, but, with a very sour countenance, was rising to go, when my name was called in the street.

Looking down, I saw my master, who doffed his cap to the daughter of the house, and begging leave to come up, fastened his horse's bridle to the ring in the wall, by the door.

Up he came, whom Charlotte welcomed very demurely, and so left us, saying that she must go about her household business; but as she departed she cast a look back at me, making a "moue," as the French say, with her red lips.

"Well, my son," cried my master, taking my hand, "why so pale? Sure thou hast had a sore bout, but thou art mending."

I could but stammer my lady's name—

"Elliot—shall I see her soon?"

He scratched his rough head and pulled his russet beard, and so laughed shamefacedly.

"Why, lad, to that very end she came, and now—St. Anthony's fire take me if I well know why—she will none of it. The Maid brought us in her company, for, as you know, she will ever have young lasses with her when she may, and as far as Orleans the roads are safe. And who so glad as Elliot when the Maid put this command on her, after we got thy letter? I myself was most eager to ride, not only for your sake, but to see how Orleans stood after the long pounding. But when we had come to our lodging, and I was now starting off to greet you, Elliot made no motion of rising. Nay, when I bade her make haste, she said that haste there was none; and when I, marvelling, asked, 'Wherefore?' answered that she was loth to spoil good company, and had seen you, as I did myself, happy enough with the lass who nursed you, and who had written to her."

Andrew Lang

"And wherefore, in Heaven's name, should we not be happy on such a day as this was an hour agone? But now the sun is out of the sky."

"I see him plainer than ever I did in the Merse," said my master, looking up where the sun was bright in the west. "But what would you? Women have been thus since Eve had a daughter, for our father Adam, I trow, had no trouble with other ladies than his wife—and that was trouble enough."

"But how am I to make my peace, and win my pardon, being innocent as I am?"

"Faith, I know not!" said he, and laughed again, which angered me some deal, for what was there to laugh at?

"May I let bring a litter, for I cannot yet walk, and so go back with you to her?"

"Indeed, I doubt if it were wise," said he; and so we stood gazing at each other, while I could have wept for very helpless anger. "I have it, I think," said he at last. "The Maid is right busy, as needs must be, gathering guns and food for her siege of Jargeau. But it is not fitting that she should visit Orleans without seeing you, nor would she wish to be so negligent. Yet if she were, I would put it in her mind, and then, when you are with her, which Elliot shall not know, I will see that Elliot comes into the chamber, and so leave all to you, and to her, and to the Maid. For she hath great power with that silly wench of mine, who has no other desire, I trow, than a good excuse to be rid of her sudden anger. If she loved you less, she would be never so fiery."

I myself could see no better hope or comfort.

Then he began to devise with me on other matters, and got

from me the story of my great peril at the hands of Brother Thomas. He laughed at the manner of my outwitting that miscreant, who had never been taken, but was fled none knew whither, and my master promised to tell the tale to the Maid, and warn her against this enemy. And so bidding me be of good cheer, he departed; but for my part, I went into my chamber, drew the bolt, and cast myself on the bed, refusing meat or drink, or to see the face of man or woman.

I was devoured by a bitter anger, considering how my lady had used me, and what was most sore of all, reflecting that I could no longer hold her for a thing all perfect, and almost without touch of mortal infirmity. Nay, she was a woman like another, and unjust, and to deem thus of her was to me the most cruel torment. We could never forgive each the other, so it seemed to me, nor be again as we had been. And all the next day no message came for me, and I kept myself quiet, apart in my chamber. Lest they who read mock at me in their hearts, and at my lady, let them remember how young we both were, and how innocent of other experience in love. For the Roman says that "the angers of lovers are love's renewal," as the brief tempests of April bring in the gladness of May. But in my heart it was all white sleet, and wind, and snow unseasonable, and so I lay, out of all comfort, tossing on my bed.

I heard the watchmen call the hours through the night, and very early, having at length fallen on sleep, I was wakened by a messenger from the Maid. It was her page, Louis de Coutes, most richly attired, but still half asleep, grumbling, and rubbing his eyes.

"My mistress bids you come with me instantly," he said, when we had saluted each other, "and I have brought a litter and men to carry it. Faith, if I lay in it, I should be asleep ere ever they had borne me ten paces. What a life it is that I lead!

Andrew Lang

Late to bed and up by prime, so busy is my mistress; and she lives as it were without sleep, and feeds on air."

Here he threw himself down in a great chair, and verily, by the time I had washed and attired myself, I had to shake him by the shoulder to arouse him. Thus I was carried to the Maid's lodging, my heart beating like a hammer with hopes and fears.

We found her already armed, for that day she was to ride to Jargeau, and none was with her but her confessor. She gave me the best of greetings, and bade me eat bread and drink wine. "And soon," she said, "if you recover the quicker, I trust to give you wine to drink in Paris."

She herself dipped a crust in wine and water, and presently, bidding her confessor, Pasquerel, wait for her in the little oratory, she asked me how I did, and told me what fear she had been in for me, as touching Brother Thomas, when she learned who he was, yet herself could not return from the field to help me.

"But now," said she, smiling with a ravishing sweetness, "I hear you are in far greater peril from a foe much harder and more cruel—ma mie Elliot. Ah! how you lovers put yourselves in jeopardy, and take me from my trade of war to play the peacemaker! Surely I have chosen the safer path in open breach and battle, though would that my war was ended, and I sitting spinning again beside my dear mother." Hereon her face grew more tender and sad than ever I had seen it, and there came over me forgetfulness of my private grief, as of a little thing, and longing to ride at the Maiden's rein, where glory was to be won.

"Would that even now I could march with you," I said; and she, smiling, made answer—

"That shall yet be; yea, verily," and here the fashion of her countenance altered wondrously, "I know, and know not how I know, that thou shalt be with me when all have forsaken me and fled."

Then she fell silent, and I also, marvelling on her face and on the words which she spoke. There came a light tap at the door, and she awoke as it were from a trance which possessed her. She drew her hands over her face, with a long sigh; she knelt down swiftly, and crossed herself, making an obeisance, for I deem that her saints had been with her, wherefore I also crossed myself and prayed. Then she rose and cried "Enter!" and ere I could speak she had passed into the oratory, and I was alone with Elliot.

Elliot gave one low cry, and cast her arms about my neck, hiding her face on my breast, and sobbing as if her heart would break.

"I have been mad, I have been bad!" she moaned. "Oh! say hard words to me, and punish me, my love."

But I had no word to say, only I fell back into a great chair for very weakness, holding my lady in my arms.

And thus, with words few enough, but great delight, the minutes went past, till she lifted her wet face and her fragrant hair; and between laughing and crying, studied on my face and caressed me, touching my thin cheek, and wept and laughed again. "I was mad," she whispered; "it seemed as if a devil entered into me. But She spoke to me and cast him out, and she bade me repent."

"And do penance," I said, kissing her till she laughed again, saying that I was a hard confessor, and that the Maid had spoken no word of penances.

"Yet one I must do and suffer," she said, "and it is more difficult to me than these austerities of thine."

Here her face grew very red, and she hid it with her hands.

"What mean you?" I asked, wondering.

"I must see her, and thank her for all her kindness to thee."

"The Maid?" I asked.

"Nay, that other, thy—fair nurse. Nay, forbid me not, I have sworn it to myself, and I must go. And the Maiden told me, when I spoke of it, that it was no more than right." Then she threw her arms about me again, in the closest embrace, and hid her head. Now, this resolve of hers gave me no little cause of apprehension, as not knowing well how things might pass in such an encounter of two ladies. But even then one touched me on the shoulder from behind, and the Maid herself stood beside us.

"O joy!" she said, "my peacemaking has been blessed! Go, you foolish folk, and sin no more, and peace and happiness be with you, long years, and glad children at your knees. Yet hereof I know nothing from my counsel. And now I must go forth about the Dauphin's business, and to do that for which I was sent. They that brought thee in the litter will carry thee back again; so farewell."

Thus saying, she stooped and kissed Elliot, who leaped up and caught the Maid in her arms, and they embraced, and parted for that time, Elliot weeping to lose her, and at the thought of the dangers of war.

CHAPTER XVII

HOW ELLIOT LOST HER JACKANAPES

The Maid's confessor, Pasquerel, stood in the chamber where we had met, with his eyes bent on the ground, so that Elliot and I had no more free speech at that time. Therefore I said farewell, not daring to ask of her when her mind was to visit my hosts, and, indeed, my trust was that she might leave this undone, lest new cause of sorrow should arise. Thus we parted, with very courtly leave-taking, the priest regarding us in his manner, and I was carried in the litter through the streets, that had been so quiet when I came forth in the morning, but now they were full of men and of noise. Herds of cattle were being driven for the food of the army marching against Jargeau; there were trains of carts full of victual, and the citizens having lent the Maid their great pieces of ordnance, the bombard called "The Shepherdess," and the gun "Montargis," these were being dragged along by clamorous companies of apprentices, and there were waggons charged with powder, and stone balls, and boxes of arrows, spades and picks for trenching, and all manner of munition of war. By reason of the troops of horses and of marching men, they that bore me were often compelled to stop. Therefore, lest any who knew me should speak with me, I drew the curtains of the litter, for I had much matter to think on, and was fain to be private. But this was to be of no avail, for I heard loud voices in my own tongue.

"What fair lady is this who travels so secretly?" and, with this, one drew the curtains, and there was the face of Randal Rutherford, with others behind him. Then he uttered a great cry—

"Faith, it is our lady of the linen-basket, and no other"; and leaning within, he gave me a rough embrace and a kiss of his bearded lips. "Why so early astir, our sick man?" he cried. "Get yourself healed anon, and be with us when we take Paris town, Norman, for there is booty enough to furnish all Scotland. Shalt thou be with us yet?"

"If my strength backs my will, Randal; and truly your face is a sight for sair eyne, and does me more good than all the powers of the apothecary."

"Then here is to our next merry meeting," he cried, "under Paris walls!"

With that the Scots gave a shout, and, some of them crowding round to press my hand, they bade me be of good cheer, and all went onward, singing in the tune of "Hey, tuttie tattie," which the pipers played when we broke the English at Bannockburn.

So I was borne back to the house of Jacques Boucher, and, in the sunny courtyard, there stood Charlotte, looking gay and fair, yet warlike, as I deemed. She was clad in a long garment of red over a white robe, and had sleeves of green, so that she wore the spring's own colours, and she was singing a French ditty concerning a lady who has a lover, and vows that she will never be a nun.

Seray-je nonnette, oui ou non,

Serray-je nonnette, je croy que non!

Seeing me, she stinted in her singing, and in feeding a falcon that was perched on her wrist.

"You are early astir for a sick man," she said. "Have you been on pilgrimage, or whither have you been faring?"

"The Maid sent for me right early, for to-day she rides to Jargeau, and to you she sends a message of her love,"—as indeed she had done, "but, for the great press of affairs she might not visit you."

"And Mistress Elliot Hume, has she forgiven her lover yet? nay, I see by your face that you are forgiven! And you go south, this very day, is it not so?"

"Indeed," I said, "if it is your will that we part, part we must, though I sorrow for it; but none has given me the word to march, save you, my fair nurse and hostess."

"Nay, it is not I who shall speed you; nevertheless the Maid is not the only prophetess in this realm of France, and something tells me that we part this day. But you are weary; will you get you to your chamber, or sit in the garden under the mulberry-tree, and I shall bring you out a cup of white wine."

Weary I was indeed, and the seat in the garden among the flowers seemed a haven most desirable. So thither I went, leaning on her shoulder, and she returned to bring the wine, but was some while absent, and I sat deep in thought. I was marvelling, not only as to what my mistress would next do, and when I should see her again (though that was uppermost in my mind), but also concerning the strange words of the Maid, that I alone should be with her when all forsook her

Andrew Lang

and fled. How might this be, and was she not to be ever victorious, and drive the English forth of France? To my thinking the Maid dwelt ever in two worlds, with her brethren of Paradise, and again with sinful men. And I have often considered that she did not always remember, in this common life, what had befallen her, and what she knew when, as the Apostle says, she "was out of the body." For I have heard her say, more than once, that she "would last but one year, or little more," and, again, she would make plans for three years to come, or four, which is a mystery.

So I was pondering, when I looked up, and saw Charlotte standing in the entrance between the court and garden, looking at me and smiling, as she shaded her eyes with her hand from the sun, and then she ran to me lightly as a lapwing.

"They are coming down the street, looking every way for our house, your lady and her father," she said, putting the wine-cup into my hand. "Now is it war or peace?" and she fled back again within the house.

My heart stood still, for now everything was on the fall of the dice. Would this mad girl be mocking or meek? Would she anger my lady to my ruin with her sharp tongue? For Charlotte was of a high temper, and wont to rule all the house by reason of her beauty and kind wild ways. Nor was Elliot the meekest of women, as well I knew, and a word, nay a smile, or a glance of mockery, might lightly turn her heart from me again for ever. Oh! the lot of a lover is hard, at least if he has set all his heart on the cast, as I had done, and verily, as our Scots saw runs, "women are kittle cattle." It is a strange thing that one who has learned not to blench from a bare blade, or in bursting of cannon-balls and flight of arrows, should so easily be daunted where a weak girl is concerned; yet so it was in my case. I know not if I feared more than now when Brother Thomas had me in the still chamber, alone at his mercy.

So the minutes went by, the sun and shade flickering through the boughs of the mulberry-tree, and the time seemed long. Perchance, I thought, there had been war, as Charlotte had said, and my lady had departed in anger with her father, and I was all undone. Yet I dared not go to seek them in the house, not knowing how matters were passing, and whether I should do good or harm. So I waited, and at length Charlotte came forth alone. Now she walked slowly, her eyes bent on the ground, and, as she drew near, I saw that they were red, and I guessed that she had been weeping. So I gave up all for lost, and my heart turned to water within me.

"I am sent to bid you come in," she said gravely.

"What has passed?" I cried. "For the saints' sake, tell me all!"

"This has passed, that I have seen such a lady as I never dreamed I should see, and she has made me weep—foolish that I am!"

"Why, what did she? Did she speak unkindly then, to my kind nurse?"

For this I could in no manner have endured, nor have abased myself to love one that was unjust, how dear soever; and none could be dearer than Elliot. Yet unjust she might have been; and this thought to me was the greatest torment.

"Speak unkind words? Oh, I remember my foolish talk, how I said that she would never forgive me while the world stands. Nay, while her father was with mine and with my mother, thanking them for what they did for you, she led me apart to devise with me, and I took her to my chamber, and

Andrew Lang

there, with tears in her eyes, and in the sweetest manner, she prayed me to pardon her for that she had been mad for a moment; and so, looking meek as an angel, she awaited my word. And I could not but weep, though to weep is never my way, and we embraced each the other, and I told her how all your converse had ever been of her, even when you were beside yourself, in your fever, and how never was so faithful a lover. Nay, I bid you be glad, for I never deemed that any woman living on earth would so repent and so confess herself to another, where she herself had first been wroth, but would blame all the world rather, and herself—never. So we women are not all alike, as I thought; for I would hardly have forgiven, if I know myself; and yet I am no worse than another. Truly, she has been much with the Maid, and has caught from her this, to be like her, who is alone among women, and of the greatest heart."

Here she ceased to speak very gravely, as she had till now done, and breaking out into a sweet laughter, she cried—

"Nevertheless I am not wholly a false prophetess, for to-day you go with them southward, to Tours, to change the air, as the physician counsels, and so now we part. O false Scot!" she said, laughing again, "how have you the ill courtesy to look so joyous? Nay, I shall change your cheer"; and with that she stooped and kissed my cheek, saying, "Go, and joy go with you, as joy abides with me, to see my sick man look so strong again. Come, they are waiting for us, and you know we must not tarry."

Then, giving me her arm, she led me in, and if one of us twain had a shamefaced guise, verify it was not Charlotte Boucher.

"I yield you back your esquire, fair lady," she said merrily, making obeisance to Elliot, who stood up, very pale, to receive us.

"He has got no ill in the bower of the enchantress," said my master; whereat, Elliot seeming some deal confused, and blushing, Charlotte bustled about, bringing wine and meat, and waiting upon all of us, and on her father and mother at table. A merry dinner it was among the elder folk, but Elliot and I were somewhat silent, and a great joy it was to me, and a heavy weight off my heart, I do confess, when, dinner being ended, and all courtesies done and said, my raiment was encased in wallets, and we all went through the garden, to Loire side; and so, with many farewells, took boat and sailed down the river, under the Bridge of Orleans, towards Blois. But Charlotte I never saw again, nor did I ever speak of her to Elliot, nor Elliot of her to me, from that day forth.

But within short space came tidings, how that Charlotte was wedding a young burgess of Orleans, with whom, as I hear, she dwelt happily, and still, for all I know, dwells in peace. As I deem, she kept her lord in a merry life, yet in great order and obedience. So now there is no more to tell of her, save that her picture comes back before me—a tall, brown girl, with black hair and eyes like the hue of hazel boughs glassed in running water, clad in white and green and red, standing smiling beneath the red-and-white blossoms of an apple-tree, in the green garden of Jacques Boucher.

Elliot was silent enough, and sat telling her beads, in the beginning of our journey down the water-way, that is the smoothest and the easiest voyaging for a sick man. She was in the stern of the boat, her fingers, when her beads were told, trailing in the smooth water, that was green with the shade of leaves. But her father stood by me, asking many questions concerning the siege, and gaping at the half-mended arch of the bridge, where through we sailed, and at the blackened walls of Les Tourelles, and all the ruin that war had wrought. But now masons and carpenters were very busy rebuilding all, and the air was full of the tinkling of trowels and hammers. Presently we passed the place where I had drawn Brother Thomas from the water; but thereof I said no word, for indeed my dreams were haunted by his hooded face, like that of the snake which, as travellers tell, wears a hood in Prester John's country, and is the most venomous of beasts serpentine. So concerning Brother Thomas I held my peace, and the barque, swinging round a corner of the bank, soon brought us into a country with no sign of war on it, and here the poplar-trees had not been felled for planks to make bulwarks, but whispered by the riverside.

The wide stream carried many a boat, and shone with sails, white, and crimson, and brown; the boat-men sang, or hailed each other from afar. There was much traffic, stores being carried from Blois to the army. Some mile or twain above Beaugency we were forced to land, and, I being borne in a litter, we took a cross-path away from the stream, joining it again two miles below Beaugency, because the English held that town, though not for long. The sun had set, yet left all his gold shining on the water when we entered Blois, and there rested at a hostel for the night. Next day—one of the goodliest of my life, so soft and clear and warm it was, yet with a cool wind on the water—we voyaged to Tours; and now Elliot was glad enough, making all manner of mirth.

Her desire, she said, was to meet a friend that she had left at their house in Tours, one that she had known as long as she knew me, my friend he was too, yet I had never spoken of him, or asked how he did. Now I, being wrapped up wholly in her, and in my joy to see her kind again, and so beautiful, had no memory of any such friend, wherefore she mocked me, and rebuked me for a hard heart and ungrateful. "This friend of mine," she said, "was the first that made us known each to other. Yea, but for him, the birds might have pecked

out your eyne, and the ants eaten your bones bare, yet"—
with a sudden anger, and tears in her eyes at the words she
spoke—"you have clean forgotten him!"

"Ah, you mean the jackanapes. And how is the little
champion?"

"Like the lads of Wamfray, aye for ill, and never for good,"
said my master; but she frowned on him, and said—

"Now you ask, because I forced you on it; but, sir, I take it
very ill that you have so short a memory for a friend. Now,
tell me, in all the time since you left us at Chinon, how often
have you thought of him?"

"Nigh as often as I thought of you," I answered. "For when
you came into my mind (and that was every minute), as in a
picture, thither too came your playfellow, climbing and
chattering, and holding out his little bowl for a comfit."

"Nay, then you thought of me seldom, or you would have
asked how he does."

Here she turned her face from me, half in mock anger. But,
just as it is with children, so it was with Elliot, for indeed my
dear was ever much of a child, wherefore her memory is now
to me so tender. And as children make pretence to be in this
humour or that for sport, and will affect to be frighted till
they really fear and weep, so Elliot scarce knew how deep
her own humour went, and whether she was acting like a
player in a Mystery, or was in good earnest. And if she knew
not rightly what her humour was, far less could I know, so
that she was ever a puzzle to me, and kept me in a hundred
pretty doubts and dreads every day. Alas! how sorely,
through all these years, have I longed to hear her rebuke me
in mirth, and put me adread, and laugh at me again I for she

was, as it were, wife and child to me, at once, and I a child with her, and as happy as a child.

Thus, nothing would now jump with her humour but to be speaking of her jackanapes, and how he would come louting and leaping to welcome her, and forsake her old kinswoman, who had followed with them to Tours. And she had much to report concerning his new tricks: how he would leap over a rod for the Dauphin or the Maid, but not if adjured in the name of the English King, or the Duke of Burgundy. Also, if you held him, he would make pretence to bite any that you called Englishman or false Frenchman. Moreover, he had now been taught to fetch and carry, and would climb into Elliot's window, from the garden, and bring her little basket of silks, or whatsoever she desired, or carry it thither, as he was commanded.

"And he wrung the cat's neck," quoth my master; but Elliot bade him hold his peace.

In such sport the hours passed, till we were safely come to Tours, and so to their house in a street running off the great place, where the cathedral stands. It was a goodly dwelling, with fair carved-work on the beams, and in the doorway stood the old Scots kinswoman, smiling wide and toothless, to welcome us. Elliot kissed her quickly, and she fondled Elliot, and held a hand out over her shoulder to greet me.

"But where is my jackanapes, that should have been here to salute his mistress?" Elliot cried.

"Out and alas!" said the old wife in our country tongue—"out and alas! for I have ill news. The poor beast is missing these three days past, and we fear he is stolen away by some gangrel bodies, for the town is full of them. There came two to our door, three days agone, and one was a blind man, and the other a one-armed soldier, maimed in the wars, and I gave them bite and sup, as a Christian should do. Now, they had not been gone but a few minutes, and I was in the spence, putting away the dishes, when I heard a whistle in the street, and anon another. I thought little of it, and so was about my business for an hour, when I missed the jackanapes. And then there was a hue and cry, and all the house was searched, and the neighbours were called on, but since that day there has been no word of the jackanapes. But, for the blind man and the armless soldier, the town guard saw them leaving by the North Gate, with a violer woman and her husband, an ill-looking loon, in their company." Elliot sat her down and wept sore. "They have stolen my little friend," she cried, "and now he that was so fat I called him Tremouille will go hungry and lean, and be whipped to make him do his tricks, and I shall never see him more."

Then she ran out of the chamber, to weep alone, as I guessed, for she was pitiful and of very tender affection, and dumb things came near about her heart, as is the manner of many women.

But I made no doubt in my mind that the husband of the ape's old mistress had stolen him, and I, too, sorrowed for the poor beast that my mistress loved, and that, in very deed, had been the saving of my own life. Then I spoke to my master, and said that we must strive to buy her a new ape, or a little messan dog, to be her playfellow.

But he shook his head. "Say nothing more of the beast," he muttered, "unless she speaks of him first, and that, methinks, will be never. For it is not her wont to speak of what lies very deep in her heart, and if you talk of the beast it will please her little."

And, indeed, I heard no word more of the jackanapes from

Andrew Lang

Elliot, save that, coming back from the minster next day, she whispered, "I have prayed for him," and so fled to her own chamber.

As then I deemed it a strange thing, and scarcely to be approved by Holy Church, that my lady should pray for a dumb beast who had no soul to be saved. But a faithful, loving prayer is not unavailing or unheard of Him who made the beasts, as well as He made us; for whose sin, or the sin of our father Adam, they now suffer, silently. And the answer to this prayer was to be known in the end.

As the week went on, tidings came that made Elliot glad again, if before she had been sad enough. For this was that great week of wonders which shall never be forgotten while France is France, and the lilies bloom.

On June the thirteenth the Maid took Jargeau, whence the famed Bastard of Orleans had been driven some weeks agone; and the Earl of Suffolk yielded him her prisoner, saying that she was "the most valiant woman in the world." Scarce had tidings of this great victory come, when messengers followed, declaring that the Maid had seized the Bridge of Meun and driven the English into the Castle.

Next she marched against Beaugency, and, at midnight of June the seventeenth, the English made terms, that they might go forth with their lives, but without baggage or arms, and with but one mark of silver apiece. Next morning came Talbot, the best knight then on ground, and Fastolf, the wariest of captains, with a great army of English. First they made for Jargeau, but they came too late, and then they rode to Meun, and would have assailed the French in the bridge-fort, but, even then, they heard how Beaugency had yielded to La Pucelle, and how the garrison was departed into Normandy, like pilgrims, without swords, and staff in hand.

Thus all the Loire and the water-way was in the power of France, wherefore the English marched off through the country called La Beauce, which then lay desert and overgrown with wild wood, by reason of the war. And there, in a place named Coynce, near Patay, the Maid overtook the English, having with her La Hire and Xaintrailles, and she charged them so rudely, that ere the English could array them in order of battle, they were already flying for their lives. There were Talbot and Warwick taken and held to ransom, but Fastolf fled as fast as his horse could carry him.

Thus in one week, between June the eleventh and June the eighteenth, the Maid had delivered three strong towns from the English, and had utterly routed them in fair field. Then, at Orleans, on June the nineteenth, the army went to the churches, thanking God, and the Blessed Virgin, and all the saints, for such great signs and marvels wrought through the Maid only.

Sorrow it is to me to write of such things by report, and not to have seen them done. But, as Talbot said to the Duc d'Alencon, when they took him at Patay, "it is fortune of war."

But, as day by day messengers came, their horses red with spurring, to the cross in the market-place of Tours, and as we that gathered round heard of some fresh victory, you may consider whether we rejoiced, feasted, filled the churches with our thanksgivings, and deemed that, in a few weeks, there would be no living Englishman on French soil. And of all that were glad my lady was the happiest, for she had believed in the Maid from the very beginning, when her father mocked. And a hard life she now led him with her sallies, day by day, as more and ever more glad tidings were brought, and we could hear Elliot singing through the house.

Yea, I found her once dancing in the garden all alone, a beautiful sight to look upon, as the sun fell on her and the shadow, she footing it as if to music, but the music was made by her own heart. Leaning against an apple-tree, I watched her, who waved her hand to me, and still danced on; this was after we had heard the news of Beaugency. As she so swayed and moved, dancing daintily, came a blast of a trumpet and a gay peal from the minster bells. Then forth rushed Elliot, and through the house, and down the street into the market-place, nor did I know where I was, till I found myself beside her, and heard the Maire read a letter to all the folk, telling how the English were routed at Pathay in open field. Thereon the whole multitude fell a-dancing, and I, for all my malady, was fain to dance with them; but Elliot led me home, her head high, and blue rays darting from her eyes. From that day my life seemed to come back to me, and I was no longer the sick man. So the weeks went by, in all delight, my master working hard, and I helping him in my degree, for new banners would be wanted when the Dauphin went for his sacring to his good town of Reims. As we all deemed, this could no longer be delayed; and thereafter our armies would fall on Paris, and so strong grew I, that I was in hopes to be with them, where, at last, fortune was to be won. But of this my hope I said little to Elliot, waiting till I could wear armour, and exercising myself thereat privately in the garden, before folk had risen in the mornings.

CHAPTER XVIII

HOW ELLIOT'S JACKANAPES WAS
SEEN AT THE KING'S CROWNING

"The hearts of kings are in His hand," says Holy Scripture, and it is of necessity to be believed that the hearts of kings, in an especial sense, are wisely governed. Yet, the blindness of our sinful souls, we often may not see, nor by deep consideration find out, the causes wherefore kings often act otherwise, and, as we might deem, less worthily than common men. For it is a truth and must be told, that neither before he was anointed with the blessed oil from the holy vessel, or ampulla, which the angel brought to St. Remigius, nor even after that anointing (which is more strange), did Charles VII., King of France, bear him kingly as regards the Maiden. Nay, I have many a time thought with sorrow that if Xaintrailles, or La Hire, ay, or any the meanest esquire in all our army, had been born Dauphin, in three months after the Maid's victories in June Paris would have been ours, and not an Englishman left to breathe the air of France. For it needed but that the King should obey the Maid, ride straight to Reims, and thence on Paris town, and every city would have opened its gates to him, as the walls of Jericho fell at the mere sound of the trumpets of Israel.

This is no foolish fancy of an old man dreaming in a cloister

Andrew Lang

about what might have been. For the Regent of the English, brother of their King Harry the Fifth, and himself a wise man, and brave, if cruel, was of this same mind. First, he left Paris and shut himself up in the strong castle of Vincennes, dreading an uproar among the people; and next, he wholly withdrew himself to Rouen, for he had now no force of men to guard the walls of Paris. Our Dauphin had but to mount and ride, and all would have been his at one blow, ay, or without a blow. The Maid, as we daily heard, kept praying him, even with tears, to do no more than this; and from every side came in men free and noble, ready to serve at their own charges. The poorest gentlemen who had lost all in the troubles, and might not even keep a horse to ride, were of goodwill to march as common foot-soldiers.

But, while all France called on her King, he was dwelling at Sully, in the castle of La Tremouille, a man who had a foot in either camp, so that neither English nor Burgundians had ever raided on his rich lands, when these lay in their power. So, what with the self-seeking, and sloth, and jealousy of La Tremouille; what with the worldly policy of the Archbishop of Reims, crying Peace, where there was no peace, the Maid and the captains were not listened to, or, if they were heard, their plans were wrought out with a faint heart, so that, at last, if it is lawful to say so, the will of men prevailed over the will of Heaven.

Never, I pray, may any prince of my own country be so bestead, and so ill-served, that, when he has won battles and gained cities two or three, and needs but to ride forward and win all his kingdom, he shall be turned back by the little faith of his counsellors! Never may such a thing befall a prince of Scotland! Concerning these matters of State, as may be believed, we devised much at Tours, while messengers were coming and going, and long, weary councils were being held at Sully and at Gien. D'Alencon, we got news, was all for striking a blow yet more bold than the march to Reims, and would have attacked the English where they were strongest, and nearest their own shores, namely, at Rouen. The counsellors of the peaceful sort were inclined to waste time in besieging La Charite, and other little towns on Loire-side. But her Voices had bidden the Maid, from the first, to carry the Dauphin to Reims, that there he might be anointed, and known to France for the very King. So at last, finding that time was sorely wasted, whereas all hope lay in a swift stroke, ere the English could muster men, and bring over the army lately raised by the Cardinal of Winchester to go crusading against the miscreants of Bohemia—the Maid rode out of Gien, with her own company, on June the twenty-seventh, and lodged in the fields, some four leagues away, on the road to Auxerre. And next day the King and the Court followed her perforce, with a great army of twelve thousand men. Thenceforth there came news to us every day in Tours, and all the news was good. Town after town opened its gates at the summons of the Maid, and notably Troyes and Chalons, in despite of the English garrisons.

We were all right glad, and could scarce sleep for joy, above all when a messenger rode in, one Thomas Scott, whom I had encountered before, as I have written, bidding my master come straightway to Reims, to join the King, and exercise his craft in designing a great picture of the coronation. So with much ado he bestowed his canvases, brushes, paints, and all other gear of his trade in wallets, and, commending his daughter to his old kinswoman, to obey her in all things, he set off on horseback with Thomas Scott. But for myself, I was to lodge, while he was at Reims, with a worthy woman of Tours, for the avoiding of evil tongues, and very tardily the time passed with me, for that I might not be, as before, always in the company of Elliot.

As for my lady, she was, during most of these days, on her

knees at the altar in the great minster, praying to the saints for the Dauphin, and the Maid, and for her father, that he might come and go safely on his journey. Nor did she pray in vain, for, no more than two days after the first tidings had arrived that the sacring was done, and that all had gone well, my master rode to his own door, weary, but glad at heart, and hobbled into his house. One was sent running to bring me this good news, and I myself ran, for now I was able, and found him seated at his meat, as well as he could eat it for Elliot, that often stopped his mouth with kisses.

He held forth his hand to me, saying, "All is as well as heart could desire, and the Maid bids you follow her, if you may, to the taking of Paris, for there she says will be your one chance to win your spurs. And now let me eat and drink, for the heat is great, the ways dusty, and I half famished. Thereafter ask me what you will, and you, Elliot, come not between a hungry man and his meat."

So he spoke, sitting at his table with his tankard in his hand, and his wallets lying about him on the floor. Elliot was therefore fain not to be embracing him, but rather to carve for him, and serve in the best manner, that he might sup the quicker and tell us all his tale. This he did at last, Elliot sitting on his knee, with her arm about his neck. But, as touches the sacring, how it was done, though many of the peers of France were not there to see, and how noble were the manners of the King and the Maid, who stood there with her banner, and of the only reward which she would take, namely, that her townsfolk should live free of tax and corvee, all this is known and written of in Chronicles. Nor did I see it myself, so I pass by. But, next to actual beholding of that glorious rite, the best thing was to hear my master tell of it, taking out his books, wherein he had drawn the King, and the Maid in her harness, and many of the great lords. From these pictures a tapestry was afterwards wrought, and hung in Reims Cathedral, where it is to this day: the Maid on horseback beckoning the King onward, the Scots archers beside him in the most honourable place, as was their lawful due, and, behind all, the father of the Maid entering Reims by another road. By great good fortune, and by virtue of being a fellow-traveller with Thomas Scott, the rider of the King's stable, my master found lodgings easily enough. So crowded was the town that, the weather being warm, in mid July, many lay in tabernacles of boughs, in the great place of Reims, and there was more singing that night than sleeping. But my master had lain at the hostelry called L'Asne Roye, in the parvise, opposite to the cathedral, where also lay Jean d'Arc, the father of the Maid. Thither she herself came to visit him, and she gave gifts to such of the people of her own countryside as were gathered at Reims.

"And, Jeannot, do you fear nothing?" one of them asked her, who had known her from a child.

"I fear nothing but treason," my master heard her reply, a word that we had afterwards too good cause to remember.

"And is she proud now that she is so great?" asked Elliot.

"She proud! No pride has she, but sat at meat, and spoke friendly with all these manants, and it was 'tu' and 'toy,' and 'How is this one? and that one?' till verily, I think, she had asked for every man, woman, child, and dog in Domremy. And that puts me in mind—"

"In mind of what?"

"Of nought. Faith, I remember not what I was going to say, for I am well weary."

"But Paris?" I asked. "When march we on Paris?" My

master's face clouded. "They should have set forth for Paris the very day after the sacring, which was the seventeenth of July. But envoys had come in from the Duke of Burgundy, and there were parleys with them as touching peace. Now, peace will never be won save at the point of the lance. But a truce of a fortnight has been made with Burgundy, and then he is to give up Paris to the King. Yet, ere a fortnight has passed, the new troops from England will have come over to fight us, and not against the heretics of Bohemia, though they have taken the cross and the vow. And the King has gone to Saint Marcoul, forsooth, seeing that, unless he goes there to do his devotions, he may not touch the sick and heal the crewels. {29} Faith, they that have the crewels might even wait till the King has come to his own again; they have waited long enough to learn patience while he was Dauphin. It should be Paris first, and Saint Marcoul and the crewels afterwards, but anything to waste time and keep out of the brunt of the battle." Here he struck his hand on the table so that the vessels leaped. "I fear what may come of it," he said. "For every day that passes is great loss to us and much gain to our enemies of England, who will anon garrison Paris."

"Faint-heart," cried Elliot, plucking his beard. "You will never believe in the Maid, who has never yet failed to help us, by the aid of the saints."

"The saints help them that help themselves," he answered. "And Paris town has walls so strong, that once the fresh English are entered in, even the saints may find it a hard bargain. But you, Elliot, run up and see if my chamber be ready, for I am well weary." She ran forth, and my master, turning to me, said in a low voice, "I have something for your own ear, but I feared to grieve her. In a booth at Reims I saw her jackanapes doing his tricks, and when he came round questing with his bowl the little beast knew me and jumped up into my arms, and wailed as if he had been a

Christian. Then I was for keeping him, but I was set on by three or four stout knaves, and, I being alone, and the crowd taking their part, I thought it not well to draw sword, and so break the King's peace that had just then begun to be King. But my heart was sore for the poor creature, and, in very truth, I bring back no light heart, save to see you twain again, for I fear me that the worst of the darg {30} is still to do. But here comes Elliot, so no word of the jackanapes."

Therewith he went off to his chamber, and I to mine, with less pleasure than I had looked for. Still, the thought came into my heart that, the longer the delay of the onslaught on Paris, the better chance I had to take part therein; and the harder the work, the greater the glory.

The boding words of my master proved over true. The King was sacred on July the sixteenth, and Paris then stood empty of English soldiers, being garrisoned by Burgundians only. But, so soon as he was anointed, the King began to parley with Burgundy, and thus they spun out the time, till, on July the twenty-fifth, a strong army of Englishmen had entered Paris. Whether their hearts were high may not be known, but on their banner they had hung a distaff, and had painted the flag with the words—

"Ores viegne la Belle,"

meaning, "Let the fair Maid come, and we shall give her wool to spin." Next we heard, and were loth to believe it, that a new truce of fifteen days more had been made with Burgundy. The Maid, indeed, said openly that she loved not the truce, and that she kept it only for the honour of the King, which was dearer to her than her life, as she proved in the end.

Then came marchings, this way and that, all about the Isle of

France, Bedford leaving Paris to fight the King, and then refusing battle, though the Maid rode up to the English palisades, and smote them with her sword, defying the English to come out, if they were men. So the English betook them back to Paris, after certain light skirmishes only. Meanwhile some of his good towns that had been in the hands of the English yielded to the King, or rather to the Maid. Among these the most notable was Compiegne, a city as great as Orleans. Many a time it had been taken and retaken in the wars, but now the burgesses swore that they would rather all die, with their wives and children, than open their gates again to the English. And this oath they kept well, as shall be seen in the end.

CHAPTER XIX

HOW NORMAN LESLIE
RODE AGAIN TO THE WARS

Tidings of these parleys, and marches, and surrenders of cities came to us at Tours, the King sending letters to his good towns by messengers. One of these, the very Thomas Scott of whom I have before spoken, a man out of Rankelburn, in Ettrick Forest, brought a letter for me, which was from Randal Rutherford.

"Mess-John Urquhart writes for me, that am no clerk," said Randal, "and, to spare his pains, as he writes for the most of us, I say no more than this: come now, or come never, for the Maid will ride to see Paris in three days, or four, let the King follow or not as he will."

There was no more but a cross marked opposite the name of Randal Rutherford, and the date of place and day, August the nineteenth, at Compiegne.

My face fired, for I felt it, when I had read this, and I made no more ado, but, covenanting with Thomas Scott to be with him when he rode forth at dawn, I went home, put my harness in order, and hired a horse from him that kept the hostelry of the "Hanging Sword," whither also I sent my harness, for that I would sleep there. This was all done in the late evening, secretly, and, after supper, I broke the matter to my master and Elliot. Her face changed to a dead white, and she sat silent, while my master took the word, saying, in our country speech, that "he who will to Cupar, maun to Cupar," and therewith he turned, and walked out and about in the garden.

We were alone, and now was the hardest of my work to do, to comfort Elliot, when, in faith, I sorely needed comfort myself. But honour at once and necessity called me to ride, being now fit to bear harness, and foreseeing no other chance to gain booty, or even, perchance, my spurs. Nor could I endure to be a malingerer. She sat there, very white, her lip quivering, but her eyes brave and steadfast.

I kneeled beside her, and in my hands I took her little hand, that was cold as ice.

"It is for the Maid, and for you, Elliot," I whispered; and she only bent her head on my shoulder, but her cold hand gripped mine firmly.

"She did say that you should come back unharmed of sword," whispered Elliot, looking for what comfort she might. "But, O my dear! you may be taken, and when shall I see you again? Oh! this life is the hardest thing for women, who must sit and tremble and pray at home. Sure no danger of war is so terrible! Ah, must you really go?"

Then she clung so closely about me, that it seemed as if I could never escape out of her arms, and I felt as if my heart must break in twain.

"How could I look men in the face, and how could I ever see the Maid again, if I go not?" I said; and, loosening her grasp, she laid her hands on my shoulders, and so gazed on me steadfastly, as if my picture could be fixed on the tablets of her brain.

"On your chin is coming a little down, at last," she said, smiling faintly, and then gave a sob, and her lips met mine, and our very souls met; but, even then, we heard my master's steps hobbling to the door, and she gave a cry, and fled to her chamber. And this was our leave-taking—brief, but I would not have had it long.

"It is ill work parting, Heaven help us," said my master. "Faith, I remember, as if it were to-day, how I set forth for Verneuil; a long time I was gone, and came back a maimed man. But it is fortune of war! The saints have you in their keeping, my son, and chiefly St. Andrew. Come back soon, and whole, and rich, for, meseems, if I lose one of you, I am to lose both."

Therewith he embraced me, and I set forth to the hostel where I was to lie that night.

Now, see how far lighter is life to men than to women, for, though I left the house with the heaviest heart of any man in Tours, often looking back at the candleshine in my lady's casement, yet, when I reached the "Hanging Sword," I found Thomas Scott sitting at his wine, and my heart and courage revived within me. He lacked nothing but one to listen, and soon was telling tales of the war, and of the road, and of how this one had taken a rich prisoner, and that one had got an arrow in his thigh, and of what chances there were to win Paris by an onslaught.

"For in no other can we take it," said he, "save, indeed, by miracle. For they are richly provisioned, and our hope is that, if we can make a breach, there may be a stir of the common folk, who are well weary of the English and the Burgundians."

Now, with his talk of adventures, and with high hopes, I was so heartened up, that, to my shame, my grief fell from me, and I went to my bed to dream of trenches and escalades, glory and gain. But Elliot, I fear me, passed a weary night, and a sorry, whereas I had scarce laid my head on my pillow, as it seemed, when I heard Thomas shouting to the grooms, and clatter of our horses' hoofs in the courtyard. So I leaped up, though it was scarce daylight, and we rode northwards before the full coming of the dawn.

Here I must needs write of a shameful thing, which I knew not then, or I would have ridden with a heavier heart, but I was told concerning the matter many years after, by Messire Enguerrand de Monstrelet, a very learned knight, and deep in the counsels of the Duke of Burgundy.

"You were all sold," he said to me, at Dijon, in the year of our Lord fourteen hundred and forty-seven—"you were all sold when you marched against Paris town. For the Maid, with D'Alencon, rode from Compiegne towards Paris, on the twenty-third of August, if I remember well"; and here he turned about certain written parchments that lay by him. "Yea, on the twenty-third she left Compiegne, but on the twenty-eighth of that month the Archbishop of Reims entered the town, and there he met the ambassadors of the Good Duke of Burgundy. There he and they made a compact between them, binding your King and the Duke, that their truce should last till Noel, but that the duke might use his men in the defence of Paris against all that might make onfall. Now, the Archbishop and the King knew well that the Maid was, in that hour, marching on Paris. To what purpose make a truce, and leave out of the peace the very point where war should be? Manifestly the French King never meant to put forth the strength of his army in helping the Maid. There was to be truce between France and Burgundy, but none between England and the Maid."

So Messire Enguerrand told me, a learned knight and a grave, and thus was the counsel of the saints defeated by the very King whom they sought to aid. But of this shameful treaty we men-at-arms knew nothing, and so hazarded our lives against loaded dice.

CHAPTER XX

CONCERNING THE MAID AND THE BIRDS

We rode northwards, first through lands that I had travelled in before to Orleans, and so into a country then strange to me, passing by way of Lagny, with intent to go to Senlis, where we deemed the King lay. The whole region being near Paris, and close under the English power, was rich and peaceful of aspect, the corn being already reaped, and standing in sheaves about the fields, whether to feed Englishmen or Frenchmen, none could tell. For the land was in a kind of hush, in expectancy and fear, no man knowing how things should fall out at Paris. Natheless the Prior of Lagny, within that very week wherein we came, had gone to St. Denis, and yielded his good town into the hands of the Duc d'Alencon for the King. And the fair Duke had sent thither Messire Ambrose de Lore, a very good knight, with Messire Jehan Foucault, and many men-at-arms.

To Messire Ambrose we were brought, that we might give and take his news. I remember well that I dropped out of the saddle at the door of his lodgings, and could scarce stand on my legs, so weary was I with the long and swift riding. Never had I ridden so far, and so fast, fresh horses standing saddled and bridled for Thomas Scott and me at every stage, but the beast which I had hired I sent back from the first stage to mine host of the "Hanging Sword." Not without labour I climbed the stairs to the chamber of Messire Ambrose, who bade us sit down, and called for wine to be given us, whereof Thomas Scott drank well, but I dared take none, lest my legs should wholly refuse their office.

When Thomas had told how all the country lay at the King's peace, and how our purpose was to ride to the King at Senlis, the knight bade us rather make what haste we might to St. Denis. "For there, by to-morrow or next day, the King is like to be, and the assault will be delivered on Paris, come of it what will."

With this he bade us good speed, but, to guess from his countenance, was in no high hopes. And, at supper, whereto we had the company of certain of his men-at-arms, I could well perceive that they were not in the best heart. For now we heard how the Maid, being sorrowful for the long delays, had bidden the Duc d'Alencon ride forth with her from Compiegne "to see Paris closer than yet she had seen it." The Duc d'Alencon, who in late days has so strangely forgotten the loyalty of his youth, was then fain to march with her, for they two were the closest friends that might be. Therefore they had passed by way of Senlis, where they were joined by some force of men-at-arms, and so, on the third day's march, they came to St. Denis, where they were now lying. Here it is that the kings of France have been buried for these eight hundred years, in the great Abbey.

"Nom Dieu!" said one of those who spoke with us. "You might deem that our King is nowise pressed to see the place where his forefathers lie. For D'Alencon is riding, now and again, to Senlis, to rouse the King, and make him march to St. Denis, with the army, that the assault may be given. But if they were bidding him to his own funeral, instead of to a gentle passage of arms, he could not make more excuses.

There are skirmishes under Paris walls, and at the gates, day by day, and the Maid rides here and there, considering of the best place for the onslaught. But the King tarries, and without him and the army they can venture on no great valiance. Nevertheless, come he must, if they bring him bound in a cart. Wherefore, if you want your part in what is toward, you do well to make no long tarrying here."

I was of the same mind, and as the King was shortly to be looked for at St. Denis, we rode thither early next morning, with what speed we might. On our left, like a cloud, was the smoke of Paris, making me understand what a great city it was, much greater than Orleans. Before us, far away, were the tall towers of the chapel of St. Denis, to be our guide! We heard, also, the noise of ordnance being fired, and therefore made the greater haste, and we so rode that, about six hours after noon, on the Eve of the Nativity of our Blessed Lady, we reached the gates of the town. Here we found great press of folk, men coming and going, some carrying the wounded, for there had been a skirmish that day, at one of the Paris gates, whence came the sound of cannon and culverins, and we had won little advantage.

At the gates of St. Denis we asked where the quarters of the Scots men-at-arms might be, and were told in the chapel, whither we needed no guide. But, as we went up the street, we saw women leaning forth from the windows, laughing with the men-at-arms, and beckoning to them, and by the tavern doors many were sitting drinking, with girls beside them, and others were playing dice, and many an oath we heard, and foul words, as is customary in a camp. Verily I saw well that this was not the army of men clean confessed and of holy life who had followed the Maid from Blois to Orleans. In place of priests, here were harlots, and, for hymns, ribald songs, for men had flocked in from every quarter; soldiers of the robber companies, Bretons, Germans,

Italians, Spaniards, all talking in their own speech, rude, foul, and disorderly. So we took our way, as best we knight, through the press, hearing oaths enough if our horses trod over near any man, and seeing daggers drawn.

It was a pleasure to come out on the great parvise, where the red, white, and green of our Scots were the commonest colours, and where the air was less foul and noisome than in the narrow wynds. High above us the great towers of the abbey shone red and golden in the light of the sinking sun, while beneath all was brown, dusk, and dim with smoke. On these towers I could gladly have looked long, and not wearied. For they are all carven with the holy company of the martyrs and saints, like the Angels whom Jacob saw ascending by the ladder into heaven; even so that blessed company seemed to scale upwards from the filth of the street, and the darkness, and the din, right on towards the golden heights of the City of God. And beneath them lie the sacred bones of all the kings of France, from the days of St. Dagobert even to our own time, all laid there to rest where no man shall disturb them, till the Angels' Trumpet calls, and the Day of Judgment is at hand. Verily it is a solemn place for a Christian man to think on, and I was gazing thereupon, as in a dream, when one plucked my sleeve, and turning, I saw Randal Rutherford, all his teeth showing in a grin.

"Welcome," he cried. "You have made good speed, and the beginning of a fray is better than the end of a feast. And, by St. Boswell, to-morrow we shall have it, lad! The King came in to-day—late is better than never—and to-morrow we go with the Maid, to give these pock-puddings a taste of Scottish steel."

"And the Maid, where is she, Randal?"

"She lodges beyond the Paris gate, at the windmill,

wherefrom she drove the English some days agone."

"Wherefore not in the town?" I asked.

"Mayhap because she likes to be near her work, and would that all were of her mind. And mayhap she loves not the sight of the wenches whom she was wont to drive from the camp, above all now that she has broken the Holy Sword of Fierbois, smiting a lass with the flat of the blade."

"I like not the omen," said I.

"Freits follow them that freits fear," said Randal, in our country speech. "And the Maid is none of these. 'Well it was,' said she, 'that I trusted not my life to a blade that breaks so easily,' and, in the next skirmish, she took a Burgundian with her own hands, and now wears his sword, which is a good cut and thrust piece. But come," he cried, "if needs you must see the Maid, you have but to walk to the Paris gate, and so to the windmill hard by. And your horse I will stable with our own, and for quarters, we living Scots men-at-arms fare as well as the dead kings of France, for to-night we lie in the chapel."

I dismounted, and he gave me an embrace, and, holding me at arms'-length, laughed—

"You never were a tall man, Norman, but you look sound, and whole, and tough for your inches, like a Highlandman's dirk. Now be off on your errand, and when it is done, look for me yonder at the sign of 'The Crane,'" pointing across the parvise to a tavern, "for I keep a word to tell in your lug that few wot of, and that it will joy you to hear. To-morrow, lad, we go in foremost."

And so, smiling, he took my horse and went his way,

whistling, "Hey, tuttie, tattie!"

Verily his was the gladdest face I had seen, and his words put some heart into me, whereas, of the rest save our own Scots, I liked neither what I saw, nor what I heard.

I had but to walk down the street, through elbowing throngs of grooms, pages, men-at-arms, and archers, till I found the Paris Gate, whence the windmill was plain to behold. It was such an old place as we see in Northern France, plain, strong, with red walls which the yellow mosses stain, and with high grey roofs. The Maid's banner, with the Holy Dove, and the Sacred Name, drooped above the gateway, and beside the door, on the mounting-stone, sat the boy, Louis des Coutes, her page. He was a lad of fifteen years, merry enough of his nature, and always went gaily clad, and wearing his yellow hair long. But now he sat thoughtful on the mounting-stone, cutting at a bit of wood with his dagger.

"So you have come to take your part," he said, when we had saluted each the other. "Faith, I hope you bring good luck with you, and more joy to my mistress, for we need all that you can bring."

"Why, what ails all of you?" I asked. "I have seen never a hopeful face, save that of one of my own countrymen. You are not afraid of a crack on your curly pate, are you?"

"Curly or not, my head knows better than to knock itself against Paris walls. They are thick, and high, and the windows of every house on the wall are piled with stones, to drop upon us. And I know not well why, but things go ill with us. I never saw Her," and he nodded towards the open gateway, "so out of comfort. When there is fighting toward, she is like herself, and she is the first to rise and the last to lie down. But, in all our waiting here, she has passed many an hour praying in the chapel, where the dead kings lie, yet her face is not glad when she comes forth. It was wont to shine strangely, when she had been praying, at the chapel in Couldray, while we were at Chinon. But now it is otherwise. Moreover, we saw Paris very close to-day, and there were over many red crosses of St. George upon the walls. And to-morrow is the Feast of the Blessed Virgin, no day for bloodshed."

"Faint heart!" said I (and, indeed, after the assault on Paris, Louis des Coutes went back, and rode no more with the maid). "The better the day, the better the deed! May I go within?"

"I will go with you," he said, "for she said that you would come, and bade me bring you to her."

We entered the gateway together, and before us lay the square of the farm, strewn with litter, and from within the byre we heard the milk ring in the pails, for the women were milking the cows. And there we both stood astonished, for we saw the Maid as never yet I had seen her. She was bareheaded, but wore the rest of her harness, holding in her hand a measure of corn. All the fowls of the air seemed to be about her, expecting their meat. But she was not throwing the grain among them, for she stood as still as a graven image, and, wonderful to tell, a dove was perched on her shoulder, and a mavis was nestling in her breast, while many birds flew round her, chiefly doves with burnished plumage, flitting as it were lovingly, and softly brushing her now and again with their wings. Many a time had I heard it said that, while she was yet a child, the wild birds would come and nestle in the bosom of the Maid, but I had never believed the tale. Yet now I saw this thing with mine own eyes, a fair sight and a marvellous, so beautiful she looked, with head unhelmeted, and the wild fowl and tame flitting about her and above her, the doves crooning sweetly in their soft voices. Then her lips moved, and she spoke—

"Tres doulx Dieu, en l'onneur de vostre saincte passion, je vous requier, se vous me aimes, que vous me revelez ce que je doy faire demain pour vostre gloire!"

So she fell silent again, and to me it seemed that I must not any longer look upon that holy mystery, so, crossing myself, I laid my hand on the shoulder of the page, and we went silently from the place.

"Have you ever seen it in this manner?" I whispered, when we were again without the farmyard.

"Never," said he, trembling, "though once I saw a stranger thing."

"And what may that have been?"

"Nay, I spoke of it to her, and she made me swear that I never would reveal it to living soul, save in confession. But she is not as other women."

What he had in his mind I know not, but I bade him good even, and went back into the town, where lights were beginning to show in the casements. In the space within the gates were many carts gathered, full of faggots wherewith to choke up the fosse under Paris, and tables to throw above the faggots, and so cross over to the assault.

CHAPTER XXI

HOW A HUNDRED SCOTS SET FORTH
TO TAKE PARIS TOWN

Entering the tavern of "The Crane," I found the doorways crowded with archers of our Guard, among whom was Randal Rutherford.

When I had come, they walked into a chamber on the ground floor, calling for wine, and bidding certain French burgesses go forth, who needed no second telling. The door was shut, two sentinels of ours were posted outside, and then Randal very carefully sounded all the panels of the room, looking heedfully lest there should be any hole whereby what passed among us might be heard in another part of the house, but he found nothing of the kind.

The room being full, some sitting and some standing, as we could, Randal bade Father Urquhart, our chaplain, tell us to what end we had been called together.

The good father thereupon stood up, and spoke in a low voice, but so that all could hear, for we were all hushed to listen.

"There is," he said, "within Paris, a certain Carmelite, a

Frenchman, and a friend of Brother Richard, the Preacher, whom, as you know, the English drove from the town."

"I saw him at Troyes," said one, "where he kneeled before the Maid, and they seemed very loving."

"That is the man, that is Brother Richard. Now, as I was busy tending the wounded, in the skirmish three days agone, this Carmelite was about the same duty for those of his party. He put into my hand a slip of paper, wherein Brother Richard commended him to any Scot or Frenchman of the King's party, as an honest man, and a friend of the King's. When I had read this, the Carmelite spoke with me in Latin, and in a low voice. His matter was this: In Paris, he said, there is a strong party of Armagnacs, who have, as we all know, a long score to settle with them of Burgundy. They are of the common folk and labourers, but among them are many rich burgesses. They have banded themselves together by an oath to take our part, within the town, if once we win a gate. Here is a cedule signed by them with their names or marks, and this he gave me as a proof of good faith."

Here he handed a long slip of parchment, all covered with writing, to Randal, and it went round among us, but few there were clerks, save myself. I looked on it, and the names, many of them attested by seals with coat armour, were plain to be read.

"Their counsel is to muster in arms secretly, and to convey themselves, one by one, into certain houses hard by the Port St. Denis, where certain of their party dwell. Now, very early to-morrow morning, before dawn, the purpose of the English is to send forth a company of a hundred men-at-arms, who will make a sudden onset on the windmill, where the Maid lies to-night, and so will take her, if they may."

"By St. Bride of Douglas," said one of us, "they will get their kail through the reek, for our guard is to lie in arms about the windmill, and be first in the field to-morrow."

"The craft is, then," Father Urquhart went on, "that we shall destroy this English company with sword or arrow, but with no alarm of culverins or cannon. Meanwhile, some five score of you will put on to-night the red cross of St. George, with plain armour, so that the English shall mistake you for their own men returning from the sally, and some few men in our own colours and coats you will hale with you as prisoners. And, if one of you can but attire himself in some gear of the Maid's, with a hucque of hers, scarlet, and dight with the Lilies of France, the English gate-wards will open to you all the more eagerly."

"By the bones of St. Boswell!" cried Randal in his loud voice, but the good Father put a hand on his mouth.

"Quiet, man!" he said.

"By the blessed bones of St. Boswell," Randal said again, as near a whisper as he could attain to, "the lady of the linen-basket shall come as the Maid. We have no man so maidenly."

They all shouted, laughing, and beating the tables with hands and tankards.

"Silence!" cried Robin Lindsay.

"Nay, the louder we laugh, the less will any suspect what is forward," said Randal Rutherford.

"Norman, will you play this part in the mumming?"

I was ashamed to say no, though I liked it not over well, and I nodded with my head.

"How maidenly he blushes!" cried one, and there was another clamour, till the walls rang.

"So be it then," says Father Urquhart, "and now you know all. The honest Armagnacs will rise so soon as you are well within the gate. They command both sides of the street that leads to the Port St. Denis, and faith, if the English want to take it, when a hundred Scots are within, they will have to sally forth by another gate, and come from the outside. And you are to run up the banner of Scotland over the Port, when once you hold it, so the French attack will be thereby."

"We played the same game before Verneuil fight, and won it," said one; "will the English have forgotten the trick?"

"By St. Bride, when once they see us haling the Maid along, they will forget old stratagems of war. This is a new device! Oh to see their faces when we cry 'St. Andrew,' and set on!"

"I am not so old as you all in the wars," I began.

"No, Mademoiselle la Lavandiere, but you are of the right spirit, with your wench's face."

"But," I said, "how if the English that are to attack the windmill in the first grey of the morning come not to hand-strokes, or take to their heels when they find us awake, and win back to Paris before us? Our craft, methinks, is to hold them in an ambush, but what if we catch them not? Let but one runaway be swift of foot, and we are undone."

"There is this to be said," quoth Father Urquhart, "that the English company is to sally forth by the Port St. Denis, and it is the Port St. Denis that our Armagnacs will be guarding. Now I speak as a man of peace, for that is my calling. But how would it be if your hundred men and Norman set forth in the dark, and lay hid not very far from the St. Denis Gate? Then some while after the lighting of the bale-fires from the windmill, to be lit when the English set on, make straight for the gate, and cry, 'St. George for England!' If you see not the bale-fires ere daylight, you will come back with what speed you may; but if you do see them, then—"

"Father, you have not lived long on the Highland line for nothing," quoth Robin Lindsay.

"A very proper stratagem indeed," I said, "but now, gentlemen, there is one little matter; how will Sir Hugh Kennedy take this device of ours? If we try it and fail, without his privity, we had better never return, but die under Paris wall. And, even if we hold the gate, and Paris town is taken, faith I would rather affront the fire of John the Lorrainer than the face of Sir Hugh."

No man spoke, there were not two minds on this matter, so, after some chaffer of words, it was agreed to send Father Urquhart with Randal to show the whole scheme to Sir Hugh, while the rest of us should await their coming back with an answer. In no long time they were with us, the father very red and shamefaced.

"He gave the good father the rough side of his tongue," quoth Randal, "for speaking first to me, and not to him. Happily we were over cunning to say aught of our gathering here. But when he had let his bile flow, he swore, and said that he could spare a hundred dyvour loons of his command, on the cast of the dice, and, now silence all! not a word or a cry," here he held up his hand, "we are to take 'fortune of war'!"

Every man grinned gladly on his neighbour, in dead stillness.

"Now," said Randal, "slip out by threes and fours, quietly, and to quarters; but you, Norman, wait with me."

CHAPTER XXII

HOW NORMAN LESLIE FARED IN PARIS TOWN

"Norman, my lad, all our fortunes are made," said Randal to me when we were left alone. "There will be gilt spurs and gold for every one of us, and the pick of the plunder."

"I like it not," I answered; whereon he caught me rudely by both shoulders, looking close into my face, so that the fume of the wine he had been drinking reached my nostrils.

"Is a Leslie turning recreant?" he asked in a low voice. "A pretty tale to tell in the kingdom of Fife!"

I stood still, my heart very hot with anger, and said no word, while his grip closed on me.

"Leave hold," I cried at last, and I swore an oath, may the Saints forgive me,—"I will not go!"

He loosed his grasp on me, and struck one hand hard into the other.

"That I should see this, and have to tell it!" he said, and stepping to the table, he drank like one thirsty, and then fell to pacing the chamber. He seemed to be thinking slowly, as he wiped and plucked at his beard.

"What is it that ails you?" he asked. "Look you, this onfall and stratagem of war may not miscarry. Perdition take the fool, it is safe!"

"Have I been seeking safety since you knew me?" I asked.

"Verily no, and therefore I wonder at you the more; but you have been long sick, and men's minds are changeful. Consider the thing, nom Dieu! If there be no two lights shown from the mill, we step back silently, and all is as it was; the English have thought worse of their night onfall, or the Carmelite's message was ruse de guerre. But if we see the two lights, then the hundred English are attempting the taking of the mill; the St. Denis Gate is open for their return, and we are looked for by our Armagnacs within Paris. We risk but a short tussle with some drowsy pock-puddings, and then the town is ours. The Gate is as strong to hold against an enemy from within as from without. Why, man, run to Louis de Coutes, and beg a cast suit of the Maid's; she has plenty, for she is a woman in this, that dearly she loves rich attire."

"Randal," I said, "I will go with you, and the gladdest lad in France to be going, but I will go in my own proper guise as a man-at-arms. To wear the raiment of the Blessed Maid, a man and a sinner like me, I will in nowise consent; it is neither seemly nor honourable. Take your own way, put me under arrest if you will, and spoil my fortunes, and make me a man disgraced, but I will not wear her holy raiment. It is not the deed of a gentleman, or of a Christian."

He plucked at his beard. "I am partly with you," he said. "And yet it were a great bourde to play off on the English, and most like to take them and to be told of in ballad and chronicle, like one of Wallace's onfalls. For, seeing the

Pucelle, as they will deem, in our hands, they will think all safe, and welcome us open armed. O Norman, can we do nothing? Stop, will you wear another woman's short kirtle over your cuisses and taslet? She shall be no saint, I warrant you, but, for a sinner, a bonny lass and a merry. As a gentleman I deem this fair stratagem of war. If I were your own brother,—the Saints have his soul in their keeping,—I would still be of this counsel. Will you, my lad?"

He looked so sad, and yet withal so comical, that I held out my hand to him, laughing.

"Disguise me as you will," I said, "I have gone mumming as Maid Marion before now, in the Robin Hood play, at St. Andrews"; and as I spoke, I saw the tall thatched roofs of South Street, and the Priory Gates open, the budding elms above the garden wall of St. Leonard's, and all the May-day revel of a year agone pouring out into the good town.

"You speak like yourself now, bless your beardless face! Come forth," he said, taking a long pull at a tankard,—"that nothing might be wasted,"—and so we went to quarters, and Randal trudged off, soon coming back, laughing, with the red kirtle. Our men had been very busy furbishing up the red cross of St. George on their breasts, and stripping themselves of any sign of our own colours. As for my busking, never had maid such rough tire-women; but by one way or another, the apparel was accommodated, and they all said that, at a little distance of ground, the English would be finely fooled, and must deem that the Maid herself was being led to them captive.

It was now in the small hours of morning, dark, save for the glimmer of stars, here and there in a cloudy sky. Father Urquhart himself went up to the roof of the mill, to say his orisons, having with him certain faggots of pitch-wood, for lighting the beacon-fires if need were; and, as it chanced, braziers to this end stood ready on the roof, as is custom on our own Border keeps.

We Scots, a hundred in all, in English colours, with three or four as prisoners, in our own badges, fared cautiously, and with no word spoken, through dewy woods, or lurking along in dry ditches where best we might, towards the St. Denis Gate of Paris. I had never been on a night surprise or bushment before, and I marvelled how orderly the others kept, as men used to such work, whereas I went stumbling and blindlings. At length, within sight of the twinkling lights of Paris, and a hundred yards or thereby off the common way, we were halted in a little wood, and bidden to lie down; no man was so much as to whisper. Some slept, I know, for I heard their snoring, but for my part, I never was less in love with sleep. When the sky first grew grey, so that we could dimly see shapes of things, we heard a light noise of marching men on the road.

"The English!" whispered he that lay next me. "Hush!" breathed Randal, and so the footsteps went by, none of us daring to stir, for fear of the rustle in the leaves.

The sound soon ceased; belike they had struck off into these very fields wherethrough we had just marched.

"Now, Robin Lindsay, climb into yonder ash-tree, and keep your eyes on the mill and the beacon-fires," said Randal.

Robin scrambled up, not easily, because of his armour, and we waited, as it seemed, for an endless time.

"What is that sound," whispered one, "so heavy and so hoarse?"

It was my own heart beating, as if it would burst my side, but I said nought, and even then Robin slid from the tree, as lightly as he might. He held up two fingers, without a word, for a sign that the beacons were lighted, and nodded.

"Down all," whispered Randal.

"Give them time, give them time."

So there we lay, as we must, but that was the hardest part of the waiting, and no sound but of the fowls and wild things arousing, and the cry of sentinels from Paris walls, came to our ears.

At length Randal said, "Up all, and onwards!"

We arose, loosened our swords in their sheaths, and so crossed to the road. We could now see Paris plainly, and were close by the farm of the Mathurins, while beyond was the level land they call "Les Porcherons," with slopes above it, and many trees.

"Now, Norman," said Randal, "when we come within clear sight of the gate, two of us shall seize you by the arms as prisoner; then we all cry 'St. George!' and set off running towards Paris. The quicker, the less time for discovery."

So, having marched orderly and speedily, while the banks of the roadway hid us, we set off to run, Randal and Robin gripping me when we were full in sight of the moat, of the drawbridge (which was down), and the gate.

Then our men all cried, "St. George for England! The witch is taken!" And so running disorderly and fast we made for the Port, while English men-at-arms might be plainly seen and heard, gazing, waving their hands, and shouting from the battlements of the two gate-towers. Down the road we ran, past certain small houses of peasants, and past a gibbet with a marauder hanging from it, just over the dry ditch.

Our feet, we three leading, with some twenty in a clump hard behind us, rang loud on the drawbridge over the dry fosse. The bridge planks quivered strangely; we were now within the gateway, when down fell the portcullis behind us, the drawbridge, creaking, flew up, a crowd of angry faces and red crosses were pressing on us, and a blow fell on my salade, making me reel. I was held in strong arms, swords shone out above me, I stumbled on a body—it was Robin Lindsay's—I heard Randal give a curse as his blade broke on a helmet, and cry, "I yield me, rescue or no rescue." Then burst forth a blast of shouts, and words of command and yells, and English curses. Cannon-shot roared overhead, and my mouth was full of sulphur smoke and dust. They were firing on those of our men who had not set foot on the drawbridge when it flew up. Soon the portcullis rose again, and the bridge fell, to let in a band of English archers, through whom our Scots were cutting their way back towards St. Denis.

Of all this I got glimpses, rather than clear sight, as the throng within the gateway reeled and shifted, crushing me sorely. Presently the English from without trooped in, laughing and cursing, welcomed by their fellows, and every man of them prying into my face, and gibing. It had been a settled plan: we were betrayed, it was over clear, and now a harsh voice behind making me turn, I saw the wolf's face of Father Thomas under his hood, and his yellow fangs.

"Ha! fair clerk, they that be no clerks themselves may yet hire clerks to work for them. How like you my brother, the Carmelite?"

Then I knew too well how this stratagem had all been laid by that devil, and my heart turned to water within me.

Randal was led away, but round me the crowd gathered in the open space, for I was haled into the greater gate tower beyond the wet fosse, and from all quarters ran soldiers, and men, women, and children of the town to mock me.

"Behold her," cried Father Thomas, climbing on a mounting-stone, as one who would preach to the people, while the soldiers that held me laughed.

"Behold this wonderful wonder of all wonders, the miraculous Maid of the Armagnacs! She boasted that, by help of the Saints, she would be the first within the city, and lo! she is the first, but she has come without her army. She is every way a miracle, mark you, for she hath a down on her chin, such as no common maidens wear; and if she would but speak a few words of counsel, methinks her tongue would sound strangely Scottish for a Lorrainer."

"Speak, speak!" shouted the throng.

"Dogs," I cried, in French, "dogs and cowards! You shall see the Maid closer before nightfall, and fly from her as you have fled before."

"Said I not so?" asked Brother Thomas.

"A miracle, a miracle, the Maid hath a Scots tongue in her head."

Therewith stones began to fall, but the father, holding up his hand, bade the multitude refrain.

"Harm her not, good brethren, for to-morrow this Maid shall

be tried by the ordeal of fire if that be the will of our governors. Then shall we see if she can work miracles or not," and so he went on gibing, while they grinned horribly upon me. Never saw I so many vile faces of the basest people come together, from their filthy dens in Paris. But as my eyes ran over them with loathing, I beheld a face I knew; the face of that violer woman who had been in our company before we came to Chinon, and lo! perched on her shoulder, chained with a chain fastened round her wrist, was Elliot's jackanapes! To see the poor beast that my lady loved in such ill company, seemed as if it would break my heart, and my head fell on my breast.

"Ye mark, brethren and sisters, she likes not the name of the ordeal by fire," cried Brother Thomas, whereon I lifted my face again to defy him, and I saw the violer woman bend her brows, and place her finger, as it were by peradventure, on her lips; wherefore I was silent, only gazing on that devil, but then rang out a trumpet-note, blowing the call to arms, and from afar came an answering call, from the quarter of St. Denis.

"Carry him, or her, or whatever the spy is, into the outer gate tower," said a Captain; "put him in fetters and manacles; lock the door and leave him; and then to quarters. And you, friar, hold your gibing tongue; lad or lass, he has borne him bravely."

Six men-at-arms he chose out to do his bidding; and while the gates were cleared of the throng, and trumpets were sounding, and church bells were rung backwards, for an alarm, I was dragged, with many a kick and blow, over the drawbridge, up the stairs of the tower, and so was thrown into a strong room beneath the battlements. There they put me in bonds, gave me of their courtesy a jug of water and a loaf of black bread by me, and then, taking my dagger, my sword, and all that was in my pouch, they left me with curses.

"You shall hear how the onfall goes, belike," they said, "and to-morrow shall be your judgment."

With that the door grated and rang, the key was turned in the lock, and their iron tread sounded on the stone stairs, going upwards. The room was high, narrow, and lit by a barred and stanchioned window, far above my reach, even if I had been unbound. I shame to say it, but I rolled over on my face and wept. This was the end of my hopes and proud heart. That they would burn me, despite their threats I scarce believed, for I had in nowise offended Holy Church, or in matters of the Faith, and only for such heretics, or wicked dealers in art-magic, is lawfully ordained the death by fire. But here was I prisoner, all that I had won at Orleans would do little more than pay my own ransom; from the end of my risk and travail I was now further away than ever.

So I mused, weeping for very rage, but then came a heavy rolling sound overhead, as of moving wheeled pieces of ordnance. Thereon (so near is Hope to us in our despair) I plucked up some heart. Ere nightfall, Paris might be in the hands of the King, and all might be well. The roar and rebound of cannon overhead told me that the fighting had begun, and now I prayed with all my heart, that the Maid, as ever, might again be victorious. So I lay there, listening, and heard the great artillery bellow, and the roar of guns in answer, the shouting of men, and clang of church bells. Now and again the walls of the tower rang with the shock of a cannon-ball, once an arrow flew through the casement and shattered itself on the wall above my head. I scarce know why, but I dragged me to the place where it fell, and, put the arrow-point in my bosom. Smoke of wood and pitch darkened the light; they had come, then, to close quarters.

But once more rang the rattle of guns; the whizzing rush of stones, the smiting with axe or sword on wooden barrier and steel harness, the cries of war, "Mont joye St. Denis!" "St. George for England!" and slogans too, I heard, as "Bellenden," "A Home! a Home!" and then I knew the Scots were there, fighting in the front. But alas, how different was the day when first I heard our own battle-cries under Orleans walls! Then I had my life and my sword in my hands, to spend and to strike; but now I lay a lonely prisoner, helpless and all but hopeless; yet even so I clashed my chains and shouted, when I heard the slogan.

Thus with noise and smoke, and trumpets blowing the charge or the recall, and our pipes shrieking the pibroch high above the din, with dust floating and plaster dropping from the walls of my cell till I was wellnigh stifled, the day wore on, nor could I tell, in anywise, how the battle went. The main onslaught, I knew, was not on the gate behind the tower in which I lay, though that tower also was smitten of cannon-balls.

At length, well past mid-day, as I deemed by the light, came a hush, and then a thicker smoke, and taste of burning pitch-wood, and a roar as if all Paris had been blown into mid-air, so that my tower shook, while heavy beams fell crashing to earth.

Again came a hush, and then one voice, clear as a clarion call, even the voice of the Maid, "Tirez en avant, en avant!" How my blood thrilled at the sound of it!

It must be now, I thought, or never, but the guns only roared the louder, the din grew fierce and fiercer, till I heard a mighty roar, the English shouting aloud as one man for joy, for so their manner is. Thrice they shouted, and my heart sank within me. Had they slain the Maid? I knew not, but for torment of soul there is scarce any greater than so to lie, bound and alone, seeing nought, but guessing at what is befalling.

After these shouts it was easy to know that the fighting waned, and was less fierce. The day, moreover, turned to thunder, and waxed lowering and of a stifling heat. Yet my worst fears were ended, for I heard, now and again, the clear voice of the Maid, bidding her men "fight on, for all was theirs." But the voice was weaker now, and other than it had been. So the day darkened, only once and again a shot was fired, and in the dusk the shouts of the English told me over clearly that for to-day our chance and hope were lost. Then the darkness grew deeper, and a star shone through my casement, and feet went up and down upon the stairs, but no man came near me. Below there was some faint cackle of mirth and laughter, and at last the silence fell.

Once more came a swift step on the stairs, as of one stumbling up in haste. The key rattled in the wards, a yellow light shone in, a man-at-arms entered; he held a torch to my face, looked to my bonds, and then gave me a kick, while one cried from below, "Come on, Dickon, your meat is cooling!" So he turned and went out, the door clanging behind him, and the key rattling in the wards.

In pain and fierce wrath I gnawed my black bread, drank some of the water, and at last I bethought me of that which should have been first in the thoughts of a Christian man, and I prayed.

Remembering the story of Michael Hamilton, which I have already told, and other noble and virtuous miracles of Madame St. Catherine of Fierbois, I commanded me to her, that, by God's grace, she would be pleased to release me from bonds and prison. And I promised that, if she would so favour me, I would go on pilgrimage to her chapel of Fierbois. I looked that my chains should now fall from my limbs, but, finding no such matter, and being very weary (for all the last night I had slept none), I fell on slumber and forgot my sorrow.

Belike I had not lain long in that blessed land where trouble seldom comes when I was wakened, as it were, by a tugging at my clothes. I sat up, but the room was dark, save for a faint light in the casement, high overhead, and I thought I had dreamed. Howbeit, as I lay down again, heavy at heart, my clothes were again twitched, and now I remembered what I had heard, but never believed, concerning "lutins" or "brownies," as we call them, which, being spirits invisible, and reckoned to have no part in our salvation, are wont in certain houses to sport with men. Curious rather than affrighted, I sat up once more, and looked around, when I saw two bright spots of light in the dark. Then deeming that, for some reason unknown to me, the prison door had been opened while I slept, and a cat let in, I stretched out my hands towards the lights, thence came a sharp, faint cry, and something soft and furry leaped on to my breast, stroking me with little hands.

It was Elliot's jackanapes, very meagre, as I could feel, and all his ribs standing out, but he made much of me, fondling me after his manner; and indeed, for my lady's sake, I kissed him, wondering much how he came there. Then he put something into my hands, almost as if he had been a Christian, for it was a wise beast and a kind. Even then there shone into my memory the thought of how my lady had prayed for her little friend when he was stolen (which I had thought strange, and scarcely warranted by our Faith), and with that, hope wakened within me. My eyes being now more accustomed to the darkness, I saw that the thing which the jackanapes gave me was a little wallet, for he had been taught to fetch and carry, and never was such a marvel at climbing. But as I was caressing him, I found a string about his neck, to which there seemed to be no end. Now, at length, I comprehended what was toward, and pulling gently at the string, I found, after some time, that it was attached to something heavy, on the outside of the casement. Therefore I set about drawing in string from above, and more string, and more, and then appeared a knot and a splice, and the end of a thick rope. So I drew and drew, till it stopped, and I could see a stout bar across the stanchions of the casement. Thereon I ceased drawing, and opening the little wallet, I found two files, one very fine, the other of sturdier fashion.

Verily then I blessed the violer woman, who at great peril of her own life, and by such witty device as doubtless Madame St. Catherine put into her heart, had sent the jackanapes up from below, and put me in the way of safety. I wasted no time, but began filing, not at the thick circlet on my wrist, but at a link of the chain whereto it was made fast. And such was the temper of the file, that soon I got the stouter weapon into the cut, and snapped the link; and so with the others, working long hours, and often looking fearfully for the first glimmer of dawn. This had not come in, when I was now free of bonds, but there was yet the casement to be scaled. With all my strength I dragged and jerked at the rope, whereby I meant to climb, lest the stanchions should be rusted through, and unable to bear my weight, but they stood the strain bravely. Then I cast off my woman's kirtle, and took from my pouch the arrow-point, and therewith scratched hastily on the plastered wall, in great letters: "Norman Leslie of Pitcullo leaves his malison on the English."

Next I bound the jackanapes within the bosom of my doublet, with a piece of the cord whereto the rope had been knotted, for I could not leave the little beast to die the death of a traitor, and bring suspicion, moreover, on the poor violer woman. Then, commanding myself to the Saints, and especially thanking Madame St. Catherine, I began to climb, hauling myself up by the rope, whereon I had made knots to this end; nor was the climbing more difficult than to scale a branchless beech trunk for a bird's nest, which, like other boys, I had often done. So behold me, at last, with my legs hanging in free air, seated on the sill of the casement. Happily, of the three iron stanchions, though together they bore my weight, one was loose in the lower socket, for lack of lead, and this one I displaced easily enough, and so passed through. Then I put the wooden bar at the rope's end, within the room, behind the two other stanchions, considering that they, by themselves, would bear my weight, but if not, rather choosing to trust my soul to the Saints than my body to the English.

The deep below me was very terrible to look upon, and the casement being above the dry ditch, I had no water to break my fall, if fall I must. Howbeit, I hardened my heart, and turning my face to the wall, holding first the wooden bar, and then shifting my grasp to the rope, I let myself down, clinging to the rope with my legs, and at first not a little helped by the knots I had made to climb to the casement. When I had passed these, methought my hands were on fire; nevertheless, I slid down slowly and with caution, till my feet touched ground.

I was now in the dry ditch, above my head creaked and swung the dead body of the hanged marauder, but he did no whit affray me. I ran, stooping, along the bed of the dry ditch, for many yards, stumbling over the bodies of men slain in yesterday's fight, and then, creeping out, I found a hollow way between two slopes, and thence crawled into a wood, where I lay some little space hidden by the boughs. The smell of trees and grass and the keen air were like wine to me; I cooled my bleeding hands in the deep dew; and

Andrew Lang

presently, in the dawn, I was stealing towards St. Denis, taking such cover of ditches and hedges as we had sought in our unhappy march of yesterday. And I so sped, by favour of the Saints, that I fell in with no marauders; but reaching the windmill right early, at first trumpet-call, I was hailed by our sentinels for the only man that had won in and out of Paris, and had carried off, moreover, a prisoner, the jackanapes. To see me, scarred, with manacles on my wrists and gyves on my ankles, weaponless, with an ape on my shoulder, was such a sight as the Scots Guard had never beheld before, and carrying me to the smith's, they first knocked off my irons, and gave me wine, ere they either asked me for my tale, or told me their own, which was a heartbreak to bear.

For no man could unfold the manner of that which had come to pass, if, at least, there were not strong treason at the root of all. For our part of the onfall, the English had made but a feigned attack on the mill, wherefore the bale-fires were lit, to our undoing. This was the ruse de guerre of the accursed cordelier, Brother Thomas. For the rest, the Maid had led on a band to attack the gate St. Honore, with Gaucourt in her company, a knight that had no great love either of her or of a desperate onslaught. But D'Alencon, whom she loved as a brother, was commanded to take another band, and wait behind a butte or knowe, out of danger of arrow-shot. The Maid had stormed all day at her gate, had taken the boulevard without, and burst open and burned the outer port, and crossed the dry ditch. But when she had led up her men, now few, over the slope and to the edge of the wet fosse, behold no faggots and bundles of wood were brought up, whereby, as is manner of war, to fill up the fosse, and so cross over. As she then stood under the wall, shouting for faggots and scaling-ladders, her standard-bearer was shot to death, and she was sorely wounded by an arbalest bolt. Natheless she lay by the wall, still crying on her men, but nought was ready that should have been, many were slain by shafts and cannon-shot, and in the dusk, she weeping and crying still that the place was theirs to take, D'Alencon carried her off by main force, set her on her horse, and so brought her back to St. Denis.

Now, my mind was, and is to this day, that there was treason here, and a black stain on the chivalry of France, to let a girl go so far, and not to follow her. But of us Scots many were slain, and more wounded, while Robin Lindsay died in Paris gate, and Randal Rutherford lay a prisoner in English hands.

Andrew Lang

CHAPTER XXIII

HOW ELLIOT'S JACKANAPES CAME HOME

Of our Blessed Lord Himself it is said in the Gospel of St. Matthew, "et non fecit ibi virtutes multas propter incredulitatem illorum." These words I willingly leave in the Roman tongue; for by the wisdom of Holy Church it is deemed that many mysteries should not be published abroad in the vulgar speech, lest the unlearned hear to their own confusion. But if even He, doubtless by the wisdom of His own will, did not many great works "propter incredulitatem," it is the less to be marvelled at that His Saints, through the person of the Blessed Maid, were of no avail where men utterly disbelieved. And that, where infidelity was, even she must labour in vain was shown anon, even on this very day of my escape out of Paris town. For I had scarce taken some food, and washed and armed myself, when the Maid's trumpets sounded, and she herself, armed and on horseback, despite her wound, rode into St. Denis, to devise with the gentle Duc d'Alencon. Together they came forth from the gate, and I, being in their company, heard her cry—

"By my baton, I will never go back till I take that city." {31}

These words Percival de Cagny also heard, a good knight, and maitre d'hotel of the house of Alencon. Thereon arose some dispute, D'Alencon being eager, as indeed he always was, to follow where the Maiden led, and some others holding back.

Now, as they were devising together, some for, some against, for men-at-arms not a few had fallen in the onfall, there came the sound of horses' hoofs, and lo! Messire de Montmorency, who had been of the party of the English, and with them in Paris, rode up, leading a company of fifty or sixty gentlemen of his house, to join the Maid. Thereat was great joy and new courage in all men of goodwill, seeing that, within Paris itself, so many gentlemen deemed ours the better cause and the more hopeful.

Thus there was an end of all dispute, our companies were fairly arrayed, and we were marching to revenge ourselves for the losses of yesterday, when two knights came spurring after us from St. Denis. They were the Duc de Bar, and that unhappy Charles de Bourbon, Comte de Clermont, by whose folly, or ill-will, or cowardice, the Scots were betrayed and deserted at the Battle of the Herrings, where my own brother fell, as I have already told. This second time Charles de Bourbon brought evil fortune, for he came on the King's part, straitly forbidding D'Alencon and the Maid to march forward another lance's length. Whereat D'Alencon swore profane, and the Maiden, weeping, rebuked him. So, with heavy hearts, we turned, all the host of us, and went back to quarters, the Maid to pray in the chapel, and the men-at-arms to drink and speak ill of the King.

All this was on the ninth of September, a weary day to all of us, though in the evening word came that we were to march early next morning and attack Paris in another quarter, crossing the river by a bridge of boats which the Duc d'Alencon had let build to that end. After two wakeful nights I was well weary, and early laid me down to sleep, rising at dawn with high hopes. And so through the grey light we marched silently to the place appointed, but bridge there was none; for the King, having heard of the Maid's intent, had caused men to work all night long, destroying that which the gentle Duke had builded. Had the King but heard the shouts and curses of our company when they found nought but the bare piles standing, the grey water flowing, and the boats and planks vanished, he might have taken shame to himself of his lack of faith. Therefore I say it boldly, it was because of men's unbelief that the Maid at Paris wrought no great works, save that she put her body in such hazard of war as never did woman, nay, nor man, since the making of the world.

I have no heart to speak more of this shameful matter, nor of these days of anger and blasphemy. It was said and believed that her voices bade the Maid abide at St. Denis till she should take Paris town, but the King, and Charles de Bourbon, and the Archbishop of Reims refused to hearken to her. On the thirteenth day of September, after dinner, the King, with all his counsellors, rode away from St. Denis, towards Gien on the Loire. The Maiden, for her part, hung up all her harness that she had worn, save the sword of St. Catherine of Fierbois, in front of the altar of Our Lady, and the blessed relics of St. Denis in the chapel. Thereafter she rode, as needs she must, and we of her company with her, to join the King, for so he commanded.

And now was the will of the Maid and of the Duc d'Alencon broken, and broken was all that great army, whereof some were free lances out of many lands, but more were nobles of France with their men, who had served without price or pay, for love of France and of the Maid. Never again were they mustered; nay when, after some weeks passed, the gentle Duc d'Alencon prayed that he might have the Maiden with him, and burst into Normandy, where the English were strongest, by the Marches of Maine, even this grace was refused to him, by the malengin and ill-will of La Tremouille and the Archbishop of Reims. And these two fair friends met never more again, neither at fray nor feast. May she, among the Saints, so work by her prayers that the late sin and treason of the gentle Duke may be washed out and made clean, for while she lived there was no man more dear to her, nor any that followed her more stoutly in every onfall.

Now concerning the times that came after this shameful treason at Paris, I have no joy to write. The King's counsellors, as their manner was, ever hankered after a peace with Burgundy, and they stretched the false truce that was to have ended at Christmas to Easter Day, "pacem clamantes quo non fuit pax." For there was no truce with the English, who took St. Denis again, and made booty of the arms which the Maid had dedicated to Our Lady. On our part La Hire and Xaintrailles plundered, for their own hand, the lands of the Duke of Burgundy, and indeed on every side there was no fair fighting, such as the Maid loved, but a war of wastry, the peasants pillaged, and the poor held to ransom. For her part, she spent her days in prayer for the poor and the oppressed, whom she had come to deliver, and who now were in worse case than before, the English harrying certain of the good towns that had yielded to King Charles.

Now her voices ever bade the Maid go back to the Isle of France, and assail Paris, where lay no English garrison, and the Armagnacs were stirring as much as they might. But Paris, being at this time under the government of the Duke of Burgundy, was forsooth within the truce. The King's counsellors, therefore, setting their wisdom against that of the Saints, bade the Maid go against the towns of St. Pierre le Moustier and La Charite, then held by the English on the Loire. This was in November, when days were short, and the weather bitter cold. The Council was held at Mehun sur

Yevre, and forthwith the Maid, glad to be doing, rode to Bourges, where she mustered her men, and so marched to St. Pierre le Moustier, a small town, but a strong, with fosses, towers, and high walls.

There we lay some two days or three, plying the town with our artillery, and freezing in the winter nights. At length, having made somewhat of a breach, the Maid gave the word for the assault, and herself leading, with her banner in hand, we went at it with what force we might. But twice and thrice we were driven back from the fosse, and to be plain, our men were fled under cover, and only the Maid stood within arrow-shot of the wall, with a few of her household, of whom I was one, for I could not go back while she held her ground. The arrows and bolts from the town rained and whistled about us, and in faith I wished myself other where. Yet she stood, waving her banner, and crying, "Tirez en avant, ils sont a nous," as was her way in every onfall. Seeing her thus in jeopardy, her maitre d'hotel, D'Aulon, though himself wounded in the heel so that he might not set foot to ground, mounted a horse, and riding up, asked her "why she abode there alone, and did not give ground like the others?"

At this the Maid lifted her helmet from her head, and so, uncovered, her face like marble for whiteness, and her eyes shining like steel, made answer—

"I am not alone; with me there are of mine fifty thousand! Hence I will not give back one step till I have taken the town."

Then I wotted well that, sinful man as I am, I was in the company of the hosts of Heaven, though I saw them not. Great heart this knowledge gave me and others, and the Maid crying, in a loud voice, "Aux fagots, tout le monde!" the very runaways heard her and came back with planks and faggots, and so, filling up the fosse and passing over, we ran into the breach, smiting and slaying, and the town was taken.

For my own part, I was so favoured that two knights yielded them my prisoners (I being the only man of gentle birth among those who beset them in a narrow wynd), and with their ransoms I deemed myself wealthy enough, as well I might. So now I could look to win my heart's desire, if no ill fortune befell. But little good fortune came in our way. From La Charite, which was beset in the last days of November, we had perforce to give back, for the King sent us no munitions of war, and for lack of more powder and ball we might not make any breach in the walls of that town. And so, by reason of the hard winter, and the slackness of the King, and the false truce, we fought no more, at that season, but went, trailing after the Court, from castle to castle.

Many feasts were held, and much honour was done to the Maid, as by gifts of coat armour, and the ennobling of all her kith and kin, but these things she regarded not, nor did she ever bear on her shield the sword supporting the crown, between the lilies of France.

If these were ill days for the Maid, I shame to confess that they were merry days with me. There are worse places than a king's court, when a man is young, and light of heart, full of hope, and with money in his purse. I looked that we should take the field again in the spring; and having gained some gold, and even some good words, as one not backward where sword-strokes were going, I know not what dreams I had of high renown, ay, and the Constable's staff to end withal. For many a poor Scot has come to great place in France and Germany, who began with no better fortune than a mind to put his body in peril. Moreover, the winning of Elliot herself for my wife seemed now a thing almost within my reach.

Therefore, as I say, I kept a merry Yule at Jargeau, going bravely clad, and dancing all night long with the merriest. Only the wan face of the Maid (that in time of war had been so gallant and glad) came between me and my pleasures. Not that she was wilfully and wantonly sad, yet now and again we could mark in her face the great and loving pity that possessed her for France. Now I would be half angered with her, but again far more wroth with myself, who could thus lightly think of that passion of hers. But when she might she was ever at her prayers, or in company of children, or seeking out such as were poor and needy, to whom she was abundantly lavish of her gifts, so that, wheresoever the Court went, the people blessed her.

In these months I had tidings of Elliot now and again; and as occasion served I wrote to her, with messages of my love, and with a gift, as of a ring or a jewel. But concerning the manner of my escape from Paris I had told Elliot nothing for this cause. My desire was, when soonest I had an occasion, to surprise her with the gift of her jackanapes anew, knowing well that nothing could make her greater joy, save my own coming, or a victory of the Maid. The little creature had been my comrade wheresoever we went, as at Sully, Gien, and Bourges, only I took him not to the leaguers of St. Pierre le Moustier and La Charite, but left him with a fair lady of the Court. He had waxed fat again, for as meagre as he was when he came to me in prison, and he was full of new tricks, warming himself at the great fire in hall, like a man.

Now in the middle of the month of January, in the year of Grace fourteen hundred and thirty, the Maid told us of her household that she would journey to Orleans, to abide for some space with certain ladies of her friends, namely, Madame de St. Mesmin and Madame de Mouchy, who loved her dearly. To the most of us she gave holiday, to see our own friends. The Maid knew surely that in France my friends were few, and well she guessed whither I was bound. Therefore she sent for me, and bidding me carry her love to Elliot, she put into my hands a gift to her friend. It was a ring of silver-gilt, fashioned like that which her own father and mother had given her. At this ring she had a custom of looking often, so that the English conceived it to be an unholy talisman, though it bore the Name that is above all names. That ring I now wear in my bosom. So, saying farewell, with many kind words on her part, I rode towards Tours, where Elliot and her father as then dwelt, in that same house where I had been with them to be healed of my malady, after the leaguer of Orleans. To Tours I rode, telling them not of my coming, and carrying the jackanapes well wrapped up in furs of the best. The weather was frosty, and folk were sliding on the ice of the flooded fields near Tours when I came within sight of the great Minster. The roads rang hard; on the smooth ice the low sun was making paths of gold, and I sang as I rode. Putting up my horse at the sign of the "Hanging Sword," I took the ape under my great furred surcoat, and stole like a thief through the alleys, towards my master's house. The night was falling, and all the casement of the great chamber was glowing with the colour and light of a leaping fire within. There came a sound of music too, as one touched the virginals to a tune of my own country. My heart was beating for joy, as it had beaten in the bushment outside Paris town.

I opened the outer door secretly, for I knew the trick of it, and I saw from the thin thread of light on the wall of the passage that the chamber door was a little ajar. The jackanapes was now fretting and struggling within my surcoat, so, opening the coat, I put him down by the chamber door. He gave a little scratch, as was his custom, for he was a very mannerly little beast, and the sound of the virginals ceased. Then, pushing the door with his little hands, he ran in, with a kind of cry of joy.

"In Our Lady's name, what is this?" came the voice of Elliot. "My dear, dear little friend, what make you here?"

Then I could withhold myself no longer, but entered, and my lady ran to me, the jackanapes clinging about her neck with his arms. But mine were round her too, and what words we said, and what cheer we made each the other, I may not write, commending me to all true lovers, whose hearts shall tell them that whereof I am silent. Much was I rebuked for that I did not write to warn them of my coming, which was yet the more joyful that they were not warned. And then the good woman, Elliot's kinswoman, must be called (though in sooth not at the very first), and then a great fire must be lit in my old chamber; and next my master came in, from a tavern where he had been devising with some Scots of his friends; and all the while the jackanapes kept such a merry coil, and played so many of his tricks, and got so many kisses from his mistress, that it was marvel. But of all that had befallen me in the wars, and of how the Maiden did (concerning which Elliot had questioned me first of all), I would tell them little till supper was brought.

And then, indeed, out came all my tale, and they heard of what had been my fortune in Paris, and how the jackanapes had delivered me from durance, whereon never, surely, was any beast of his kind so caressed since our father Adam gave all the creatures their names. But as touching the Maid, I told how she had borne herself at St. Pierre le Moustier, and of all the honours that had been granted to her, and I bade them be of good heart and hope, for that her banner would be on the wind in spring, after Easter Day. All the good news that might be truly told I did tell, as how La Hire had taken Louviers town, and harried the English up to the very gates of Rouen. And I gave to Elliot the ring which the Maid had sent to her, fashioned like that she herself wore, but of silver gilt, whereas the Maid's was of base metal, and it bore the

Holy Names MARI. IHS. Thereon Elliot kissed it humbly, and avowed herself to be, that night, the gladdest damsel in all France.

"For I have gotten you, mon ami, and my little friend that I had lost, beyond all hope, and I have a kind word and a token from Her, la fille de Dieu," whereat her speech faltered, and her eyes swam in tears. But some trick of her jackanapes brought back her mirth, and so the hours passed, as happy as any in my life. Truly the memory of these things tells me how glad this world might be, wherein God has placed us, were it not troubled by the inordinate desires of men. In my master's house of Tours, then, my days of holiday went merrily by, save for one matter, and that of the utmost moment. For my master would in no manner permit me to wed his daughter while this war endured; and Elliot herself, blushing like any rose, told me that, while the Maid had need of me, with the Maid I must abide at my duty, and that she herself had no mind for happiness while her friend was yet labouring in the cause of France. Howbeit, I delivered me of my vow, by pilgrimage to the chapel in Fierbois. {32}

Andrew Lang

CHAPTER XXIV

HOW THE MAID HEARD ILL TIDINGS FROM HER VOICES, AND OF THE SILENCE OF THE BIRDS

Eastertide came at last, and that early, Easter Day falling on March the twenty-seventh. Our King kept his Paques at Sully with great festival, but his deadly foe, the Duke of Burgundy, lay at the town of Peronne. So soon as Eastertide was over, the Duke drew all the force he had to Montdidier, a town which lies some eight leagues to the north and west of Compiegne. Hence he so wrought that he made a pact with the captain of the French in Gournay, a town some four leagues north and west of Compiegne, whereby the garrison there promised to lie idle, and make no onslaught against them of Burgundy, unless the King brought them a rescue. Therefore the Duke went back to Noyon on the Oise, some eight leagues north and east of Compiegne, while his captain, Jean de Luxembourg, led half his army west, towards Beauvais. There he took the castle of Provenlieu, an old castle, and ruinous, that the English had repaired and held. And there he hanged certain English, who were used to pillage all the country about Montdidier. Thence Jean de Luxembourg came back to the Duke, at Noyon, and took and razed Choisy, which was held for France.

Now all these marchings, and takings of towns, were

designed to one end, namely, that the Duke might have free passage over the river Oise, so that his men and his victual might safely come and go from the east. For, manifestly, it was his purpose to besiege and take the good town of Compiegne, which lies on the river Oise some fifteen leagues north and east of Paris. This town had come in, and yielded to the Maid, some weeks before the onfall of Paris, and it was especially dear to her, for the people had sworn that they would all die, and see their wives and children dead, rather than yield to England or Burgundy. Moreover, whosoever held Compiegne was like, in no long time, to be master of Paris. But as now Guillaume de Flavy commanded in Compiegne for the King, a very good knight and skilled captain, but a man who robbed and ravished wheresoever he had power. His brother, Louis de Flavy, also joined him after Choisy fell, as I have told.

All this I have written that men may clearly know how the Maid came by her end. For, so soon as Eastertide was over, and the truce ended, she made no tarrying, nor even said farewell to the King, who might have held her back, but drew out all her company, and rode northward, whither she knew that battle was to be. Her mind was to take some strong place on the Oise, as Pont l'Eveque, near Noyon, that she might cut off them of Burgundy from all the country eastward of Oise, and so put them out of the power to besiege Compiegne, and might destroy all their host at Montdidier and in the Beauvais country. For the Maid was not only the first of captains in leading a desperate onslaught, but also (by miracle, for otherwise it might not be) she best knew how to devise deep schemes and subtle stratagem of war.

Setting forth, therefore, early in April, on the fifteenth day of the month she came to Melun, a town some seven leagues south of Paris, that had lately yielded to the King. Bidding me walk with her, she went afoot about the walls, considering what they lacked of strength, and how they might best be repaired, and bidding me write down all in a little book. Now we two, and no other, were walking by the dry fosse of Melun, the day being very fair and warm for that season, the flowers blossoming, and the birds singing so sweet and loud as never I heard them before or since that day.

The Maid stood still to listen, holding up her hand to me for silence, when, lo! in one moment, in the midst of merry music, the birds hushed suddenly.

As I marvelled, for there was not a cloud in the sky, nor a breath of cold wind, I beheld the Maid standing as I had seen her stand in the farmyard of the mill by St. Denis. Her head was bare, and her face was white as snow. So she stood while one might count a hundred, and if ever any could say that he had seen the Maid under fear, it was now. As I watched and wondered, she fell on her knees, like one in prayer, and with her eyes set and straining, and with clasped hands, she said these words—"Tell me of that day, and that hour, or grant me, of your grace, that in the same hour I may die."

Then she was silent for short space, and then, having drawn herself upon her knees for three paces or four, she very reverently bowed down, and kissed the ground.

Thereafter she arose, and beholding me wan, I doubt not, she gently laid her hand upon my shoulder, and, smiling most sweetly, she said—

"I know not what thou hast seen or heard, but promise, on thine honour, that thou wilt speak no word to any man, save in confession only, while I bear arms for France."

Then humbly, and with tears, I vowed as she had bidden me,

whereto she only said—

"Come, we loiter, and I have much to do, for the day is short."

But whether the birds sang again, or stinted, I know not, for I marked it not.

But she set herself, as before, to consider the walls and the fosses, bidding me write down in my little book what things were needful. Nor was her countenance altered in any fashion, nor was her wit less clear; but when we had seen all that was to be looked to, she bade me call the chief men of the town to her house, after vespers, and herself went into the Church of St. Michael to pray.

Though I pondered much on this strange matter, which I laid up in my heart, I never knew what, belike, the import was, till nigh a year thereafter, at Rouen.

But there one told me how the Maid, before her judges, had said that, at Melun, by the fosse, her Saints had told her how she should be made prisoner before the feast of St. John. And she had prayed them to warn her of that hour, or in that hour might she die, but they bade her endure all things patiently, and with a willing mind. At that coming, then, of the Saints, I was present, though, being a sinful man, I knew not that the Holy Ones were there. But the birds knew, and stinted in their singing.

Now that the Maid, knowing by inspiration her hour to be even at the doors, and wotting well what the end of her captivity was like to be, yet had the heart to put herself in jeopardy day by day, this I deem the most valiant deed ever done by man or woman since the making of the world. For scarce even Wallace wight would have stood to his standard had he known, by teaching of them who cannot lie, what end awaited him beyond all hope. Nay, he would have betaken him to France, as once he did in time of less danger.

Now, I pray you, consider who she was that showed this courage and high heart. She was but the daughter of a manant, a girl of eighteen years of age. Remember, then, what manner of creature such a girl is of her nature; how weak and fearful; how she is discomfited and abashed by the company of even one gentleman or lady of noble birth; how ignorant she is of war; how fond to sport and play with wenches of her own degree; how easily set on fire of love; and how eager to be in the society of young men amorous. Pondering all these things in your hearts, judge ye whether this Maid, the bravest leader in breach, the wisest captain, having foreknowledge of things hidden and of things to come, the most courteous lady who ever with knights sat in hall, not knowing carnal love, nor bodily fear, was aught but a thing miraculous, and a sister of the Saints.

CHAPTER XXV

OF THE ONFALL AT PONT L'EVEQUE,
AND HOW NORMAN LESLIE WAS HURT

I have now shown wherefore the fighting, in this spring, was to be up and down the water of Oise, whence the villagers had withdrawn themselves, of necessity, into the good towns. For the desire of the Duke of Burgundy was to hold the Oise, and so take Compiegne, the better to hold Paris. And on our side the skill was to cut his army in two, so that from east of the water of Oise neither men nor victual might come to him.

Having this subtle device of war in her mind, the Maid rode north from Melun, by the King's good towns, till she came to Compiegne, that was not yet beleaguered. There they did her all the honour that might be, and thither came to her standard Messire Jacques de Chabennes, Messire Rigault de Fontaines, Messire Poton de Xaintrailles, the best knight then on ground, and many other gentlemen, some four hundred lances in all. {33} With these lances the Maid consorted to attack Pont l'Eveque by a night onfall. This is a small but very strong hold, on the Oise, some six leagues from Compiegne, as you go up the river, and it lies near the town of Noyon, which was held by the English. In Pont l'Eveque there was a garrison of a hundred lances of the English, and our skill was to break on them in the grey of dawn, when men least fear a surprise, and are most easily taken. By this very device La Hire had seized Compiegne but six years agone, wherefore our hope was the higher. About five of the clock on an April day we rode out of Compiegne, a great company,—too great, perchance, for that we had to do. For our army was nigh a league in length as it went on the way, nor could we move swiftly, for there were waggons with us and carts, drawing guns and couleuvrines and powder, fascines wherewith to fill the fosses, and ladders and double ladders for scaling the walls. So the captains ordered it to be, for ever since that day by Melun fosse, when the Saints foretold her captivity, the Maid submitted herself in all things to the captains, which was never her manner before.

As we rode slowly, she was now at the head of the line, now in the midst, now at the rear, wherever was need; and as I rode at her rein, I took heart to say—

"Madame, it is not thus that we have taken great keeps and holds, in my country, from our enemies of England."

"Nay," said she, checking her horse to a walk, and smiling on me in the dusk with her kind eyes. "Then tell me how you order it in your country."

"Madame," I said, "it was with a little force, and lightly moving, that Messire Thomas Randolph scaled the Castle rock and took Edinburgh Castle out of the hands of the English, a keep so strong, and set on a cliff so perilous, that no man might deem to win it by sudden onfall. And in like manner the good Messire James Douglas took his own castle, more than once or twice, by crafty stratagem of war, so that the English named it Castle Perilous. But in every such onfall few men fought for us, of such as could move secretly and swiftly, not with long trains of waggons that cover a league of road, and by their noise and number give warning to an enemy."

"My mind is yours," she said, with a sigh, "and so I would have made this onslaught. But I submitted me to the will of the captains."

Through the night we pushed our way slowly, for in such a march none may go swifter than the slowest, namely, the carts and the waggons. Thus it befell that the Maid and the captains were in more thoughts than one to draw back to Compiegne, for the night was clear, and the dawn would be bright. And, indeed, after stumbling and wandering long, and doubting of the way, we did, at last, see the church towers and walls of Pont l'Eveque stand out against the clear sky of morning, a light mist girdling the basement of the walls. Had we been a smaller and swifter company, we should have arrived an hour before the first greyness shows the shapes of things. But now, alas! we no sooner saw the town than we heard the bells and trumpets calling the townsfolk and men-at-arms to be on their ward. The great guns of the keep roared at us so soon as we were in reach of shot; nevertheless, Pothon and the Maid set companies to carry the double ladders, for the walls were high, and others were told off to bring up the fascines, and so, leaving our main battle to wait out of shot, and come on as they were needed, the Maid and Pothon ran up the first rampart, she waving her standard and crying that all was ours. As we ran, for I must needs be by her side, the din of bells and guns was worse than I had heard at Orleans, and on the top of the church towers were men-at-arms waving flags, as if for a signal. Howbeit, we sprang into the fosse, under shield, wary of stones cast from above, and presently three ladders were set against the wall, and we went up, the Maid leading the way.

Now of what befell I know but little, save that I had so climbed that I looked down over the wall, when the ladder whereon I stood was wholly overthrown by two great English knights, and one of them, by his coat armour, was

Messire de Montgomery himself, who commanded in Pont l'Eveque. Of all that came after I remember no more than a flight through air, and the dead stroke of a fall on earth with a stone above me. For such is the fortune of war, whereof a man knows but his own share for the most part, and even that dimly. The eyes are often blinded with swift running to be at the wall, and, what with a helm that rings to sword-blows, and what with smoke, and dust, and crying, and clamour, and roar of guns, it is but little that many a man-at-arms can tell concerning the frays wherein, may be, he has borne himself not unmanly.

This was my lot at Pont l'Eveque, and I knew but little of what passed till I found myself in very great anguish. For I had been laid in one of the carts, and so was borne along the way we had come, and at every turn of the wheels a new pang ran through me. For my life I could not choose but groan, as others groaned that were in the same cart with me. For my right leg was broken, also my right arm, and my head was stounding as if it would burst. It was late and nigh sunset or ever we won the gates of Compiegne, having lost, indeed, but thirty men slain, but having wholly failed in our onfall. For I heard in the monastery whither I was borne that, when the Maid and Xaintrailles and their men had won their way within the walls, and had slain certain of the English, and were pushing the others hard, behold our main battle was fallen upon in the rear by the English from Noyon, some two miles distant from Pont l'Eveque. Therefore there was no help for it but retreat we must, driving back the English to Noyon, while our wounded and all our munitions of war were carried orderly away.

As to the pains I bore in that monastery of the Jacobins, when my broken bones were set by a very good surgeon, there is no need that I should write. My fortune in war was like that of most men-at-arms, or better than that of many who are slain outright in their first skirmish. Some good fortune I had, as at St. Pierre, and again, bad fortune, of which this was the worst, that I could not be with the Maid: nay, never again did I ride under her banner.

She, for her part, was not idle, but, after tarrying certain days in Compiegne with Guillaume de Flavy, she rode to Lagny, "for there," she said, "were men that warred well against the English," namely, a company of our Scots. And among them, as later I heard in my bed, was Randal Rutherford, who had ransomed himself out of the hands of the French in Paris, whereat I was right glad. At Lagny, with her own men and the Scots, the Maid fought and took one Franquet d'Arras, a Burgundian "routier," or knight of the road, who plundered that country without mercy. Him the Maid would have exchanged for an Armagnac of Paris, the host of the Bear Inn, then held in duresse by the English, for his share in a plot to yield Paris to the King. But this burgess died in the hands of the English, and the echevins {34} of Lagny, claiming Franquet d'Arras as a common thief, traitor, and murderer, tried him, and, on his confession, put him to death. This was counted a crime in the Maid by the English and Burgundian robbers, nay, even by French and Scots. "For," said they, "if a gentleman is to be judged like a manant, or a fat burgess by burgesses, there is no more profit or glory in war." Nay, I have heard gentlemen of France cry out that, as the Maid gave up Franquet to such judges as would surely condemn him, so she was rightly punished when Jean de Luxembourg sold her into the hands of unjust judges. But I answer that the Maid did not sell Franquet d'Arras, as I say De Luxembourg sold her: not a livre did she take from the folk of Lagny. And as for the slaying of robbers, this very Jean de Luxembourg had but just slain many English of his own party, for that they burned and pillaged in the Beauvais country.

Yet men murmured against the Maid not only in their hearts, but openly, and many men-at-arms ceased to love her cause, both for the slaying of Franquet d'Arras, and because she was for putting away the leaguer-lasses, and, when she might, would suffer no plundering. Whether she was right or wrong, it behoves me not to judge, but this I know, that the King's men fought best when she was best obeyed. And, like Him who sent her, she was ever of the part of the poor and the oppressed, against strong knights who rob and ravish and burn and torture, and hold to ransom. Therefore the Archbishop of Reims, who was never a friend of the Maid, said openly in a letter to the Reims folk that "she did her own will, rather than obeyed the commandments of God." But that God commands knights and gentlemen to rob the poor and needy (though indeed He has set a great gulf between a manant and a gentleman born) I can in nowise believe. For my part, when I have been where gentlemen and captains lamented the slaying of Franquet d'Arras, and justified the dealings of the English with the Maid, I have seemed to hear the clamour of the cruel Jews: "Tolle hunc, et dimitte nobis Barabbam." {35} For Barabbas was a robber. Howbeit on this matter, as on all, I humbly submit me to the judgment of my superiors and to Holy Church.

Meantime the Maid rode from Lagny, now to Soissons, now to Senlis, now to Crepy-en-Valois, and in Crepy she was when that befell which I am about to relate.

CHAPTER XXVI

HOW, AND BY WHOSE DEVICE,
THE MAID WAS TAKEN AT COMPIEGNE

"Verily and indeed the Maid is of wonderful excellence," quoth Father Francois to me, in my chamber at the Jacobins, where I was healing of my hurts.

"Any man may know that, who is in your company," the father went on speaking.

"And how, good father?" I asked him; "sure I have caught none of her saintliness."

"A saint I do not call you, but I scarce call you a Scot. For you are a clerk."

"The Maid taught me none of my clergy, father, nor have I taught her any of mine."

"She needs it not. But you are peaceful and gentle; you brawl not, nor drink, nor curse . . . "

"Nay, father, with whom am I to brawl, or how should I curse in your good company? Find you Scots so froward?"

"But now, pretending to be our friends, a band of them is harrying the Sologne country . . . "

"They will be Johnstons and Jardines, and wild wood folk of Galloway," I said. "These we scarce reckon Scots, but rather Picts, and half heathen. And the Johnstons and Jardines are here belike, because they have made Scotland over hot to hold them. We are a poor folk, but honest, let by the clans of the Land Debatable and of Ettrick Forest, and the Border freebooters, and the Galloway Picts, and Maxwells, and Glendinnings, and the red-shanked, jabbering Highlanders and Islesmen, and some certain of the Angus folk, and, maybe, a wild crew in Strathclyde."

"Yours, then, is a very large country?"

"About the bigness of France, or, may be, not so big. And the main part of it, and the most lawful and learned, is by itself, in a sort, a separate kingdom, namely Fife, whence I come myself. The Lothians, too, and the shire of Ayr, if you except Carrick, are well known for the lands of peaceful and sober men."

"Whence comes your great captain, Sir Hugh Kennedy?"

"There you name an honourable man-at-arms," I said, "the glory of Scotland; and to show you I was right, he is none of your marchmen, or Highlanders, but has lands in Ayrshire, and comes of a very honourable house."

"It is Sir Hugh that hath just held to ransom the King's good town of Tours, where is that gracious lady the mother of the King's wife, the Queen of Sicily."

Hereat I waxed red as fire.

"He will be in arrears of his pay, no doubt," I made answer.

"It is very like," said Father Francois: "but considering all that you tell me, I crave your pardon if I still think that the Blessed Maid has won you from the common ways of your countrymen."

To which, in faith, I had no answer to make, but that my fortune was like to be the happier in this world and the next.

"Much need have all men of her goodness, and we of her valour," said the father, and he sighed. "This is now the fourth siege of Compiegne I have seen, and twice have the leads from our roofs and the metal of our bells been made into munition of war. Absit omen Domine! And now they say the Duke of Burgundy has sworn to slay all, and spare neither woman nor child."

"A vaunt of war, father. Call they not him the Good Duke? When we lay before Paris, the English put about a like lying tale concerning us, as if we should sack and slay all."

"I pray that you speak sooth," said Father Francois.

On the next day, being May the twentieth, he came to me again, with a wan face.

"Burgundians are in Claroix," said he, "across the river, and yet others, with Jean de Luxembourg, at Margny, scarce a mile away, at the end of the causeway through the water meadows, beyond the bridge. And the Duke is at Coudun, a league off to the right of Claroix, and I have clomb the tower-top, and thence seen the English at Venette, on the left hand of the causeway. All is undone."

"Nay, father, be of better cheer. Our fort at the bridge end is stronger than Les Tourelles were at Orleans. The English shot can scarce cross the river. Bridge the enemy has none, and northward and eastward all is open. Be of better heart, Heaven helps France."

"We have sent to summon the Maid," said he, "from Crepy-en-Valois. In her is all my hope; but you speak lightly, for you are young, and war is your trade."

"And praying is yours, father, wherefore you should be bolder than I."

But he shook his head.

So two days passed, and nothing great befell, but in the grey dawn of May the twenty-third I was held awake by clatter of horsemen riding down the street under the window of my chamber. And after matins came Father Francois, his face very joyful, with the tidings that the Maid, and a company of some three hundred lances of hers, had ridden in from Crepy-en-Valois, she making her profit of the darkness to avoid the Burgundians.

Then I deemed that the enemy would soon have news of her, and all that day I heard the bells ring merry peals, and the trumpets sounding. About three hours after noonday Father Francois came again, and told me that the Maid would make a sally, and cut the Burgundians in twain; and now nothing would serve me but I must be borne in a litter to the walls, and see her banner once more on the wind.

So, by the goodwill of Father Francois, some lay brethren bore me forth from the convent, which is but a stone's-throw from the bridge. They carried me across the Oise to a mill hard by the boulevard of the Bridge fort, whence, from a window, I beheld all that chanced. No man sitting in the gallery of a knight's hall to see jongleurs play and sing could have had a better stance, or have seen more clearly all the mischief that befell.

The town of Compiegne lies on the river Oise, as Orleans on the Loire, but on the left, not the right hand of the water. The bridge is strongly guarded, as is custom, by a tower at the further end, and, in front of that tower, a boulevard. All the water was gay to look on, being covered with boats, as if for a holiday, but these were manned by archers, whom Guillaume de Flavy had set to shoot at the enemy, if they drove us back, and to rescue such of our men as might give ground, if they could not win into the boulevard at the bridge end.

Beyond the boulevard, forth to the open country, lay a wide plain, and behind it, closing it in, a long, low wall of steep hills. On the left, a mile and a half away, Father Francois showed me the church tower of Venette, where the English camped; to the right, a league off, was the tower of Clairoix; and at the end of a long raised causeway that ran from the bridge across the plain, because of the winter floods, I saw the tower and the village of Margny. All these towns and spires looked peaceful, but all were held by the Burgundians. Men-at-arms were thick on the crest of our boulevard, and on the gate-keep, all looking across the river towards the town, whence the Maid should sally by way of the bridge. So there I lay on a couch in the window and waited, having no fear, but great joy.

Nay, never have I felt my spirit lighter within me, so that I laughed and chattered like a fey man. The fresh air, after my long lying in a chamber, stirred me like wine. The May sun shone warm, yet cooled with a sweet wind of the west. The room was full of women and maids, all waiting to throw flowers before the Maid, whom they dearly loved.

Everything had a look of holiday, and all was to end in joy and great victory. So I laughed with the girls, and listened to a strange tale, how the Maid had but of late brought back to life a dead child at Lagny, so that he got his rights of Baptism, and anon died again.

So we fleeted the time, till about the fifth hour after noon, when we heard the clatter of horses on the bridge; and some women waxed pale. My own heart leaped up. The noise drew nearer, and presently She rode across and forth, carrying her banner in the noblest manner, mounted on a grey horse, and clad in a rich hucque of cramoisie; she smiled and bowed like a queen to the people, who cried, "Noel! Noel!" Beside her rode Pothon le Bourgignon (not Pothon de Xaintrailles, as some have falsely said), her confessor Pasquerel on a palfrey; her brother, Pierre du Lys, with his new arms bravely blazoned; and her maitre d'hotel, D'Aulon. But of the captains in Compiegne no one rode with her. She had but her own company, and a great rude throng of footmen of the town that would not be said nay. They carried clubs, and they looked, as I heard, for no less than to take prisoner the Duke of Burgundy himself. Certain of these men also bore spades and picks and other tools; for the Maid, as I deem, intended no more than to take and hold Margny, that so she might cut the Burgundians in twain, and sunder from them the English at Venette. Now as the night was not far off, then at nightfall would the English be in sore straits, as not knowing the country and the country roads, and not having the power to join them of Burgundy at Clairoix. This, one told me afterwards, was the device of the Maid.

Be this as it may, and a captain of hers, Barthelemy Barrette, told me the tale, the Maid rode gallantly forth, flowers raining on her, while my heart longed to be riding at her rein. She waved her hand to Guillaume de Flavy, who sat on his horse by the gate of the boulevard, and so, having arrayed her men, she cried, "Tirez avant!" and made towards Margny, the foot-soldiers following with what speed they might, while I and Father Francois, and others in the chamber, strained our eyes after them. All the windows and roofs of the houses and water-mills on the bridge were crowded with men and women, gazing, and it came into my mind that Flavy had done ill to leave these mills and houses standing. They wrought otherwise at Orleans. This was but a passing thought, for my heart was in my eyes, straining towards Margny. Thence now arose a great din, and clamour of trumpets and cries of men-at-arms, and we could see tumult, blown dust, and stir of men, and so it went for it may be half of an hour. Then that dusty cloud of men and horses drove, forward ever, out of our sight.

The sun was now red and sinking above the low wall of the western hills, and the air was thicker than it had been, and confused with a yellow light. Despite the great multitude of men and women on the city walls, there came scarcely a sound of a voice to us across the wide river, so still they kept, and the archers in the boats beneath us were silent: nay, though the chamber wherein I lay was thronged with the people of the house pressing to see through the open casement, yet there was silence here, save when the father prayed.

A stronger wind rising out of the west now blew towards us with a sweet burden of scent from flowers and grass, fragrant upon our faces. So we waited, our hearts beating with hope and fear.

Then I, whose eyes were keen, saw, blown usward from Margny, a cloud of flying dust, that in Scotland we call stour. The dust rolled white along the causeway towards Compiegne, and then, alas! forth from it broke little knots of our men, foot-soldiers, all running for their lives. Behind them came more of our men, and more, all running, and then mounted men-at-arms, spurring hard, and still more and more of these; and ever the footmen ran, till many riders and some runners had crossed the drawbridge, and were within the boulevard of the bridge. There they stayed, sobbing and panting, and a few were bleeding. But though the foremost runaways thus won their lives, we saw others roll over and fall as they ran, tumbling down the sides of the causeway, and why they fell I knew not.

But now, in the midst of the causeway, between us and Margny, our flying horsemen rallied under the Maiden's banner, and for the last time of all, I heard that clear girl's voice crying, "Tirez en avant! en avant!"

Anon her horsemen charged back furiously, and drove the Picards and Burgundians, who pursued, over a third part of the raised roadway.

But now, forth from Margny, trooped Burgundian men-at-arms without end or number, the banner of the Maid waved wildly, now up, now down, in the mad mellay, and ever they of Burgundy pressed on, and still our men, being few and outnumbered, gave back. Yet still some of the many clubmen of the townsfolk tumbled over as they ran, and the drawbridge was choked with men flying, thrusting and thronging, wild and blind with the fear of death. Then rose on our left one great cry, such as the English give when they rejoice, or when they charge, and lo! forth from a little wood that had hidden them, came galloping and running across the heavy wet meadowland between us and Venette, the men-at-arms and the archers of England. Then we nigh gave up all for lost, and fain I would have turned my eyes away, but I might not.

Now and again the English archers paused, and loosed a

flight of clothyard shafts against the stream of our runaways on the bridge. Therefore it was that some fell as they ran. But the little company of our horsemen were now driven back so near us that I could plainly see the Maid, coming last of all, her body swung round in the saddle as she looked back at the foremost foemen, who were within a lance's length of her. And D'Aulon and Pierre du Lys, gripping each at her reins, were spurring forward. But through the press of our clubmen and flying horsemen they might not win, and now I saw, what never man saw before, the sword of the Maid bare in battle! She smote on a knight's shield, her sword shivered in that stroke, she caught her steel sperthe into her hand, and struck and hewed amain, and there were empty saddles round her.

And now the English in the meadow were within four lances' lengths of the causeway between her and safety. Say it I must, nor cannon-ball nor arrow-flight availed to turn these English. Still the drawbridge and the inlet of the boulevard were choked with the press, and men were leaping from bank and bridge into the boats, or into the water, while so mixed were friends and foes that Flavy, in a great voice, bade archers and artillerymen hold their hands.

Townsfolk, too, were mingled in the throng, men who had come but to gape as curious fools, and among them I saw the hood of a cordelier, as I glanced from the fight to mark how the Maid might force her way within. Still she smote, and D'Aulon and Pierre du Lys smote manfully, and anon they gained a little way, backing their horses, while our archers dared not shoot, so mixed were French, English, and Burgundians.

Flavy, who worked like a man possessed, had turned about to give an order to the archers above him; his back, I swear, was to the press of flying men, to the inlet of the boulevard, and to the drawbridge, when his own voice, as all deemed who heard it, cried aloud, "Up drawbridge, close gates, down portcullis!" The men whose duty it was were standing ready at the cranks and pulleys, their tools in hand, and instantly, groaning, the drawbridge flew up, casting into the water them that were flying across, down came the portcullis, and slew two men, while the gates of the inlet of the boulevard were swung to and barred, all, as it might he said, in the twinkling of an eye.

Flavy turned in wrath and great amaze: "In God's name, who cried?" he shouted. "Down drawbridge, up portcullis, open gates! To the front, men-at-arms, lances forward!"

For most of the mounted men who had fled were now safe, and on foot, within the boulevard.

All this I heard and saw, in a glance, while my eyes were fixed on the Maid and the few with her. They were lost from our sight, now and again, in a throng of Picards, Englishmen, Burgundians, for all have their part in this glory. Swords and axes fell and rose, steeds countered and reeled, and then, they say, for this thing I myself did not see, a Picard archer, slipping under the weapons and among the horses' hoofs, tore the Maid from saddle by the long skirts of her hucque, and they were all upon her. This befell within half a stone's-throw of the drawbridge. While Flavy himself toiled with his hands, and tore at the cranks and chains, the Maid was taken under the eyes of us, who could not stir to help her. Now was the day and the hour whereof the Saints told her not, though she implored them with tears. Now in the throng below I heard a laugh like the sound of a saw on stone, and one struck him that laughed on the mouth. It was the laugh of that accursed Brother Thomas!

I had laid my face on my hands, being so weak, and was

weeping for very rage at that which my unhappy eyes had seen, when I heard the laugh, and lifting my head and looking forth, I beheld the hood of the cordelier.

"Seize him!" I cried to Father Francois, pointing down at the cordelier. "Seize that Franciscan, he has betrayed her! Run, man, it was he who cried in Flavy's voice, bidding them raise drawbridge and let fall portcullis. The devil gave him that craft to counterfeit men's voices. I know the man. Run, Father Francois, run!"

"You are distraught with very grief," said the good father, the tears running down his own cheeks; "that is Brother Thomas, the best artilleryman in France, and Flavy's chief trust with the couleuvrine. He came in but four days agone, and there was great joy of his coming."

Thus was the Maid taken, by art and device of the devil and Brother Thomas, and in no otherwise. They who tell that Flavy sold her, closing the gates in her face, do him wrong; he was an ill man, but loyal to France, as was seen by the very defence he made at Compiegne, for there was none like it in this war. But of what avail was that to us who loved the Maid? Rather, many times, would I have died in that hour than have seen what I saw. For our enemies made no more tarrying, nor any onslaught on the boulevard, but rode swiftly back with the prize they had taken, with her whom they feared more than any knight or captain of France. This page whereon I work, in a hand feeble and old, and weary with much writing, is blotted with tears that will not be held in. But we must bow humbly to the will of God and of His Saints. "Dominus dedit, et Dominus abstulit; benedictum sit nomen Domini."

Wherefore should I say more? They carried me back in litter over the bridge, through the growing darkness. Every church was full of women weeping and praying for her that was the friend of them, and the playmate of their children, for all children she dearly loved.

Concerning Flavy, it was said, by them who loved him not, that he showed no sign of sorrow. But when his own brother Louis fell, later in the siege, a brother whom he dearly loved, none saw him weep, or alter the fashion of his countenance; nay, he bade musicians play music before him.

I besought the Prior, when I was borne home, that I might be carried to Flavy, and tell him that I knew. But he forbade me, saying that, in very truth, I knew nought, or nothing that could be brought against a Churchman, and one in a place of trust. For I had not seen the lips of the cordelier move when that command was given—nay, at the moment I saw him not at all. Nor could I even prove to others that he had this devilish art, there being but my oath against his, and assuredly he would deny the thing. And though I might be assured and certain within myself, yet other witness I had none at all, nor were any of my friends there who could speak with me. For D'Aulon, and Pasquerel, and Pierre du Lys had all been taken with the Maid. It was long indeed before Pierre du Lys was free, for he had no money to ransom himself withal. Therefore Flavy, knowing me only for a wounded Scot of the Maid's, would think me a brainsick man, and as like as not give me more of Oise river to drink than I craved.

With these reasonings it behoved me to content myself. The night I passed in prayers for the Maid, and for myself, that I might yet do justice on that devil, or, at least, might see justice done. But how these orisons were answered shall be seen in the end, whereto I now hasten.

CHAPTER XXVII

HOW NORMAN LESLIE FARED IN COMPIEGNE, WITH THE END OFTHAT LEAGUER

About all that befell in the besieged city of Compiegne, after that wicked day of destiny when the Maid was taken, I heard for long only from the Jacobin brothers, and from one Barthelemy Barrette. He was a Picardy man, more loyal than most of his country, who had joined the Maid after the fray at Paris. Now he commanded a hundred of her company, who did not scatter after she was taken, and he was the best friend I then had.

"The burgesses are no whit dismayed," said he, coming into my chamber after the day of the Ascension, which was the second after the capture of the Maid. "They have sent a messenger to the King, and expect succour."

"They sue for grace at a graceless face," said I, in the country proverb; for my heart was hot against King Charles.

"That is to be seen," said be. "But assuredly the Duke of Burgundy is more keen about his own business."

"How fare the Burgundians?" I asked, "for, indeed, I have heard the guns speak since dawn, but none of the good fathers cares to go even on to the roof of the church tower and bring me tidings, for fear of a stray cannon-ball."

"For holy men they are wondrous chary of their lives," said Barthelemy, laughing. "Were I a monk, I would welcome death that should unfrock me, and let me go a-wandering in Paradise among these fair lady saints we see in the pictures."

"It is written, Barthelemy, that there is neither marrying nor giving in marriage."

"Faith, the more I am fain of it," said Barthelemy, "and may be I might take the wrong track, and get into the Paradise of Mahound, which, I have heard, is no ill place for a man-at-arms."

This man had no more faith than a paynim, but, none the less, was a stout carl in war.

"But that minds me," quoth he, "of the very thing I came hither to tell you. One priest there is in Compiegne who takes no keep of his life, a cordelier. What ails you, man? does your leg give a twinge?"

"Ay, a shrewd twinge enough."

"Truly, you look pale enough."

"It is gone," I said. "Tell me of that cordelier."

"Do you see this little rod?" he asked, putting in my hand a wand of dark wood, carven with the head of a strange beast in a cowl.

"I see it."

"How many notches are cut in it?"

"Five," I said. "But why spoil you your rod?"

"Five men of England or Burgundy that cordelier shot this day, from the creneaux of the boulevard where the Maid," crossing himself, "was taken. A fell man he is, strong and tall, with a long hooked nose, and as black as Sathanas."

"How comes he in arms?" I asked.

"Flavy called him in from Valenciennes, where he was about some business of his own, for there is no greater master of the culverin. And, faith, as he says, he 'has had rare sport, and will have for long.'"

"Was there an onfall of the enemy?"

"Nay, they are over wary. He shot them as they dug behind pavises. {36} For the Duke has moved his quarters to Venette, where the English lay, hard by the town. And, right in the middle of the causeway to Margny, two arrow-shots from our bridge end, he is letting build a great bastille, and digging a trench wherein men may go to and fro. The cordelier was as glad of that as a man who has stalked a covey of partridges. 'Keep my tally for me,' he said to myself; 'cut a notch for every man I slay'; and here," said Barthelemy, waving his staff, "is his first day's reckoning."

Now I well saw what chance I had of bringing that devil to justice, for who would believe so strange a tale as mine against one so serviceable in the war? Nor was D'Aulon here to speak for me, the enemy having taken him when they took the Maid. Thinking thus, I groaned, and Barthelemy, fearing that he had wearied me, said farewell, and went out.

Every evening, after sunset, he would come in, and partly cheer me, by telling how hardily our people bore them, partly break my heart with fresh tidings of that devil, Brother Thomas.

"Things go not ill, had we but hope of succour," he said. "The Duke's bastille is rising, indeed, and the Duke is building taudis {37} of oaken beams and earth, between the bastille and our boulevard. The skill is to draw nearer us, and nearer, till he can mine beneath our feet. Heard you any new noise of war this day?"

"I heard such a roar and clatter as never was in my ears, whether at Orleans or Paris."

"And well you might! This convent is in the very line of the fire. They have four great bombards placed, every one of them with a devilish Netherland name of its own. There is Houpembiere,—that means the beer-barrel, I take it,—and La Rouge Bombarde, and Remeswalle and Quincequin, every one shooting stone balls thirty inches in girth. The houses on the bridge are a heap of stones, the mills are battered down, and we must grind our meal in the city, in a cellar, for what I can tell. Nom Dieu! when they take the boulevard we lose the river, and if once they bar our gates to the east, whence shall viands come?"

"Is there no good tidings from the messenger?"

"The King answers ever like a drawer in a tavern, 'Anon, anon, sir!' He will come himself presently, always presently, with all his host."

"He will never come," I said. "He is a . . . "

"He is my King," said Barthelemy. "Curse your own King of

Scots, if you will. Scots, by the blood of Iscariot, traitors are they; well, I crave your pardon, I spake in haste and anger. Know you Nichole Cammet?"

"I have heard of the man," I said. "A town's messenger, is he not?"

"The same. But a week agone, Cammet was sent on a swift horse to Chateau Thierry. The good town craved of Pothon de Xaintrailles, who commands there, to send them what saltpetre he could spare for making gunpowder. The saltpetre came in this day by the Pierrefonds Gate, and Cammet with it, but on another horse, a jade."

"Well, and what have the Scots to do with that?"

"No more than this. A parcel of them, routiers and brigands, have crept into an old castle on the road, and hold it for their own hands. Thence they sallied forth after Cammet, and so chased him that his horse fell down dead under him in the gateway of Chateau Thierry."

"They would be men of the Land Debatable," I cried: "Elliots and Armstrongs, they never do a better deed, being corrupted by dwelling nigh our enemies of England. Fain would I pay for that horse; see here," and I took forth my purse from under my pillow, "take that to the attournes, and say a Scot atones for what Scots have done."

"Norman, I take back my word; I crave your pardon, and I am shamed to have spoken so to a sick man of his own country-folk. But for your purse, I am ill at carrying purses; I have no skill in that art, and the dice draw me when I hear the rattle of them. But look at the cordelier's tally: four men to-day, three yesterday; faith, he thins them!"

Indeed, to shorten a long story, by the end of Barthelemy's count there were two hundred and thirty-nine notches on the rod. That he kept a true score (till he stinted and reckoned no more), I know, having proof from the other side. For twelve years thereafter, I falling into discourse with Messire Georges Chastellain, an esquire of the Duke of Burgundy, and a maker both of verse and prose, he told me the same tale to a man, three hundred men. And I make no doubt but that he has written it in his book of the praise of his prince, and of these wars, to witness if I lie.

Consider, then, what hope I had of being listened to by Flavy, or by the attournes (or, as we say, bailies), of the good town, if, being recovered from my broken limbs, I brought my witness to their ears.

None the less, the enemy battered at us every day with their engines, destroying, as Barthelemy had said, the houses on the bridge, and the mills, so that they could no longer grind the corn.

And now came the Earls of Huntingdon and Arundel, with two thousand Englishmen, while to us appeared no succour. So at length, being smitten by balls from above, and ruined by mines dug under earth from below, our company that held the boulevard at the bridge end were surprised in the night, and some were taken, some drowned in the river Oise. Wherefore was great sorrow and fear, the more for that the Duke of Burgundy let build a bridge of wood from Venette, to come and go across Oise, whereby we were now assailed on both hands, for hitherto we had been free to come and go on the landward side, and through all the forest of Pierrefonds. We had but one gate unbeleaguered, the Chapel Gate, leading to Choisy and the north-east. Now were we straitened for provender, notably for fresh meat, and men were driven, as in a city beleaguered, to eat the flesh of dead horses, and even of rats and dogs, whereof I have partaken, and it is ill food.

None the less we endured, despite the murmuring of the commons, so strong are men's hearts; moreover, all France lay staked on this one cast of the dice, no less than at Orleans in the year before.

Somewhat we were kept in heart by tidings otherwise bitter. For word came that the Maid, being in ward at Beaurevoir, a strong place of Jean de Luxembourg, had leaped in the night from the top of the tower, and had, next morning, been taken up all unhurt, as by, miracle, but astounded and bereft of her senses. For this there was much sorrow, but would to God that He had taken her to Himself in that hour!

Nevertheless, when she was come to herself again, she declared, by inspiration of the Saints, that Compiegne should be delivered before the season of Martinmas. Whence I, for one, drew great comfort, nor ever again despaired, and many were filled with courage when this tidings came to our ears, hoping for some miracle, as at Orleans.

Now, too, God began to take pity upon us; for, on August the fifteenth, the eighty-fifth day of the siege, came news to the Duke of Burgundy that Philip, Duke of Brabant, was dead, and he must go to make sure of that great heritage. The Duke having departed, the English Earls had far less heart for the leaguer; I know not well wherefore, but now, at least, was seen the truth of that proverb concerning the "eye of the master." The bastille, too, which our enemies had made to prevent us from going out by our Pierrefonds Gate on the landward side, was negligently built, and of no great strength. All this gave us some heart, so much that my hosts, the good Jacobins, and the holy sisters of the Convent of St. John, stripped the lead from their roofs, and bestowed it on the town, for munition of war. And when I was in case to walk upon the walls, and above the river, I might see men and boys diving in the water and searching for English cannon-balls, which we shot back at the English.

It chanced, one day, that I was sitting and sunning myself in the warm September weather, on a settle in a secure place hard by the Chapel Gate. With me was Barthelemy Barrette, for it was the day of Our Lady's Feast, that very day whereon we had failed before Paris last year, and there was truce for the sacred season. We fell to devising of what had befallen that day year, and without thought I told Barthelemy of my escape from prison, and so, little by little, I opened my heart to him concerning Brother Thomas and all his treasons.

Never was man more astounded than Barthelemy; and he bade me swear by the Blessed Trinity that all this tale was true.

"Mayhap you were fevered," he said, "when you lay in the casement seat, and saw the Maid taken by device of the cordelier."

"I was no more fevered than I am now, and I swear, by what oath you will, and by the bones of St. Andrew, which these sinful hands have handled, that Flavy's face was set the other way when that cry came, 'Down portcullis, up drawbridge, close gates!' And now that I have told you the very truth, what should I do?"

"Brother Thomas should burn for this," quoth Barthelemy; "but not while the siege endures. He carries too many English lives in his munition-box. Nor can you slay him in single combat, or at unawares, for the man is a priest. Nor would Flavy, who knows you not, listen to such a story."

So there he sat, frowning, and plucking at his beard. "I have it," he said; "D'Aulon is no further off than Beaulieu, where Jean de Luxembourg holds him till he pays his ransom. When the siege is raised, if ever we are to have succour, then purchase safe-conduct to D'Aulon, take his testimony, and bring it to Flavy."

As he spoke, some stir in the still air made me look up, and suddenly throw my body aside; and it was well, for a sword swept down from the low parapet above our heads, and smote into the back of that settle whereon we were sitting.

Ere I well knew what had chanced, Barthelemy was on his feet, his whinger flew from his hand, and he, leaping up on to the parapet, was following after him who smote at me.

In the same moment a loud grating voice cried—

"The Maid shall burn, and not the man," and a flash of light went past me, the whinger flying over my head and clipping into the water of the moat below.

Rising as I best might, but heedfully, I spied over the parapet, and there was Barthelemy coming back, his naked sword in his hand.

"The devil turned a sharp corner and vanished," he said. "And now where are we? We have a worse foe within than all the men of Burgundy without. There goes the devil's tally!" he cried, and threw the little carven rod far from him into the moat, where it fell and floated.

"No man saw this that could bear witness; most are in church, where you and I should have been," I said.

Then we looked on each other with blank faces.

"My post is far from his, and my harness is good," said Barthelemy; "but for you, beware!" Thenceforth, if I saw any cowl of a cordelier as I walked, I even turned and went the other way.

I was of no avail against this wolf, whom all men praised, so serviceable was he to the town.

Once an arbalest bolt struck my staff from my hand as I walked, and I was fain to take shelter of a corner, yet saw not whence the shot came.

Once a great stone fell from a turret, and broke into dust at my feet, and it is not my mind that a cannon-ball had loosened it.

Thus my life went by in dread and watchfulness. No more bitter penance may man dree than was mine, to be near this devil, and have no power to avenge my deadly quarrel. There were many heavy hearts in the town; for, once it was taken, what man could deem his life safe, or what woman her honour? But though they lay down and rose up in fear, and were devoured by desire of revenge, theirs was no such thirst as mine.

So the days went on, and darkened towards the promised season of Martinmas, but there dawned no light of hope. Now, on the Wednesday before All Saints, I had clambered up into the tower of the Church of the Jacobins, on the north-east of the city, whence there was a prospect far and wide. With me were only two of the youngest of the fathers. I looked down into the great forest of Pierrefonds, and up and down Oise, and beheld the army of our enemies moving in divers ways. The banners of the English and their long array were crossing the Duke of Burgundy's new bridge of wood, that he had builded from Venette, and with them the men of

Jean de Luxembourg trooped towards Royaulieu. On the crest of their bastille, over against our Pierrefonds Gate, matches were lighted and men were watching in double guard, and the same on the other side of the water, at the Gate Margny. Plainly our foes expected a rescue sent to us of Compiegne by our party. But the forest, five hundred yards from our wall, lay silent and peaceable, a sea of brown and yellow leaves.

Then, while the English and Burgundian men-at-arms, that had marched south and east, were drawn up in order of battle away to the right between wood and water, behold, trumpets sounded, faint enough, being far off. Then there was a glitter of the pale sun on long lines of lance-points, under the banners of French captains, issuing out from the forest, over against the enemy. We who stood on the tower gazed long at these two armies, which were marshalled orderly, with no more than a bowshot and a half between them, and every moment we looked to see them charge upon each other with the lance. Much we prayed to the Saints, for now all our hope was on this one cast. They of Burgundy and of England dismounted from their horses, for the English ever fight best on foot, and they deemed that the knights of France would ride in upon them, and fall beneath the English bows, as at Azincour and Crecy. We, too, looked for nought else; but the French array never stirred, though here and there a knight would gallop forth to do a valiance. Seldom has man seen a stranger sight in war, for the English and Burgundians could not charge, being heavy-armed men on foot, and the French would not move against them, we knew not wherefore.

All this spectacle lay far off, to the south, and we could not be satisfied with wondering at it nor turn away our eyes, when, on the left, a trumpet rang out joyously. Then, all of us wheeling round as one man, we saw the most blessed sight, whereto our backs had been turned; for, into the Chapel

Andrew Lang

Gate—that is, far to the left of the Pierrefonds Gate on the north-east—were streaming cattle, sheep and kine, pricked on and hastened by a company of a hundred men-at-arms. They had come by forest paths from Choisy way, and anon all our guns on the boulevard of the Pierrefonds Gate burst forth at once against the English bastille over against it. Now this bastille, as I have said, had never been strongly builded, and, in some sort, was not wholly finished.

After one great volley of guns against the bastille, we, looking down into our boulevard of the Pierrefonds Gate, saw the portcullis raised, the drawbridge lowered, and a great array of men-at-arms carrying ladders rush out, and charge upon the bastille. Then, through the smoke and fire, they strove to scale the works, and for the space of half an hour all was roar of guns; but at length our men came back, leaving many slain, and the running libbards grinned on the flag of England.

I might endure no longer, but, clambering down the tower stairs as best I might, for I was still lame, I limped to my lodgings at the Jacobins, did on my harness, and, taking a horse from the stable, I mounted and rode to the Pierrefonds Gate. For Brother Thomas and his murderous ways I had now no care at all.

Never, sure, saw any man such a sight. Our boulevard was full, not only of men-at-arms, but of all who could carry clubs, burgesses armed, old men, boys, yea, women and children, some with rusty swords, some with carpenters' axes, some bearing cudgels, some with hammers, spits, and knives, all clamouring for the portcullis to rise and let them forth. Their faces were lean and fierce, their eyes were like eyes of wolves, for now, they cried, was the hour, and the prophecy of the Maid should be fulfilled! Verily, though she lay in bonds, her spirit was with us on that day!

But still our portcullis was down, and the long tail of angry people stretched inwards, from the inner mouth of the boulevard, along the street, surging like a swollen loch against its barrier.

On the crest of the boulevard was Flavy, baton in hand, looking forth across field and forest, watching for I knew not what, while still the people clamoured to be let go. But he stood like the statue of a man-at-arms, and from the bastille of the Burgundians the arrows rained around him, who always watched, and was still. Now the guards of the gate had hard work to keep the angry people back, who leaped and tore at the men-at-arms arrayed in front of them, and yelled for eagerness to issue forth and fight.

Suddenly, on the crest of the boulevard, Flavy threw up his arm and gave one cry—

"Xaintrailles!"

Then he roared to draw up portcullis and open gates; the men-at-arms charged forth, the multitude trampled over each other to be first in field, I was swept on and along with them through the gate, and over the drawbridge, like a straw on a wave, and, lo! a little on our left was the banner of Pothon de Xaintrailles, his foremost men dismounting, the rearguard just riding out from the forest. The two bands joined, we from Compiegne, the four hundred of Xaintrailles from the wood, and, like two swollen streams that meet, we raced towards the bastille, under a rain of arrows and balls. Nothing could stay us: a boy fell by my side with an arrow thrilling in his breast, but his brother never once looked round. I knew not that I could run, but run I did, though not so fast as many, and before I reached the bastille our ladders were up, and the throng was clambering, falling, rising again, and flowing furiously into the fort. The townsfolk had no thought but to slay and slay; five or six would be at the throat of one Burgundian man-at-arms; hammers and axes were breaking up armour, knives were scratching and searching for a crevice; women, lifting great stone balls, would stagger up to dash them on the heads of the fallen. Of the whole garrison, one-half, a hundred and sixty men-at-arms, were put to the sword. Only Pothon de Xaintrailles, and the gentlemen with him, as knowing the manner of war, saved and held to ransom certain knights, as Messire Jacques de Brimeu, the Seigneur de Crepy, and others; while, for my own part, seeing a knight assailed by a knot of clubmen, I struck in on his part, for gentle blood must ever aid gentle blood, and so, not without shrewd blows on my salade, I took to ransom Messire Collart de Bertancourt.

Thereafter, very late, and in the twilight of October the twenty-fifth, we turned back to Compiegne, leaving the enemies' bastille in a flame behind us, while in front were blazing the bonfires of the people of the good town. And, in Compiegne, we heard how the English and the main army of Burgundians had turned, late in the day, and crossed by the Duke of Burgundy's bridge, leaving men to keep guard there. So our victory was great, and wise had been the prudence of the French captains, subtlety being the mother of victory; for, without a blow struck, they had kept Jean de Luxembourg, and the Earls of Huntingdon and Arundel, waiting idle all day, while their great bastille was taken by Xaintrailles and the townsfolk, and food was brought into Compiegne. Thus for the second time I passed a night of joy in a beleaguered town, for there was music in every street, the churches full of people praising God for this great deliverance, men and maids dancing around bonfires, yet good watch was kept at the gates and on the towers. Next day we expected battle, but our spies brought in tidings that Burgundians and English had decamped in the dawn, their men deserting. That day was not less joyful than the night had been; for at Royaulieu, in the abbey where Jean de Luxembourg had lain, the townsfolk found all manner of meat, and of wine great plenty, so right good cheer we made, for it cost us nothing.

Andrew Lang

CHAPTER XXVIII

HOW THE BURGUNDIANS HUNTED HARES, WITH THE END OF THAT HUNTING

"Tell me, what tidings of him?" Barthelemy Barrette asked me, on the day after that unbought feast at Royaulieu.

He was sitting in the noonday sun on the bridge of Compiegne, and strange it was to see the place so battered yet so peaceful after five months of war. The Oise sliding by and rippling on the piers was not more quiet than this bridge of many battles, yet black in places with dried-up blood of men slain. "Tidings can I find none," I answered. "He who saw the cordelier last was on guard in the boulevard during the great charge. He marked Brother Thomas level his couleuvrine now and again, as we ran for the bastille, and cried out to him to aim higher, for that the ball would go amongst us."

"You were his target, I make no doubt," said Barthelemy, "but by reason of the throng he had no certain aim."

"After we broke into the bastille, I can find no man who has set eyes on him," and I cursed the cordelier for very rage.

"He is well away, if he stays away: you and I need scarce

any longer pray for eyes in the backs of our heads. But what make we next?"

"I have but one thought," I said: "to pluck the Maid out of the hands of the English, for now men say that she is sold to them by Jean of Luxembourg. They mean to take her to Arras, and so by Crotoy at the mouth of Seine, and across Normandy to Rouen. Save her France must, for the honour of France."

"My mind is the same," he said, and fell into a muse. "Hence the straight road, and the shortest," he said at last, "is by Beauvais on to Rouen, where she will lie in chains," and drawing his dagger he scratched lines on the bridge parapet with its point. "Here is Compiegne; there, far to the west, is the sea, and here is Rouen. That straight line," which he scratched, "goes to Rouen from Compiegne. Here, midway, is Beauvais, whereof we spoke, which town we hold. But there, between us and Beauvais, is Clermont, held by Crevecoeur for the Burgundians, and here, midway between Beauvais and Rouen, is Gournay, where Kyriel and the Lord Huntingdon lie with a great force of English. Do you comprehend? We must first take Clermont ere we can ride to rescue the Maid at Rouen!"

"The King should help us," I said. "For what is the army that has delivered Compiegne but a set of private bands, under this gentleman's flag or that, some with Boussac, some with Xaintrailles, some with a dozen others, and victuals are hard to come by."

"Ay, many a peaceful man sits by the fire and tells how great captains should have done this, and marched there, never thinking that men fight on their bellies. And the King should help us, and march with D'Alencon through Normandy from the south, while our companies take Clermont if we may, and drive back the English and Burgundians. But you know the King, and men say that the Archbishop of Reims openly declares that the Maid is rightly punished for her pride. He has set up a mad shepherd-boy to take her place, Heaven help him! who can fight as well as that stone can swim," and he dropped a loose stone over the bridge into the water.

"Whoever stays at home, we take the field," I said; "let us seek counsel of Xaintrailles."

We rose and went to the Jacobins, where Xaintrailles was lodged, and there found him at his dejeuner.

He was a tall young knight, straight as a lance, lean as a greyhound; for all his days his sword had won his meat; and he was hardy, keen, and bright, with eyes of steel in a scarred face, and his brow was already worn bald with the helmet. When he walked his legs somewhat straggled apart, by reason of his much riding.

Xaintrailles received us in the best manner, we telling him that we had ridden with the Maid, that I was of her own household, and that to save her we were willing to go far, and well knew that under no banner could we be so forward as under his.

"I would all my company were as honest as I take you twain to be," he said, "and I gladly receive you under my colours with any men you can bring."

"Messire, I have a handful of horse of the Maid's company," said Barthelemy, hardily; "but when do we march, for to-day is better than to-morrow."

"As soon as may be," said the knight; "the Marechal de Boussac leads us against Clermont. That town we cannot leave behind us when we set forth from Beauvais. But, with these great bombards, which we have won from the Burgundians, we may have reason of Clermont, and then," clapping his hands together, and looking up, "then for Rouen! We shall burst the cage and free the bird, God willing!"

He stood like one in prayer, crossing himself, and our hearts turned to him in loyalty.

"If but the King will send a force to join hands with La Hire in Louviers, the English shall have news of you, Messire!" I made bold to say.

"Ay, if!" quoth Xaintrailles, and his face grew darker, "but we must make good speedy for the midwinter draws nigh."

Therewith we left him, and, in few days, were marching on Clermont, dragging with long trains of horses the great bombards of the Burgundians.

To our summons Messire de Crevecoeur answered knightly, that Clermont he would hold till death or rescue, so we set to battering his house about his ears. But, alas! after four days a sentinel of ours saw, too late, an English knight with nine men slip through the vines, under cover of darkness, and win a postern gate in the town wall. Soon we heard a joy-fire of guns within Clermont town, and foreboded the worst. At midnight came a peasant to Xaintrailles, with tidings that a rescue was riding to Clermont, and next morning it was boots and saddles and away, so hastily that we left behind us the great bombards of the Burgundians. On this they made much mirth; but they laugh best who laugh last, as shall he seen.

And the cause of our going was that the Earl of Huntingdon had ridden out of Gournay, in Normandy, with a great force of English, to deliver Clermont. Against foes within the town and foes without the town the captains judged that we were of no avail. So we departed, heavy at heart. Now the companies scattered, and Barthelemy and I, sorry enough, rode behind Xaintrailles, due north to Guermigny, whence we threatened Amiens.

At Guermigny, then, for a short season, lay Xaintrailles, gathering all the force he might along the Picardy marches, for the Duke of Burgundy was in Peronne, full of wrath and sorrow, so many evils had befallen him. For ourselves, we were in no gentler temper, having lost our hope of pushing on to Rouen.

I was glad, therefore, when Xaintrailles himself rode one day to the door of our lodging in Guermigny, strode clanging into our chamber, and asked if we were alone? We telling him that none was within ear-shot, he sat him down on the table, playing with his dagger hilt, and, with his hawk's eye on Barthelemy, asked, "You know this land well?"

"I have ridden over it, in war or peace, since I was a boy."

"How far to Lihons?"

"A matter of two leagues."

"What manner of country lies between?"

"Chiefly plain, rude and untilled, because of the distresses of these times. There is much heath and long grasses, a great country for hares."

"Know you any covert nigh the road?"

"There runs a brook that the road crosses by a bridge,

midway between Guermigny and Lihons. The banks are steep, and well wooded with such trees and undergrowth as love water."

"You can guide me thither?"

"There is no missing the road."

"God could not have made this land better for me, if He had asked my counsel," said Xaintrailles. "You can keep your own?"

"Nom Dieu, yea!" said Barthelemy.

"And your Scots friend I can trust. A good-day to you, and thanks many."

Thereupon he went forth.

"What has he in his mind?" I asked Barthelemy.

"Belike an ambush. The Duke of Burgundy lies at Peronne, and has mustered a great force. Lihons is midway between us and Peronne, and is in the hands of Burgundy. I deem Xaintrailles has tidings that they intend to ride from Peronne to Lihons to-night, and thence make early onfall on us to-morrow. Being heavy-pated men of war, and bemused with their strong wine, they know not, belike, that we have more with us than the small garrison of Guermigny. And we are to await them on the road, I doubt not. You shall see men that wear your cross of St. Andrew, but not of your colour."

I shame not to say that of bushments in the cold dawn I had seen as much as I had stomach for, under Paris. But if any captain was wary in war, and knew how to discover whatso-ever his enemy designed, that captain was Xaintrailles. None

Andrew Lang

the less I hoped in my heart that his secret tidings of the Burgundian onfall had not come through a priest, and namely a cordelier.

Dawn found us mounted, and riding at a foot's-pace through the great plain which lies rough and untilled between Guermigny and Lihons. All grey and still it was, save for a cock crowing from a farmstead here and there on the wide wold, broken only by a line of trees that ran across the way.

Under these trees, which were mainly poplars and thick undergrowth of alders about the steep banks of a little brook, we were halted, and here took cover, our men lying down.

"Let no man stir, or speak, save when I speak to him, whatever befalls, on peril of his life," said Xaintrailles, when we were all disposed in hiding. Then touching me on the shoulder that I should rise, he said—

"You are young enough to climb a tree; are your eyes good?"

"I commonly was the first that saw the hare in her form, when we went coursing at home, sir."

"Then up this tree with you! keep outlook along the road, and hide yourself as best you may in the boughs. Throw this russet cloak over your harness." It was shrewdly chill in the grey November morning, a hoarfrost lying white on the fields. I took the cloak gladly and bestowed myself in the tree, so that I had a wide view down Lihons way, whence we expected our enemies, the road running plain to see for leagues, like a ribbon, when once the low sun had scattered the mists. It was a long watch, and a weary, my hands being half frozen in my steel gauntlets. Many of our men slept; if ever a wayfarer crossed the bridge hard by he was stopped, gagged, and trussed in a rope's end. But wayfarers were few, and all were wandering afoot. I was sorry for two lasses, who crossed on some business of their farm, but there was no remedy.

These diversions passed the time till nigh noon, when I whispered to Xaintrailles that I saw clouds of dust (the roads being very dry) a league away. He sent Barthelemy and another to waken any that slept, and bade all be ready at a word.

Now there came shouts on the wind, cries of venerie, loud laughter, and snatches of songs.

And now, up in my perch, I myself broke into a laugh at that I saw.

"Silence, fool!" whispered Xaintrailles. "Why laugh you, in the name of Behemoth?"

"The Burgundians are hunting hares," I whispered; "they are riding all disorderly, some on the road, some here and there about the plain. One man has no lance, another is unhelmeted, many have left their harness behind with the baggage!" Even as I spoke rose up a great hunting cry, and a point of the chase was blown on a trumpet. The foremost Burgundians were spurring like madmen after some beast, throwing at it with their lances, and soon I saw a fox making our way for its very life.

"To horse," cried Xaintrailles, and, leaving thirty men to hold the bridge, the whole of our company, with spears in rest, drove down on these hare-hunters of Burgundy.

Two hundred picked men in all, fully armed, were we, and we scattered the foremost riders as they had scattered the hares. Saddles were emptied, archers were cut down or speared ere they could draw bows, the Burgundians were spurring for their lives, many cried mercy, and were taken to ransom, of whom I had my share, as I shall tell.

But a few men made a right good end. Thomas Kyriel, a knight of England, stood to his banner, his archers rallied about it, with three or four knights of Burgundy. There, unhelmeted for the most part, they chose the way of honour, but they were of no avail where so many lances were levelled and so many swords were hewing at so few. There was a great slaughter, but Geoffrey de Thoisy, nephew to the Bishop of Tournay, plucked from danger fortune, for he so bore him that he being fully armed we took him for Messire Antoine de Vienne, a very good knight. For his courage we spared him, but Antoine, being unhelmeted and unknown, was smitten on the head by Barthelemy Barrette, with a blow of a casse-tete.

For this Barthelemy made much sorrow, not only that so good a knight was slain, but that he had lost a great ransom, whereby he should have been a rich man. Yet such is the fortune of war! Which that day was strangely seen; for a knight having yielded to me because his horse threw him, and he lost for a moment all sense with the fall and found my boot on his neck when he came to himself, who should he be but Messire Robert Heron, the same whom I took at Orleans!

Who, when he knew me, took off his salade for greater ease, and, sitting down on a rock by the way, swore as never I heard man swear, French, English, Spaniard, or Scot; and at length laughed, and said it was fortune of war, and so was content. This skirmish being thus ended, we returned, blithe and rich men every one of us, what with prisoners, horses, arms, and all manner of treasure taken with the baggage. That night we slept little in Guermigny, but feasted and drank deep. For my own part, I know not well where I did sleep, or how I won to what bed, which shames me some deal after all these years.

On the morrow we left Guermigny to the garrison of the place for their ill-fortune, and rode back towards Compiegne.

And this was the sport that the Burgundians had in hare-hunting.

This Battle of the Hares was the merriest passage of arms for our party, and bourdes were made on it, and songs sung, as by the English on that other Battle of the Herrings. Now, moreover, I might be called rich, what with ransoms, what with my share of the plunder in horses, rings, chains of gold, jewels, silver dishes, and rich cloths, out of the baggage of the enemy. Verily lack of wealth could no more sunder Elliot and me! For Pothon was as open of hand as he was high of heart, and was no greedy captain, wherefore men followed him the more gladly.

CHAPTER XXIX

SHOWETH HOW VERY NOBLE
WAS THE DUKE OF BURGUNDY

All this was well, but we were no nearer Rouen, and the freeing of the Maid, on this twentieth of November, than we had been when the siege of Compiegne broke up, on the twenty-sixth of October.

The Duke of Burgundy, we learned, was like a man mad when he heard of the Battle of the Hares. Nothing would serve him that day but to lead all his host to Guermigny from Peronne, whence he would have got little comfort of vengeance, for we were in a place of safety. But Jean de Luxembourg told him that he must not venture his nobility among routiers like us, wherein he pleased the Duke, but spoke foolishly. For no man, be he duke or prince, can be of better blood than we of the House of Rothes, not to speak of Xaintrailles and many other gentlemen of our company.

The Duke, then, put not his noble person in any jeopardy, but, more wisely, he sent messengers after my Lord of Huntingdon that he should bring up the English to aid the Burgundian hare-hunters. But Huntingdon had departed to Rouen, where then lay Henry, King of England, a boy on whom and on whose House God has avenged the Maid with terrible judgments, and will yet the more avenge her, blessed be His name!

The Duke of Burgundy comforted himself after his kind, for when he did pluck up heart to go against Guermigny, he, finding us departed, sacked the place, and razed it to the very ground, and so withdrew to Roye, and there waited for what help England would send him. Now Roye is some sixteen leagues due north of Compiegne.

So the days went by, for Messire Lefebvre Saint-Remy, the pursuivant, was hunting for my Lord of Huntingdon, all up and down Normandy, and at last came to Rouen, and to the presence of the Duke of Bedford, the uncle of the English King. All this I myself heard from Messire Saint-Remy, who is still a pursuivant, and a learned man, and a maker of books.

Bedford then, who was busy hounding that devil, Cauchon, sometime Bishop of Beauvais, against the Maid, sent the Comte de Perche and Messire Loys Robsart, to bid the Duke of Burgundy be of what courage he might, for succour of England he should have. Wherein Bedford was no true prophet.

Of all this we, in Compiegne, knew so much as that it was wiser to strike the Duke at Roye, before he could add English talbots to his Burgundian harriers. Therefore all the captains of companies, as Boussac, Xaintrailles, Alain Giron, Amadee de Vignolles, and Loys de Naucourt, mustered their several companies, to the number of some five thousand men-at-arms. We had news of six hundred English marching to join the Duke, and on them we fell at Couty, hard by Amiens, and there slew Loys Robsart, a good knight, of the Order of the Garter, and drove the English that fled into the castle of Couty, and we took all their horses, leaving them shamed, for they kept no guard.

Thence we rode to within a league of Roye, and thence sent a herald, in all due form, to challenge the Duke to open battle for his honour's sake. This we did, because we had no store of victual, and must fight or ride home.

The Duke received the herald, and made as if he would hear him as beseems a gentleman under challenge. But his wise counsellors forbade him, because he was so noble.

We were but "routiers," they said, and had no Prince in all our company; so we must even tarry till the morrow, and then the Duke would fight. In truth he expected the English, who were footing it to Castle Couty.

I stood by Xaintrailles when the pursuivant bore back this message.

Pothon spat on the ground.

"Shall we be more noble to-morrow than to-day, or to-morrow can this huxter of maids, the Duke, be less noble than he is, every day that he soils knighthood?"

Thereon he sent the herald back, to say that the Duke should have battle at his gates if he gave no better answer, for that wait for his pleasure we could not, for want of victuals.

And so we drew half a league nearer to Roye.

The Duke sent back our herald with word that of victuals he would give us half his own store; for he had read, as I deem, the romance of Richard Lion-Heart, another manner of man than himself. We said nought to this, not choosing to dine in such high company, but rode up under the walls of Roye, defying the Duke with open ribaldry, such as no manant could bear but he would take cudgel in hand to defend his honour. Our intent was, if the Duke accepted battle, to fight with none but him, if perchance we might take him, and hold him as hostage for the Maid's life.

Howbeit, so very noble was the Duke this day, that he did not put lance in rest (as belike he would have done on the morrow), but, drawing up his men on foot, behind certain mosses and marshes, all in firm array, he kept himself coy behind them, and not too far from the gate of Roye.

To cross these mosses and marshes was beyond our cunning, nor could we fast all that night, and see if the Duke would feel himself less noble, and more warlike, on the morrow.

So, with curses and cries of shame, we turned bridle, and, for that we could not hold together, being in lack of meat, the companies broke up, and went each to his own hold.

I have heard Messire Georges Chastellain tell, in times that were still to come, how fiercely the Duke of Burgundy bore him in council that night, after that we had all gone, and how he blamed his people who would not let him fight. But, after he had well supped, he even let this adventure slip by, as being ordained by the will of God, who, doubtless, holds in very high honour men of birth princely, and such, above all, as let sell young virgins to the tormentors. And thus ended our hope to save the Maid by taking captive the Duke of Burgundy.

CHAPTER XXX

HOW NORMAN LESLIE TOOK
SERVICE WITH THE ENGLISH

"What make we now?" I asked of Barthelemy Barrette, one day, after the companies had scattered, as I have said, and we had gone back into Compiegne. "What stroke may France now strike for the Maid?" He hung his head and plucked at his beard, ere he spoke.

"To be as plain with you as my heart is with myself, Norman," he answered at last, "deliverance, or hope of deliverance, see I none. The English have the bird in the cage, and Rouen is not a strength that can be taken by sudden onslaught. And, were it so, where is our force, in midwinter? I rather put my faith, that can scarce move mountains, in some subtle means, if any man might devise them."

"We cannot sit idle here," I said. "And for three long months there will be no moving of armies in open field."

"And in three months these dogs of false French doctors of Paris will have tried and condemned the Maid. For my part, I ride with my handful of spears to the Loire. Perchance there is yet some hope in the King."

"Then I ride with you, granted your goodwill, for I must needs to Tours, and I have overmuch treasure in my wallet to ride alone."

Indeed, I was now a rich man, more by luck than by valour; and though I said nought of it, I hoped that my long wooing might now come to a happy end.

Barthelemy clasped hands gladly on that offer; and not to make a long tale, he and his men were my escort to Tours, and thence he rode to Sully to see the King.

I had no heart for glad surprises this time, but having sent on a letter to my master, by a King's messenger who rode from Compiegne ere we did, I was expected and welcomed by Elliot and my master, with all the joy that might be, after our long severance. And in my master's hands I laid my newly gotten gear, and heard privily from him that, with his goodwill, I and his daughter might wed so soon as she would.

"For she is pining with grief, and prayer, and fasting, and marriage is the best remede for such maladies."

Of this grace I was right glad; yet Christmas went by and I dared not speak, for Elliot seemed set on far other things than mirth, and was ever and early in the churches, above all when service and prayer were offered up for the Maid. She was very willing to hear all the tale of the long siege, and her face, that was thin and wan, unlike her bright countenance of old, flushed scarlet when she heard how we had bearded and shamed the noble Duke of Burgundy, and what words Xaintrailles had spoken concerning his nobleness.

"There is one true knight left in France!" she said, and fell silent again.

Then, we being alone in the chamber, I tried to take her hand, but she drew it away.

"My dear love," she said, "I know all that is in your heart, and all my love that is in mine you know well. But in mine there is no care for happiness and joy, and to speak as plain as a maiden may, I have now no will to marry. While the Sister of the Saints lies in duresse, or if she be unjustly slain, I have set up my rest to abide unwed, for ever, as the Bride of Heaven. And, if the last evil befall her, as well I deem it must, I shall withdraw me from the world into the sisterhood of the Clarisses."

Had the great mid-beam of the roof fallen and smitten me, I could not have been stricken more dumb and dead. My face showed what was in my mind belike, for, looking fearfully and tenderly on me, she took my hand between hers and cherished it.

"My love," I said at last, "you see in what case I am, that can scarce speak for sorrow, after all I have ventured, and laboured, and won, for you and for the Maid."

"And I," she answered, "being but a girl, can venture and give nothing but my poor prayers; and if she now perish, then I must pray the more continually for the good rest of her soul, and the forgiveness of her enemies and false friends."

"Sure, she hath already the certain promise of Paradise, and even in this world her life is with the Saints. And if men slay her body, we need her prayers more than she needs ours."

But Elliot said no word, being very wilful.

"Consider what manner of friend the Maid is," I said, "who desires nothing but joy and happy life to all whom she loves, as she loves you. Verily, I am right well assured that, could she see us in this hour, she would bid you be happy with me, and not choose penance for love of her."

"If she herself bids me do as you desire," said Elliot at last, "then I would not be disobedient to that Daughter of God."

Here I took some comfort, for now a thought came into my mind.

"But," said Elliot, "as we read of the rich man and Lazarus, between her and us is a great gulf fixed, and none may come from her to us, or from us to her."

"Elliot!" I said, "if either the Maid be delivered, or if she sends you sure and certain tidings under her own hand that she wills you to put off this humour, will you then be persuaded, and make no more delay!"

"Indeed, if either of these miracles befall, or both, right gladly will I obey both you and her. But now her Saints, methinks, have left her, wearied by the wickedness of France."

"I ask no more," I answered, "for, Elliot, either the Maid shall be free, or she shall send you this command, or you shall see my face no more."

My purpose was now clear before me, even as I executed it, as shall be seen.

"Indeed, if my vow must be kept, never may I again behold you; for oh! my love, my heart would surely break in twain, being already weak with grief and fasting, and weary with prayer."

Whereon she laid her kind arms about my neck, and, despite my manhood, I wept no less than she.

For Holy Writ says well, that hope deferred maketh the heart sick; and mine was sick unto death.

Of my resolve I spoke no word more to Elliot, lest her counsel should change when she knew the jeopardy whereinto I was firmly minded to go. And to my master I said no more than that I was minded to ride to the Court, and for that end I turned into money a part of my treasure, for money I should need more than arms.

One matter in especial, which I deemed should stand me in the greatest stead, I purchased for gold of the pottinger at Tours, the same who had nursed me after my wound. This draught I bestowed in a silver phial, graven with strange signs, and I kept it ever close and secret, for it was my chief mainstay.

Secretly as I wrought, yet I deem that my master had some understanding of what was in my mind, though I told him nothing of the words between me and Elliot. For I was in no way without hope that, when the bitterness of her grief was overpast, Elliot might change her counsel. And again, I would not have him devise and dispute with her, as now, whereby I very well knew that she would be but the more unhappy, and the more set on taking her own wilful way. I therefore said no more than that it behoved me to see such captains as were about the King.

Thereafter I bade them farewell, nor am I disposed to write concerning what passed at the parting of Elliot and me. For thrice ere now I had left her to pass into the mouth of war, but now I went into other peril, and with fainter hope.

I did indeed ride to the Court, which was at Sully, and there I met, as I desired, Barthelemy Barrette. He greeted me well, and was richly clad, and prosperous to behold. But it gave me greater joy that he spoke of some secret enterprise which should shortly be put in hand, when the spring came.

"For I have good intelligence," he said, "that the Bastard of Orleans will ride privily to Louviers with men-at-arms. Now Louviers, where La Hire lies in garrison, is but seven leagues from Rouen town, and what secret enterprise can he purpose there, save to break the cage and set free the bird?"

In this hope I tarried long, intending to ride with the spears of Barthelemy, and placing my trust on two knights so good and skilled in war as La Hire and the Bastard, the Maid's old companions in fight.

But the days waxed long, and it was March the thirteenth ere we rode north, and already the doctors had begun to entrap the Maid with their questions, whereof there could be but one end.

Without adventure very notable, riding much at night, through forests and byways, we came to Louviers, where they received us joyfully. For it was very well known that the English were minded to besiege this town, that braved them so near their gates at Rouen, and that they only held back till they had slain the Maid. While she lived they dared not stir against us, knowing well that their men feared to follow their flag.

Now, indeed, I was in good hope, but alas! there were long counsels of the captains, there was much harrying of Normandy, and some outlying bands of English were trapped, and prisoners were taken. But of an assault on Rouen we heard no word, and, indeed, the adventure was desperate, though, for the honour of France, I marvel yet that it was not put to the touch.

"There is nought to be done," Barthelemy said to me; "I cannot take Rouen with a handful of spears, and the captains will not stir."

"Then," said I, "farewell, for under the lilies I fight never again. One chance remains, and I go to prove it."

"Man, you are mad," he answered me. "What desperate peril are you minded to run?"

"I am minded to end this matter," I said. "My honour and my very life stand upon it. Ask me not why, and swear that you will keep this secret from all men, if you would do the last service to me, and to Her, whom we both love. I tell you that, help me or hinder me, I have no choice but this; yet so much I will say to you, that I put myself in this jeopardy for my honour and the honour of Scotland, and for my lady."

"The days are past for the old chivalry," he said; "but no more words. I swear by St. Ouen to keep your counsel, and if more I can do, without mere madness and risk out of all hope, I will do it."

"This you can do without risk. Let me have the accoutrements of one of the Englishmen who lie in ward, and let me ride with your band at daybreak to-morrow. It is easy to tell some feigned tale, when you ride back without me."

"You will not ride into Rouen in English guise? They will straightway hang you for a spy, and therein is little honour."

"My purpose is some deal subtler," I said, with a laugh, "but let me keep my own counsel."

"So be it," said he, "a wilful man must have his way. And now I drink to your better wisdom, and may you escape that rope on which your heart seems to be set!"

I grasped his hand on it, and by point of day we were riding out seawards. We made an onslaught on a village, burned a house or twain, and seized certain wains of hay, so, in the confusion, I slipped forward, and rode alone into a little wood. There I clad myself in English guise, having carried the gear in a wallet on my saddle-bow, and so pushed on, till at nightfall I came to a certain little fishing-village. There, under cover of the dark, I covenanted with a fisherman to set me across the Channel, I feigning to be a deserter who was fleeing from the English army, for fear of the Maid.

"I would well that I had to carry all the sort of you," said the boat-master, for I had offered him my horse, and a great reward in money, part down, and the other part to be paid when I set foot in England. Nor did he make any tarrying, but, taking his nets on board, as if he would be about his lawful business, set sail, with his two sons for a crew. The east wind served us to a miracle, and, after as fair a passage as might be, they landed me under cloud of night not far from the great port of Winchelsea.

That night I slept none, but walking fast and warily, under cover of a fog, I fetched a compass about, and ended by walking into the town of Rye by the road from the north. Here I went straight to the best inn of the place, and calling aloud for breakfast, I bade the drawer bring mine host to me instantly. For, at Louviers, we were so well served by spies, the country siding with us rather than with the English, that I knew how a company of the Earl of Warwick's men was looked for in Winchelsea to sail when they had a fair wind for Rouen.

Mine host came to me in a servile English fashion, and asked me what I would?

"First, a horse," said I, "for mine dropped dead last night, ten miles hence on the north road, in your marshes, God damn them, and you may see by my rusty spur and miry boot that I have walked far. Here," I cried, pulling off my boots, and flinging them down on the rushes of the floor, "bid one of your varlets clean them! Next, breakfast, and a pot of your ale; and then I shall see what manner of horses you keep, for I must needs ride to Winchelsea."

"You would join the men under the banner of Sir Thomas Grey of Falloden, I make no doubt?" he answered. "Your speech smacks of the Northern parts, and the good knight comes from no long way south of the border. His men rode through our town but few days agone."

"And me they left behind on the way," I answered, "so evil is my luck in horse-flesh. But for this blessed wind out of the east that hinders them, my honour were undone."

My tale was not too hard of belief, and before noon I was on my way to Winchelsea, a stout nag enough between my legs.

The first man-at-arms whom I met I hailed, bidding him lead me straight to Sir Thomas Grey of Falloden. "What, you would take service?" he asked, in a Cumberland burr that I knew well, for indeed it came ready enough on my own tongue.

"Yea, by St. Cuthbert," I answered, "for on the Marches nothing stirs; moreover, I have slain a man, and fled my own country."

With that he bade God damn his soul if I were not a good

fellow, and so led me straight to the lodgings of the knight under whose colours he served. To him I told the same tale, adding that I had heard late of his levying of his men, otherwise I had ridden to join him at his setting forth.

"You have seen war?" he asked.

"Only a Warden's raid or twain, on the moss-trooping Scots of Liddesdale. Branxholme I have seen in a blaze, and have faced fire at the Castle of the Hermitage."

"You speak the tongue of the Northern parts," he said; "are you noble?"

"A poor cousin of the Storeys of Netherby," I answered, which was true enough; and when he questioned me about my kin, I showed him that I knew every name and scutcheon of the line, my mother having instructed me in all such lore of her family. {38}

"And wherefore come you here alone, and in such plight?"

"By reason of a sword-stroke at Stainishawbank Fair," I answered boldly.

"Faith, then, I see no cause why, as your will is so good, you should not soon have your bellyful of sword-strokes. For, when once we have burned that limb of the devil, the Puzel" (for so the English call the Maid), "we shall shortly drive these forsworn dogs, the French, back beyond the Loire."

I felt my face reddening at these ill words, so I stooped, as if to clear my spur of mire.

"Shortly shall she taste the tar-barrel," I answered, whereat he swore and laughed; then, calling a clerk, bade him write my indenture, as is the English manner. Thus, thanks to my northern English tongue, for which I was sore beaten by the other boys when I was a boy myself, behold me a man-at-arms of King Henry, and so much of my enterprise was achieved.

I make no boast of valour, and indeed I greatly feared for my neck, both now and later. For my risk was that some one of the men-at-arms in Rouen, whither we were bound, should have seen my face either at Orleans, at Paris (where I was unhelmeted), or in the taking of the Bastille at Compiegne. Yet my visor was down, both at Orleans and Compiegne, and of those few who marked me in girl's gear in Paris none might chance to meet me at Rouen, or to remember me in changed garments. So I put a bold brow on it, for better might not be. None cursed the Puzel more loudly than I, and, without feigning, none longed so sorely as I for a fair wind to France, wherefore I was ever going about Winchelsea with my head in the air, gazing at the weather-cocks. And, as fortune would have it, the wind went about, and we on board, and with no long delay were at Rouen town.

CHAPTER XXXI

HOW NORMAN LESLIE SAW THE
MAID IN HER PRISON

On arriving in the town of Rouen, three things were my chief care, whereof the second helped me in the third. The first was to be lodged as near as I might to the castle, wherein the Maid lay, being chained (so fell was the cruelty of the English) to her bed. The next matter was to purvey me three horses of the fleetest. Here my fortune served me well, for the young esquires and pages would ever be riding races outside of the gates, they being in no fear of war, and the time till the Maid was burned hung heavy on their hands. I therefore, following the manner of the English Marchmen, thrust myself forward in these sports, and would change horses, giving money to boot, for any that outran my own. My money I spent with a very free hand, both in wagers and in feasting men-at-arms, so that I was taken to be a good fellow, and I willingly let many make their profit of me. In the end, I had three horses that, with a light rider in the saddle, could be caught by none in the whole garrison of Rouen.

Thirdly, I was most sedulous in all duty, and so won the favour of Sir Thomas Grey, the rather that he counted cousins with me, and reckoned that we were of some far-off kindred, wherein he spoke the truth. Thus, partly for our common blood, partly for that I was ever ready at call, and forward to do his will, and partly because none could carry a message swifter, or adventure further to spy out any bands of the French, he kept me close to him, and trusted me as his galloper. Nay, he gave me, on occasion, his signet, to open the town gates whensoever he would send me on any errand. Moreover, the man (noble by birth, but base by breeding) who had the chief charge and custody of the Maid, was the brother's son of Sir Thomas. He had to name John Grey, and was an esquire of the body of the English King, Henry, then a boy. This miscreant it was often my fortune to meet, at his uncle's table, and to hear his pitiless and cruel speech. Yet, making friends, as Scripture commands us, of the Mammon of unrighteousness, I set myself to win the affection of John Grey by laughing at his jests and doing him what service I might.

Once or twice I dropped to him a word of my great desire to see the famed Puzel, for the trials that had been held in open hall were now done in the dungeon, where only the bishop, the doctors of law, and the notaries might hear them. Her noble bearing, indeed, and wise answers (which were plainly put into her mouth by the Saints, for she was simple and ignorant) had gained men's hearts.

One day, they told me, an English lord had cried—"The brave lass, pity she is not English." For to the English all the rest of God's earth is as Nazareth, out of which can come no good thing. Thus none might see the Maid, and, once and again, I let fall a word in John Grey's ear concerning my desire to look on her in prison. I dared make no show of eagerness, though now the month of May had come, which was both her good and ill month. For in May she first went to Vaucouleurs and prophesied, in May she delivered Orleans, and in May she was taken at Compiegne. Wherefore

I deemed, as men will, that in May she should escape her prison, or in May should die. Moreover, on the first day of March they had asked her, mocking her—

"Shalt thou be delivered?"

And she had answered—

"Ask me on this day three months, and I shall declare it to you."

The English, knowing this, made all haste to end her ere May ended, wherefore I had the more occasion for speed.

Now, on a certain day, being May the eighth, the heart of John Grey was merry within him. He had well drunk, and I had let him win of me, at the dice, that one of my three horses which most he coveted.

He then struck me in friendly fashion on the back, and cried—

"An unlucky day for thee, and for England. This very day, two years agone, that limb of the devil drove us by her sorceries from before Orleans. But to-morrow—" and he laughed grossly in his beard. "Storey, you are a good fellow, though a fool at the dice."

"Faith, I have met my master," I said. "But the lesson you gave me was worth bay Salkeld," for so I had named my horse, after a great English house on the Border who dwell at the Castle of Corby.

"I will do thee a good turn," he said. "You crave to see this Puzel, ere they put on her the high witch's cap for her hellward journey."

"I should like it not ill," I said; "it were something to tell my grandchildren, when all France is English land."

"Then you shall see her, for this is your last chance to see her whole."

"What mean you, fair sir?" I asked, while my heart gave a turn in my body, and I put out my hand to a great tankard of wine.

"To-morrow the charity of the Church hath resolved that she shall be had into the torture-chamber."

I set my lips to the tankard, and drank long, to hide my face, and for that I was nigh swooning with a passion of fear and wrath.

"Thanks to St. George," I said, "the end is nigh!"

"The end of the tankard," quoth he, looking into it, "hath already come. You drink like a man of the Land Debatable."

Yet I was in such case that, though by custom I drink little, the great draught touched not my brain, and did but give me heart.

"You might challenge at skinking that great Danish knight who was with us under Orleans, Sir Andrew Haggard was his name, and his bearings were . . . " {39}

So he was running on, for he himself had drunk more than his share, when I brought him back to my matter.

"But as touching this Puzel, how may I have my view of her, that you graciously offered me?"

"My men change guard at curfew," he said; "five come out and five go in, and I shall bid them seek you here at your lodgings. So now, farewell, and your revenge with the dice you shall have when so you will."

"Nay, pardon me one moment: when relieve you the guard that enters at curfew?"

"An hour after point of day. But, now I bethink me, you scarce will care to pass all the night in the Puzel's company. Hast thou paper or parchment?"

I set paper and ink before him, who said—

"Nay, write yourself; I am no great clerk, yet I can sign and seal."

Therewith, at his wording, I set down an order to the Castle porter to let me forth as early in the night as I would. This pass he signed with his name, and sealed with his ring, bearing his arms.

"So I wish you joy of this tryst and bonne fortune," he said, and departed.

I had two hours before me ere curfew rang, and the time was more than I needed. Therefore I went first to the Church of St. Ouen, which is very great and fair, and there clean confessed me, and made my orisons that, if it were God's will, this enterprise might turn to His honour, and to the salvation of the Maid. And pitifully I besought Madame St. Catherine of Fierbois, that as she had delivered me, a sinner, she would deliver the Sister of the Saints.

Next I went back to my lodgings, and there bade the hostler to have my two best steeds saddled and bridled in stall, by point of day, for a council was being held that night in the Castle, and I and another of Sir Thomas's company might be sent early with a message to the Bishop of Avranches. This holy man, as then, was a cause of trouble and delay to the Regent and Pierre Cauchon, Bishop of Beauvais, because he was just, and fell not in with their treasons.

Next I clad myself in double raiment, doublet above doublet, and hose over hose, my doublets bearing the red cross of St. George. Over all I threw a great mantle, falling to the feet, as if I feared the night chills. Thereafter I made a fair copy of my own writing in the pass given to me by John Grey, and copied his signature also, and feigned his seal with a seal of clay, for it might chance that two passes proved better than one. Then I put in a little wallet hanging to my girdle the signet of Sir Thomas Grey, and the pass given to me by John Grey, also an inkhorn with pen and paper, and in my hand, secretly, I held that phial which I had bought of the apothecary in Tours. All my gold and jewels I hid about my body; I sharpened my sword and dagger, and then had no more to do but wait till curfew rang.

This was the weariest part of all; for what, I thought, if John Grey had forgotten his promise, the wine being about his wits. Therefore I walked hither and thither in my chamber, in much misdoubt; but at the chime of curfew I heard rude voices below, and a heavy step on the stairs. It was a man-at-arms of the basest sort, who, lurching with his shoulder against my door, came in, and said that he and his fellows waited my pleasure. Thereon I showed him the best countenance, and bade my host fill a pannier with meat and cakes and wine, to pass the hours in the prison merrily. I myself ran down into the host's cellar, and was very busy in tasting wine, for I would have the best. And in making my choice, while the host stooped over a cask to draw a fresh tankard, I poured all the drugs of my phial into a large pewter vessel with a lid, filled it with wine, and, tasting it, swore it would serve my turn. This flagon, such as we call a 'tappit hen' in my country, but far greater, I bore with me up the cellar stairs, and gave it to one of the guard, bidding him spill not a drop, or he should go thirsty.

The lourdaud, that was their captain, carried the pannier, and, laughing, we crossed the street and the moat, giving the word "Bedford." To the porter I showed my pass, telling him that, though I was loath to disturb him, I counted not to watch all night in the cell, wherefore I gave him a gold piece for the trouble he might have in letting me go forth at an hour untimely. Herewith he was well content, and so, passing the word to the sentinel at each post, we entered.

And now, indeed, my heart beat so that my body seemed to shake with hope and fear as I walked. At the door of the chamber wherein the Maid lay we met her guards coming forth, who cried roughly, bidding her good even, and to think well of what waited her, meaning the torments. They tumbled down the stairs laughing, while we went in, and I last. It was a dark vaulted chamber with one window near the roof, narrow and heavily barred. In the recess by the window was a brazier burning, and casting as much shadow as light by reason of the smoke. Here also was a rude table, stained with foul circles of pot-rims, and there were five or six stools. On a weighty oaken bed lay one in man's raiment, black in hue, her face downwards, and her arms spread over her neck. It could scarce be that she slept, but she lay like one dead, only shuddering when the lourdaud, the captain of the guard, smote her on the shoulder, asking, in English, how she did?

"Here she is, sir, surly as ever, and poor company for Christian men. See you how cunningly all her limbs are gyved, and chained to the iron bolts of the bed? What would my lady Jeanne give me for this little master-key?"

Here he showed a slender key, hung on a steel chain about his neck.

"Never a saint of the three, Michael, Margaret, and Catherine, can take this from me; nay, nor the devils who wear their forms."

"Have you seen this fair company of hers?" I whispered in English, crossing myself.

"No more than she saw the white lady that goes with that other witch, Catherine of La Rochelle. But, sir, she is sullen; it is her manner. With your good leave, shall we sup?"

This was my own desire, so putting the pannier on the table, I carved the meat with my dagger, and poured out the wine in cups, and they fell to, being hungry, as Englishmen are at all times. They roared over their meat, eating like wolves and drinking like fishes, and one would sing a lewd song, and the others strike in with the over-word, but drinking was their main avail.

"This is better stuff," says the lourdaud, "than our English ale. Faith, 'tis strong, my lads! Wake up, Jenkin; wake up, Hal," and then he roared a snatch, but stopped, looking drowsily about him.

O brothers in Christ, who hear this tale, remember ye that, for now four months and more, the cleanest soul in Christenty, and the chastest lady, and of manners the noblest, had endured this company by night and by day!

"Nay, wake up," I cried; "ye are dull revellers; what say ye to the dice?"

Therewith I set out my tablier and the dice. Then I filled up the cup afresh, pretending to drink, and laid on the foul table a great shining heap of gold. Their dull eyes shone like the metal when I said—

"Myself will be judge and umpire; play ye, honest fellows, for I crave no gains from you. Only, a cup for luck!"

They camped at the table, all the five of them, and some while their greed kept them wakeful, and they called the mains, but their drought kept them drinking. And, one by one, their heads fell heavy on the table, or they sprawled on their stools, and so sank on to the floor, so potent were the poppy and mandragora of the leech in Tours.

At last they were all sound on sleep, one man's hand yet clutching a pile of my gold that now and again would slip forth and jingle on the stone floor.

Now all this time she had never stirred, but lay as she had lain, her face downwards, her arms above her neck.

Stealthily I took the chain and the key from about the neck of the sleeping lourdaud, and then drew near her on tiptoe.

I listened, and, from her breathing, I believe that she slept, as extreme labour and weariness and sorrow do sometimes bring their own remede.

Then a thought came into my mind, how I should best awake her, and stooping, I said in her ear—

"Fille De!"

Instantly she turned about, and, sitting up, folded her hands as one in prayer, deeming, belike, that she was aroused by the voices of her Saints. I kneeled down beside the bed, and whispered—"Madame, Jeanne, look on my face!"

She gazed on me, and now I saw her brave face, weary and thin and white, and, greater than of old, the great grey eyes.

"I said once," came her sweet voice, "that thou alone shouldst stand by me when all had forsaken me. Fair Saints, do I dream but a dream?"

"Nay, Madame," I said, "thou wakest and dost not dream. One has sent me who loves thee, even my lady Elliot; and now listen, for the time is short. See, here I have the master-key, and when I have unlocked thy bonds . . . "

"Thou hast not slain these men?" she asked. "That were deadly sin."

"Nay, they do but sleep, and will waken belike ere the fresh guard comes, wherefore we must make haste."

"When I have freed thee, do on thy body, above thy raiment, this doublet of mine, for it carries the cross of England, and, I being of little stature, you may well pass for me. Moreover, this cloak and its hood, which I wore when I came in, will cover thee. Then, when thou goest forth give the word 'Bedford' to the sentinels; and, to the porter in the gate, show this written pass of John Grey's. He knows it already, having seen it this night. Next, when thou art without the castle, fare to the hostelry called 'The Rose and Apple,' which is nearest the castle gate, and so straight into the stable, where stand two steeds, saddled and bridled. Choose the black, he is the swifter. If the hostler be awake, he expects me, and will take thee for me; mount, with no word, and ride to the eastern port. There show to the gate ward this signet of Sir Thomas Grey, and he will up with portcullis and down with drawbridge, for he has often done no less for me and that signet.

"Then, Madame, ride for Louviers, and you shall break your fast with the Bastard and La Hire." Her white face changed to red, like the morning light, as on that day at Orleans, before she took Les Tourelles.

Then the flush faded, and she grew ashen pale, while she said—

"But thou, how shalt thou get forth?"

"Madame," I said, "fear not for me. I will follow after thee, and shame the sleepy porter to believe that he has dreamed a dream. And I have written this other pass, on seeing which he will needs credit me, being adrowse, and, moreover, I will pay him well. And I shall be at the stable as soon almost as thou, and I have told the hostler that belike I shall ride with a friend, carrying a message to the Bishop of Avranches. For I have beguiled the English to believe me of their party, as Madame Judith wrought to the tyrant Holofernes."

"Nay," she answered simply, "this may not be. Even if the porter were to be bought or beguiled, thou couldst not pass the sentinels. It may not be."

"The sentinels, belike, are sleeping, or wellnigh sleeping, and I have a dagger. O Madame! for the sake of the fortune of France, and the honour of the King"—for this, I knew, was my surest hope—"delay not, nor reck at all of me. I have but one life, and it is thine freely."

"They will burn thee, or slay thee with other torments."

"Not so," I said; "I shall not be taken alive."

"That were deadly sin," she answered. "I shall not go and leave thee to die for me. Then were my honour lost, and I could not endure to live. Entreat me not, for I will not go forth, as now. Nay more, I tell thee as I have told my judges, that which the Saints have spoken to me. 'Bear this thy martyrdom gently,' they say, 'tu t'en viendras en royaume du Paradis.' Moreover, this I know, that I am to be delivered with great victory!"

Here she clasped her hands, looking upwards, and her face was as the face of an angel.

"Fair victory it were to leave thee in my place, and so make liars of my brethren of Paradise."

Then, alas! I knew that I was of no more avail to move her; yet one last art I tried.

"Madame," I said, "I have prayed you in the name of the fortune of France, and the honour of the King, which is tarnished for ever if you escape not."

"I shall be delivered," she answered.

"I pray you in the dear name of your lady mother, Madame du Lys."

"I shall be delivered," she said, "and with great victory!"

"Now I pray thee in my own name, and in that of thy first friend, my lady. She has made a vow to give her virginity to Heaven unless either thou art set free, or she have tidings from thee that thou willest her to wed me, without whom I have no desire to live, but far rather this very night to perish. For I am clean confessed, within these six hours, knowing that I was like to be in some jeopardy."

"Then," she said, smiling sweetly, and signing that I should take her hand—"Then live, Norman Leslie, for this is to me an easy thing and a joyous. Thou art a clerk, hast thou wherewithal to write?"

"Yes, Madame, here in my wallet."

"Then write as I tell thee:—

"JHESU MARIA"

"'I, Jehanne la Pucelle, send from prison here in Rouen my tidings of love to Elliot Hume, my first friend among women, and bid her, for my sake, wed him who loves her, Norman Leslie of Pitcullo, my faithful servant, praying that all happiness may go with them. In witness whereto, my hand being guided to write, I set my name, Jehanne la Pucelle, this ninth day of May, in the year Fourteen hundred and thirty-one.'

"So guide my hand," she said, taking the pen from my fingers; and thus guided, while my tears fell on her hand, she wrote JEHANNE LA PUCELLE.

"Now," quoth she, smiling as of old, "we must seal this missive. Cut off one lock of my hair with your dagger, for my last gift to my first friend, and make the seal all orderly."

I did as she bade, and, bringing a lighted stick from the brazier, I melted wax. Then, when it was smooth, she laid on it two hairs from the little sundered lock (as was sometimes her custom), and bade me seal with my own signet, and put the brief in my wallet.

"Now, all is done," she said.

"Nay, nay," I said, "to die for thee is more to me than to live in love. Ah, nay, go forth, I beseech thee!"

"With victory shall I go forth, and now I lay my last commands on the last of all my servants. If in aught I have ever offended thee, in word or deed, forgive me!"

I could but bow my head, for I was weeping, though her eyes were dry.

"And so, farewell," she said—

"As thou art leal and true, begone; it is my order, and make no tarrying. To-morrow I have much to do, and needs must I sleep while these men are quiet. Say to thy lady that I love her dearly, and bid her hope, as I also hope. Farewell!"

She moved her thin hand, which I kissed, kneeling.

Again she said "Farewell," and turned her back on me as if she would sleep.

Then I hung the chain and key again on the neck of the lourdaud; I put some of the fallen coins in the men's pouches, but bestowed the dice and tablier in my wallet. I opened the door, and went forth, not looking back; and so from the castle, showing my pass, and giving the porter another coin. Then I went home, in the sweet dawn of May, and casting myself on my bed, I wept bitterly, for to-day she should be tormented.

* * * * *

Of the rest I have no mind to tell (though they had not the heart to torture the Maid), for it puts me out of charity with a people who have a name to be Christians, and it is my desire, if I may, to forgive all men before I die.

At Rouen I endured to abide, even until the day of unjust doom, and my reason was that I ever hoped for some miracle, even as her Saints had promised. But it was their will that she should be made perfect through suffering, and being set free through the gate of fire, should win her victory over unfaith and mortal fear. Wherefore I stood afar off at the end, seeing nothing of what befell; yet I clearly heard, as did all men there, the last word of her sweet voice, and the cry of JHESUS!

Then I passed through the streets where men and women, and the very English, were weeping, and, saddling my swiftest horse, I rode to the east port. When the gate had closed behind me, I turned, and, lifting my hand, I tore the cross of St. George from my doublet.

"Dogs!" I cried, "ye have burned a Saint! A curse on cruel English and coward French! St Andrew for Scotland!" The shafts and bolts hailed past me as I wheeled about; there was mounting of steeds, and a clatter of hoofs behind me, but the sound died away ere I rode into Louviers.

There I told them the tale which was their shame, and so betook me to Tours, and to my lady.

CHAPTER XXXII

THE END OF THIS CHRONICLE

It serves not to speak of my later fortunes, being those of a private man, nor have I the heart to recall old sorrows. We were wedded when Elliot's grief had in some sort abated, and for one year we were happier than God has willed that sinful men should long be in this world. Then that befell which has befallen many. I may not write of it: suffice it that God took from me both her and her child. Then, after certain weeks and days of which I am blessed enough to keep little memory, I forswore arms, and served in the household of the Lady Margaret of Scotland, who married the Dauphin on an unhappy day. I have known much of Courts and of the learned, I have seen the wicked man exalted, and Brother Thomas Noiroufle in great honour with Charles VII. King of France, and offering before him, with his murderous hands, the blessed sacrifice of the Mass.

The death of the Lady Margaret, slain by lying tongues, and the sudden sight of that evil man, Brother Thomas, raised to power and place, drove me from France, and I was certain years with the King's ambassadors at the Courts of Italy. There I heard how the Holy Inquisition had reversed that false judgment of the English and false French at Rouen, which made me some joy. And then, finding old age come upon me, I withdrew to my own country, where I have lived in religion, somewhile in the Abbey of Dunfermline, and this year gone in our cell of Pluscardine, where I now write, and where I hope to die and be buried.

Here ends my tale, in my Latin Chronicle left untold, of how a Scots Monk was with the Maid both in her victories and recoveries of towns, and even till her death.

For myself, I now grow old, and the earthly time to come is short, and there remaineth a rest for all souls Christian. Miscreants I have heard of, men misbelieving and heretics, who deny that the spirit abides after the death of the body, for in the long years, say they, the spirit with the flesh wanes, and at last dies with the bodily death. Wherein they not only make Holy Church a liar, but are visibly confounded by this truth which I know and feel, namely, that while my flesh wastes hourly towards old age, and of many things my memory is weakened, yet of that day in Chinon I mind me as clearly, and see my love as well, and hear her sweet voice as plain, as if she had but now left the room.

Herein my memory does not fail, nor does love faint, growing stronger with the years, like the stream as it races to the fall. Wherefore, being more strong than Time, Love shall be more strong than Death. The river of my life speeds yearly swifter, the years like months go by, the months like weeks, the weeks like days. Even so fleet on, O Time, till I rest beside her feet! Nay, never, being young, did I more desire my love's presence when we were apart than to-day I desire it, the memory of her filling all my heart as fragrance of flowers fills a room, till it seems as if she were not far away, but near me, as I write of her. And, foolish that I am! I look up as if I might see her by my side. I know not if this be so with all men, for, indeed, I have asked none, nor spoken to any of the matter save in confession. For I have loved this once, and no more; wherefore I deem me happier than most, and more certain of a good end to my love, where the blessed dwell in the Rose of Paradise, beholding the Beatific Vision.

To this end I implore the prayers of all Christian souls who read this book, and of all the Saints, and of that Sister of the Saints whom, while I might, I served in my degree.

VENERABILIS JOHANNA

ORA PRO NOBIS

APPENDIX A

NORMAN'S MIRACLE

(See "Livre des Miracles de Madame Sainte Katherine de Fierboys". MSS. Bib. Nat. 7335, fol. lxxxiv.)

Le xvi jour du moys de janvier, l'an mil cccc. xxx., vint en la chapelle de ceans Norman Leslie de Pytquhoulle, escoth, escuyer de la compagnie de Hugues Cande, capitaine. {40} Lequel dist et afferma par serment estre vray le miracle cy apres declaire. C'est assavoir que le dit Leslie fut prins des Anglois a Paris le jour de la Nativite de Nostre Dame de l'an dernier passe. Lequel Norman Leslie avoit entre dans la ville de Paris avec c. Escossoys en guise d'Angloys, lesqueuls Escossoys furent prins des Angloys, et ledit Norman fut mis en fers et en ceps. Et estoit l'intention de ceux qui l'avoient pris de le faire lendemain ardre, parce qu'il portoit robe de femme par maniere de ruse de guerre.

Si s'avint que ledit Norman se voua a Madame Sainte Katherine, qu'il luy pleust prier Dieu qu'il le voulsist delivrer de la prison ou il estoit; et incontinent qu'il pourroit estre dehors, il yroit mercier Madame Sainte Katherine en sa chapelle de Fierboys. Et incontinent son veu fait si s'en dormit, et au reveiller trouva en la tour avecques luy un Singe, qui lui apporta deux files, et un petit cousteau. Ainsi il trouva maniere de se deferrer, et adoncques s'en sortit de la prison emportant avecques luy le singe. Si se laissoit cheoir a val en priant Madame Sainte Katherine et chut a bas, et oncques ne se fist mal, et se rendit a Saint Denys ou il trouvoit des compagnons Escossoys.

Et ainsy ledit Norman Leslie s'en est venu audit lieu de Fierboys, tout sain et sauf, emportant avecques luy ledit singe, qui est beste estrange et fol de son corps. Et a jure ledit Norman ce estre vray par la foy et serment de son corps.

Presens messire Richart Kyrthrizian, frere Giles Lacourt, prestres gouverneurs de la dite chapelle, et messire Hauves Polnoire, peintre du Roy, et plusieurs aultres.

APPENDIX B

ELLIOT'S RING

The Ring of the Maid, inscribed with the Holy Names, is often referred to in her Trial ("Proces," i. 86, 103, 185, 236, 238), and is mentioned by Bower, the contemporary Scottish chronicler ("Proces," iv. 480), whose work was continued in the "Liber Pluscardensis." We have also, in the text, Norman's statement that a copy of this ring was presented by the Maid to Elliot Hume.

While correcting the proof-sheets of this Chronicle, the Translator received from Mr. George Black, Assistant Keeper of the National Museum of Antiquities in Edinburgh, a copy of his essay on "Scottish Charms and Amulets" ("Proceedings of the Society of Antiquaries of Scotland," May 8, 1893, p. 488). There, to his astonishment, the Translator read: "The formula MARI. IHS. occurs on two finger-rings of silver-gilt, one of which was found at Pluscarden, Elginshire, and the other in an old graveyard near Fintray House, Aberdeenshire." Have we in the Pluscarden ring a relic of the Monk of Pluscarden, the companion of Jeanne d'Arc, the author of "Liber Pluscardensis"?

FOOTNOTES

{1} Several copies of this book, the Liber Pluscardensis, are extant, but the author's original MS. is lost.

{2} This was written after the Act of the Scots Parliament of 1457.

{3} Daggers.

{4} Rude wall surrounding a keep.

{5} Sisters in the rule of St. Francis.

{6} These tricks of sleight-of-hand are attributed by Jean Nider, in his "Formicarium," to the false Jeanne d'Arc.—A. L.

{7} Very intimate.

{8} When the sky falls and smothers the larks,

{9} This quotation makes it certain that Scott's ballad of Harlaw, in "The Antiquary," is, at least in part, derived from tradition.

{10} This description confirms that of the contemporary

town-clerk of La Rochelle.

{11} The staircase still exists.

{12} "My neck would learn the weight of my more solid proportions."

{13} Neck.

{14} "Frightened by a ghost."

{15} "Airt," i.e. "quarter."

{16} "Fright for fright."

{17} Lameter, a lame.

{18} Bor-brief, certificate of gentle birth.

{19} Howlet, a young owl; a proverb for voracity.

{20} Battle-axe.

{21} Bougran, lustrous white linen.

{22} There are some slight variations, as is natural, in the Fierbois record.

{23} Equipped for battle.

{24} That is, in the "Liber Pluscardensis."

{25} Englishman.

{26} Heavy and still.

{27} Daughter of God, go on, and I will be thine aid. Go on!

{28} Lyrat, grey.

{29} The king's evil: "ecrouelles," scrofula.

{30} Darg, day's work.

{31} "Par mon martin," the oath which she permitted to La Hire.

{32} See Appendix A, 'Norman's Miracle,' Appendix B, 'Elliot's Ring.'

{33} That in to say, some two thousand combatants.

{34} Echevins—magistrates.

{35} "Away with this man, and release unto us Barabbas."

{36} Pavises—large portable shelters.

{37} Block-houses.

{38} The Grahames had not yet possessed themselves of Netherby.—A. L.

{39} Substituting 'or' for 'argent,' his bearings were those of the distinguished modern novelist of the same name.—A. L.

{40} Cande = Kennedy.

ABOUT THE AUTHOR

 **Andrew Lang** Born in Selkirk, Scotland (March 31, 1844 – July 20, 1912) was a prolific Scots man of letters. He was a poet, novelist, and literary critic, and contributor to anthropology. He now is best known as the collector of folk and fairy tales.

The Andrew Lang lectures at St Andrews University are named for him.

Lang is now chiefly known for his publications on folklore, mythology, and religion. The earliest of his publications is Custom and Myth (1884). In Myth, Ritual and Religion (1887) he explained the "irrational" elements of mythology as survivals from more primitive forms. Lang's Making of Religion was heavily influenced by the 18th century idea of the "noble savage": in it, he maintained the existence of high spiritual ideas among so-called "savage" races, drawing parallels with the contemporary interest in occult phenomena in England. His Blue Fairy Book (1889) was a beautifully produced and illustrated edition of fairy tales that has become a classic. This was followed by many other collections of fairy tales, collectively known as Andrew Lang's Fairy Books. Lang examined the origins of totemism in Social Origins (1903).

Choose from Thousands of 1stWorldLibrary Classics By

A. M. Barnard
Ada Leverson
Adolphus William Ward
Aesop
Agatha Christie
Alexander Aaronsohn
Alexander Kielland
Alexandre Dumas
Alfred Gatty
Alfred Ollivant
Alice Duer Miller
Alice Turner Curtis
Alice Dunbar
Allen Chapman
Alleyne Ireland
Ambrose Bierce
Amelia E. Barr
Amory H. Bradford
Andrew Lang
Andrew McFarland Davis
Andy Adams
Angela Brazil
Anna Alice Chapin
Anna Sewell
Annie Besant
Annie Hamilton Donnell
Annie Payson Call
Annie Roe Carr
Annonaymous
Anton Chekhov
Archibald Lee Fletcher
Arnold Bennett
Arthur C. Benson
Arthur Conan Doyle
Arthur M. Winfield
Arthur Ransome
Arthur Schnitzler
Arthur Train
Atticus
B.H. Baden-Powell
B. M. Bower
B. C. Chatterjee
Baroness Emmuska Orczy
Baroness Orczy
Basil King
Bayard Taylor
Ben Macomber
Bertha Muzzy Bower
Bjornstjerne Bjornson

Booth Tarkington
Boyd Cable
Bram Stoker
C. Collodi
C. E. Orr
C. M. Ingleby
Carolyn Wells
Catherine Parr Traill
Charles A. Eastman
Charles Amory Beach
Charles Dickens
Charles Dudley Warner
Charles Farrar Browne
Charles Ives
Charles Kingsley
Charles Klein
Charles Hanson Towne
Charles Lathrop Pack
Charles Romyn Dake
Charles Whibley
Charles Willing Beale
Charlotte M. Braeme
Charlotte M. Yonge
Charlotte Perkins Stetson
Clair W. Hayes
Clarence Day Jr.
Clarence E. Mulford
Clemence Housman
Confucius
Coningsby Dawson
Cornelis DeWitt Wilcox
Cyril Burleigh
D. H. Lawrence
Daniel Defoe
David Garnett
Dinah Craik
Don Carlos Janes
Donald Keyhoe
Dorothy Kilner
Dougan Clark
Douglas Fairbanks
E. Nesbit
E. P. Roe
E. Phillips Oppenheim
E. S. Brooks
Earl Barnes
Edgar Rice Burroughs
Edith Van Dyne
Edith Wharton

Edward Everett Hale
Edward J. O'Biren
Edward S. Ellis
Edwin L. Arnold
Eleanor Atkins
Eleanor Hallowell Abbott
Eliot Gregory
Elizabeth Gaskell
Elizabeth McCracken
Elizabeth Von Arnim
Ellem Key
Emerson Hough
Emilie F. Carlen
Emily Bronte
Emily Dickinson
Enid Bagnold
Enilor Macartney Lane
Erasmus W. Jones
Ernie Howard Pie
Ethel May Dell
Ethel Turner
Ethel Watts Mumford
Eugene Sue
Eugenie Foa
Eugene Wood
Eustace Hale Ball
Evelyn Everett-green
Everard Cotes
F. H. Cheley
F. J. Cross
F. Marion Crawford
Fannie E. Newberry
Federick Austin Ogg
Ferdinand Ossendowski
Fergus Hume
Florence A. Kilpatrick
Fremont B. Deering
Francis Bacon
Francis Darwin
Frances Hodgson Burnett
Frances Parkinson Keyes
Frank Gee Patchin
Frank Harris
Frank Jewett Mather
Frank L. Packard
Frank V. Webster
Frederic Stewart Isham
Frederick Trevor Hill
Frederick Winslow Taylor

Friedrich Kerst	Hayden Carruth	James Branch Cabell
Friedrich Nietzsche	Helent Hunt Jackson	James DeMille
Fyodor Dostoyevsky	Helen Nicolay	James Joyce
G.A. Henty	Hendrik Conscience	James Lane Allen
G.K. Chesterton	Hendy David Thoreau	James Lane Allen
Gabrielle E. Jackson	Henri Barbusse	James Oliver Curwood
Garrett P. Serviss	Henrik Ibsen	James Oppenheim
Gaston Leroux	Henry Adams	James Otis
George A. Warren	Henry Ford	James R. Driscoll
George Ade	Henry Frost	Jane Abbott
Geroge Bernard Shaw	Henry James	Jane Austen
George Cary Eggleston	Henry Jones Ford	Jane L. Stewart
George Durston	Henry Seton Merriman	Janet Aldridge
George Ebers	Henry W Longfellow	Jens Peter Jacobsen
George Eliot	Herbert A. Giles	Jerome K. Jerome
George Gissing	Herbert Carter	Jessie Graham Flower
George MacDonald	Herbert N. Casson	John Buchan
George Meredith	Herman Hesse	John Burroughs
George Orwell	Hildegard G. Frey	John Cournos
George Sylvester Viereck	Homer	John F. Kennedy
George Tucker	Honore De Balzac	John Gay
George W. Cable	Horace B. Day	John Glasworthy
George Wharton James	Horace Walpole	John Habberton
Gertrude Atherton	Horatio Alger Jr.	John Joy Bell
Gordon Casserly	Howard Pyle	John Kendrick Bangs
Grace E. King	Howard R. Garis	John Milton
Grace Gallatin	Hugh Lofting	John Philip Sousa
Grace Greenwood	Hugh Walpole	John Taintor Foote
Grant Allen	Humphry Ward	Jonas Lauritz Idemil Lie
Guillermo A. Sherwell	Ian Maclaren	Jonathan Swift
Gulielma Zollinger	Inez Haynes Gillmore	Joseph A. Altsheler
Gustav Flaubert	Irving Bacheller	Joseph Carey
H. A. Cody	Isabel Cecilia Williams	Joseph Conrad
H. B. Irving	Isabel Hornibrook	Joseph E. Badger Jr
H.C. Bailey	Israel Abrahams	Joseph Hergesheimer
H. G. Wells	Ivan Turgenev	Joseph Jacobs
H. H. Munro	J.G.Austin	Jules Vernes
H. Irving Hancock	J. Henri Fabre	Julian Hawthrone
II. R. Naylor	J. M. Barrie	Julie A Lippmann
H. Rider Haggard	J. M. Walsh	Justin Huntly McCarthy
H. W. C. Davis	J. Macdonald Oxley	Kakuzo Okakura
Haldeman Julius	J. R. Miller	Karle Wilson Baker
Hall Caine	J. S. Fletcher	Kate Chopin
Hamilton Wright Mabie	J. S. Knowles	Kenneth Grahame
Hans Christian Andersen	J. Storer Clouston	Kenneth McGaffey
Harold Avery	J. W. Duffield	Kate Langley Bosher
Harold McGrath	Jack London	Kate Langley Bosher
Harriet Beecher Stowe	Jacob Abbott	Katherine Cecil Thurston
Harry Castlemon	James Allen	Katherine Stokes
Harry Coghill	James Andrews	L. A. Abbot
Harry Houidini	James Baldwin	L. T. Meade

L. Frank Baum
Latta Griswold
Laura Dent Crane
Laura Lee Hope
Laurence Housman
Lawrence Beasley
Leo Tolstoy
Leonid Andreyev
Lewis Carroll
Lewis Sperry Chafer
Lilian Bell
Lloyd Osbourne
Louis Hughes
Louis Joseph Vance
Louis Tracy
Louisa May Alcott
Lucy Fitch Perkins
Lucy Maud Montgomery
Luther Benson
Lydia Miller Middleton
Lyndon Orr
M. Corvus
M. H. Adams
Margaret E. Sangster
Margret Howth
Margaret Vandercook
Margaret W. Hungerford
Margret Penrose
Maria Edgeworth
Maria Thompson Daviess
Mariano Azuela
Marion Polk Angellotti
Mark Overton
Mark Twain
Mary Austin
Mary Catherine Crowley
Mary Cole
Mary Hastings Bradley
Mary Roberts Rinehart
Mary Rowlandson
M. Wollstonecraft Shelley
Maud Lindsay
Max Beerbohm
Myra Kelly
Nathaniel Hawthrone
Nicolo Machiavelli
O. F. Walton
Oscar Wilde

Owen Johnson
P.G. Wodehouse
Paul and Mabel Thorne
Paul G. Tomlinson
Paul Severing
Percy Brebner
Percy Keese Fitzhugh
Peter B. Kyne
Plato
Quincy Allen
R. Derby Holmes
R. L. Stevenson
R. S. Ball
Rabindranath Tagore
Rahul Alvares
Ralph Bonehill
Ralph Henry Barbour
Ralph Victor
Ralph Waldo Emmerson
Rene Descartes
Ray Cummings
Rex Beach
Rex E. Beach
Richard Harding Davis
Richard Jefferies
Richard Le Gallienne
Robert Barr
Robert Frost
Robert Gordon Anderson
Robert L. Drake
Robert Lansing
Robert Lynd
Robert Michael Ballantyne
Robert W. Chambers
Rosa Nouchette Carey
Rudyard Kipling
Saint Augustine
Samuel B. Allison
Samuel Hopkins Adams
Sarah Bernhardt
Sarah C. Hallowell
Selma Lagerlof
Sherwood Anderson
Sigmund Freud
Standish O'Grady
Stanley Weyman
Stella Benson
Stella M. Francis

Stephen Crane
Stewart Edward White
Stijn Streuvels
Swami Abhedananda
Swami Parmananda
T. S. Ackland
T. S. Arthur
The Princess Der Ling
Thomas A. Janvier
Thomas A Kempis
Thomas Anderton
Thomas Bailey Aldrich
Thomas Bulfinch
Thomas De Quincey
Thomas Dixon
Thomas H. Huxley
Thomas Hardy
Thomas More
Thornton W. Burgess
U. S. Grant
Upton Sinclair
Valentine Williams
Various Authors
Vaughan Kester
Victor Appleton
Victor G. Durham
Victoria Cross
Virginia Woolf
Wadsworth Camp
Walter Camp
Walter Scott
Washington Irving
Wilbur Lawton
Wilkie Collins
Willa Cather
Willard F. Baker
William Dean Howells
William le Queux
W. Makepeace Thackeray
William W. Walter
William Shakespeare
Winston Churchill
Yei Theodora Ozaki
Yogi Ramacharaka
Young E. Allison
Zane Grey

www.ingramcontent.com/pod-product-compliance
Lightning Source LLC
Chambersburg PA
CBHW032258260626
47157CB00022B/380